FEAR AGENT™

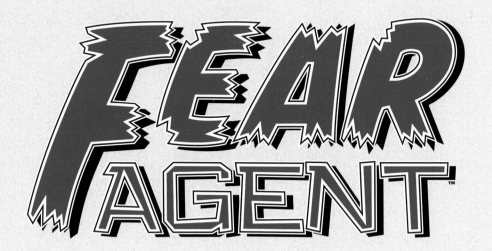

SENSES-SHATTERING!

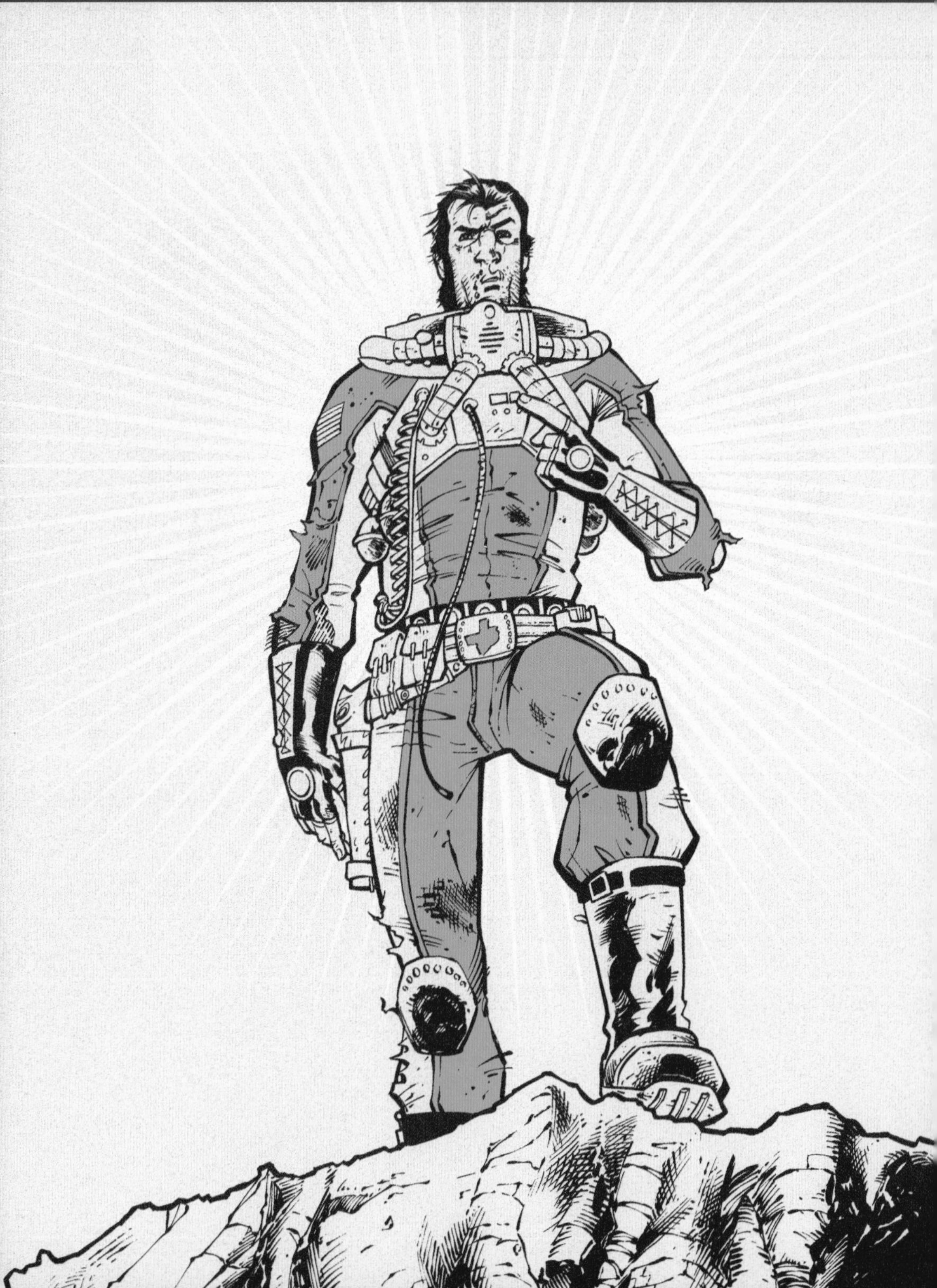

Space thrills and chills

FEAR AGENT™

Volume One

RE-IGNITION

story **RICK REMENDER**

pencils **TONY MOORE**

inks Sean Parsons & Mike Manley

colors Lee Loughridge

letters Rus Wooton

covers Tony Moore

pencil assists on chapter 4 Jerome Opeña

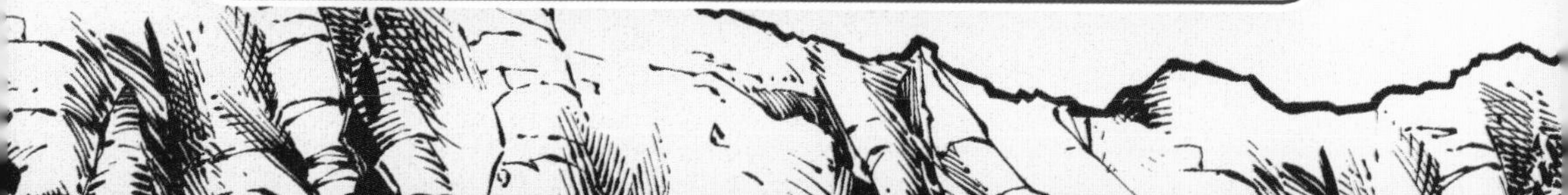

DARK HORSE BOOKS®

Publisher ⁄⁄ Mike Richardson
Art Director ⁄⁄ Lia Ribacchi
Designer ⁄⁄ M. Joshua Elliott
Assistant Editor ⁄⁄ Katie Moody
Editor ⁄⁄ Dave Land

Dark Horse Books
A division of Dark Horse Comics, Inc.
10956 SE Main Street
Milwaukie, OR 97222

darkhorse.com

To find a comics shop in your area call the Comic Shop
Locator Service toll-free at (888) 266-4226

First edition: May 2007
ISBN 978-1-59307-764-8

5 7 9 10 8 6
Printed at Midas Printing International, Ltd., Huizhou, China

FEAR AGENT: RE-IGNITION

This book collects issues one through four of the comic-book series *Fear Agent* originally published by Image Comics.

LOVING DEDICATIONS!

For Danni—

It's the simple things that are so hard to grasp can't find myself in all these days that pass but I can feel it when it shines.

—Rick

For Kara—

Because your belief in me far exceeds my belief in myself, I always pick myself up and dust myself off, no matter how bad the fall. I don't have the words to thank you enough.

—Tony

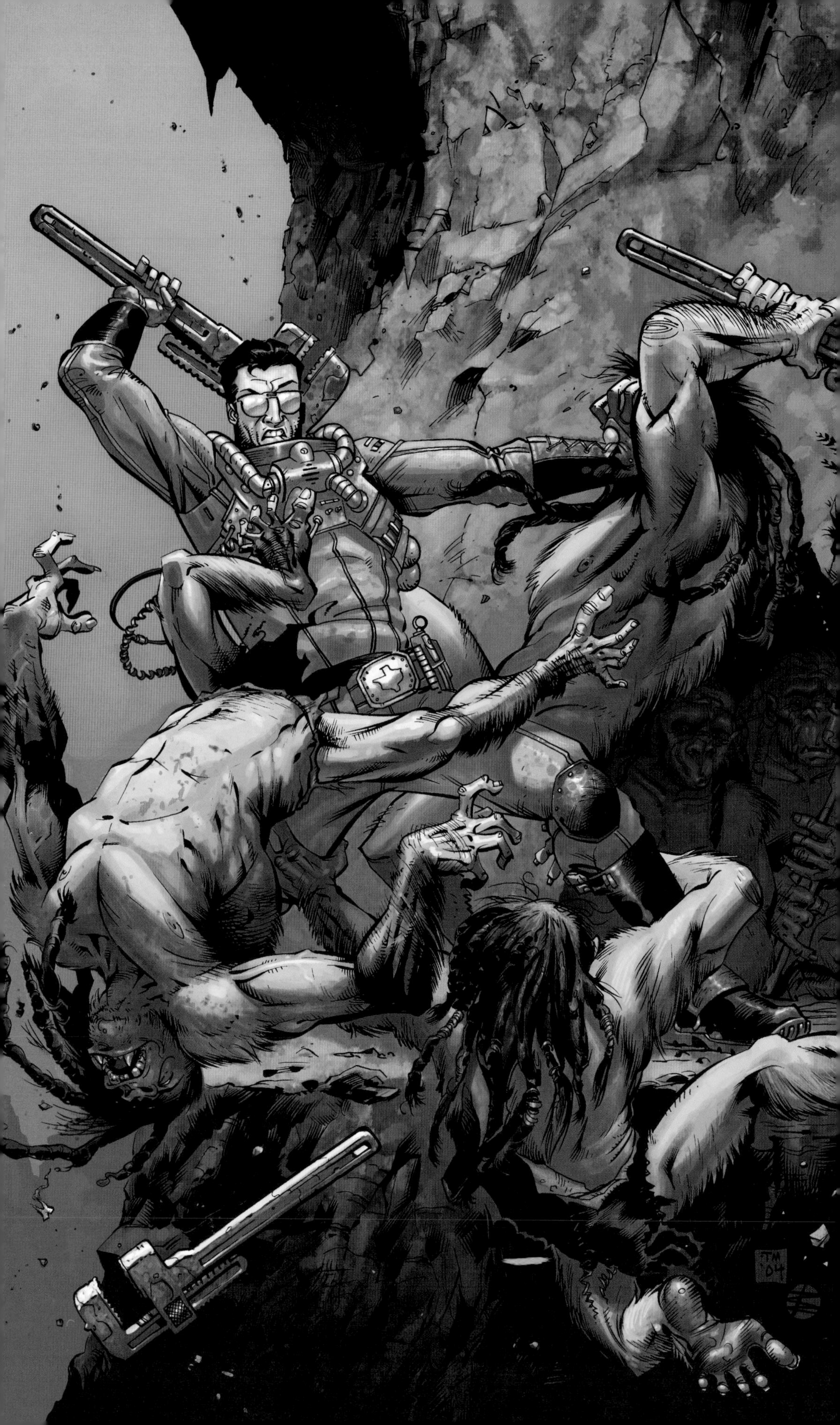

RE-IGNITION CHAPTER 1

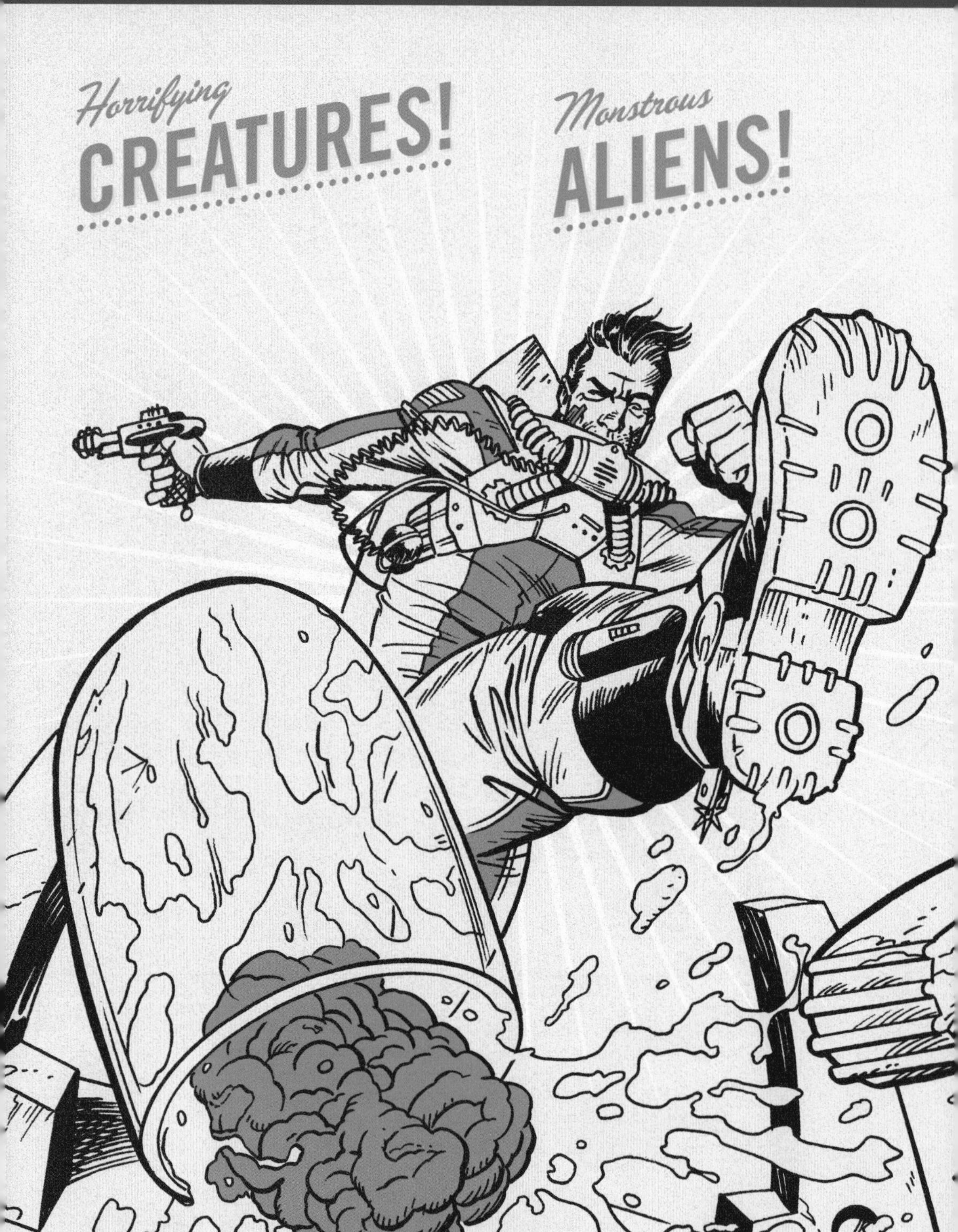
Horrifying
CREATURES!
Monstrous
ALIENS!

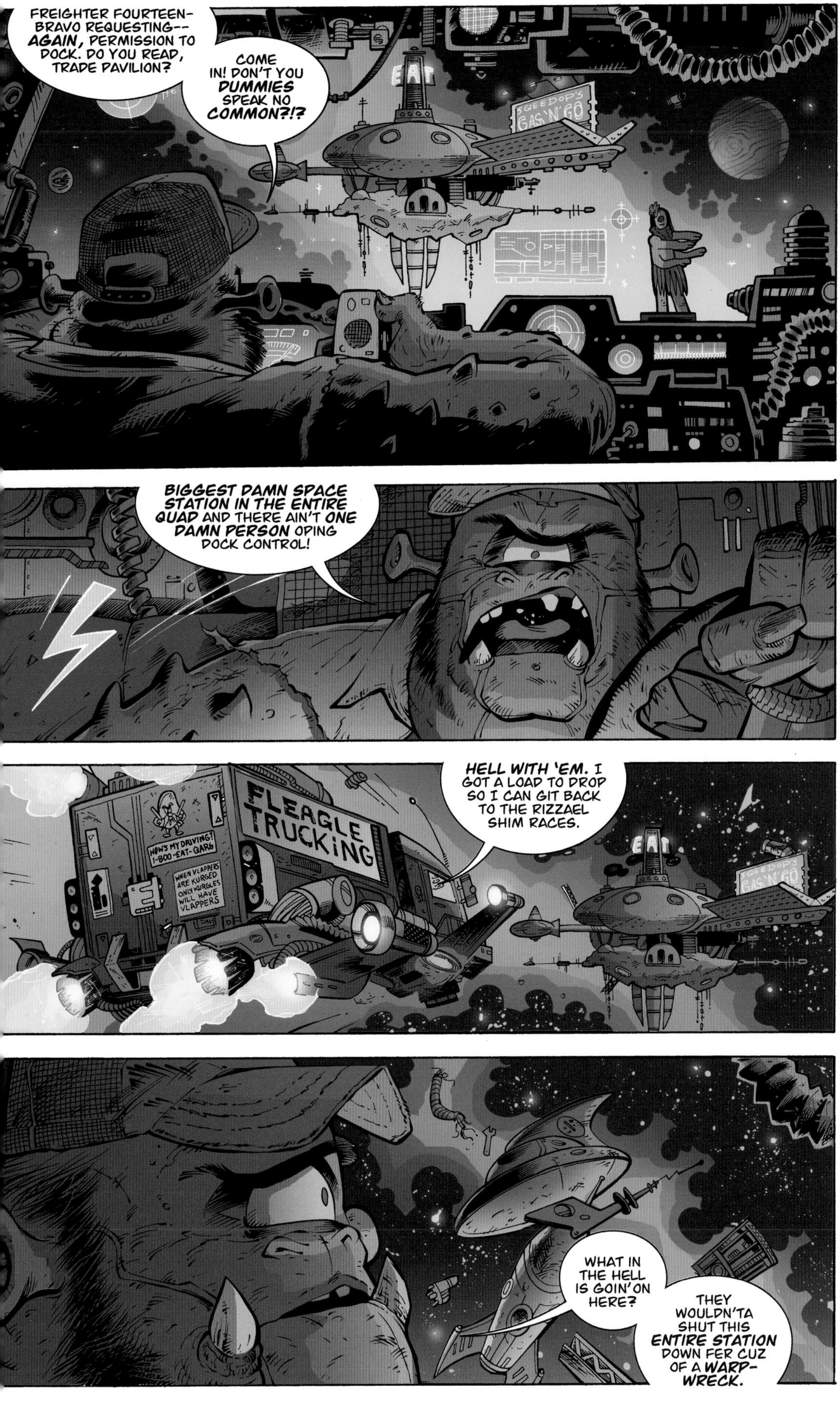
FREIGHTER FOURTEEN-BRAVO REQUESTING-- AGAIN, PERMISSION TO DOCK. DO YOU READ, TRADE PAVILION?
COME IN! DON'T YOU DUMMIES SPEAK NO COMMON?!?
EAT
SGEEDOP'S GAS 'N' GO
BIGGEST DAMN SPACE STATION IN THE ENTIRE QUAD AND THERE AIN'T ONE DAMN PERSON OPING DOCK CONTROL!
FLEAGLE TRUCKING
HOW'S MY DRIVING? 1-800-EAT-GARG
WHEN VLAPPERS ARE KURGED ONLY KURGLES WILL HAVE VLAPPERS
HELL WITH 'EM. I GOT A LOAD TO DROP SO I CAN GIT BACK TO THE RIZZAEL SHIM RACES.
EAT
SGEEDOP'S GAS 'N' GO
WHAT IN THE HELL IS GOIN' ON HERE?
THEY WOULDN'TA SHUT THIS ENTIRE STATION DOWN FER CUZ OF A WARP-WRECK.

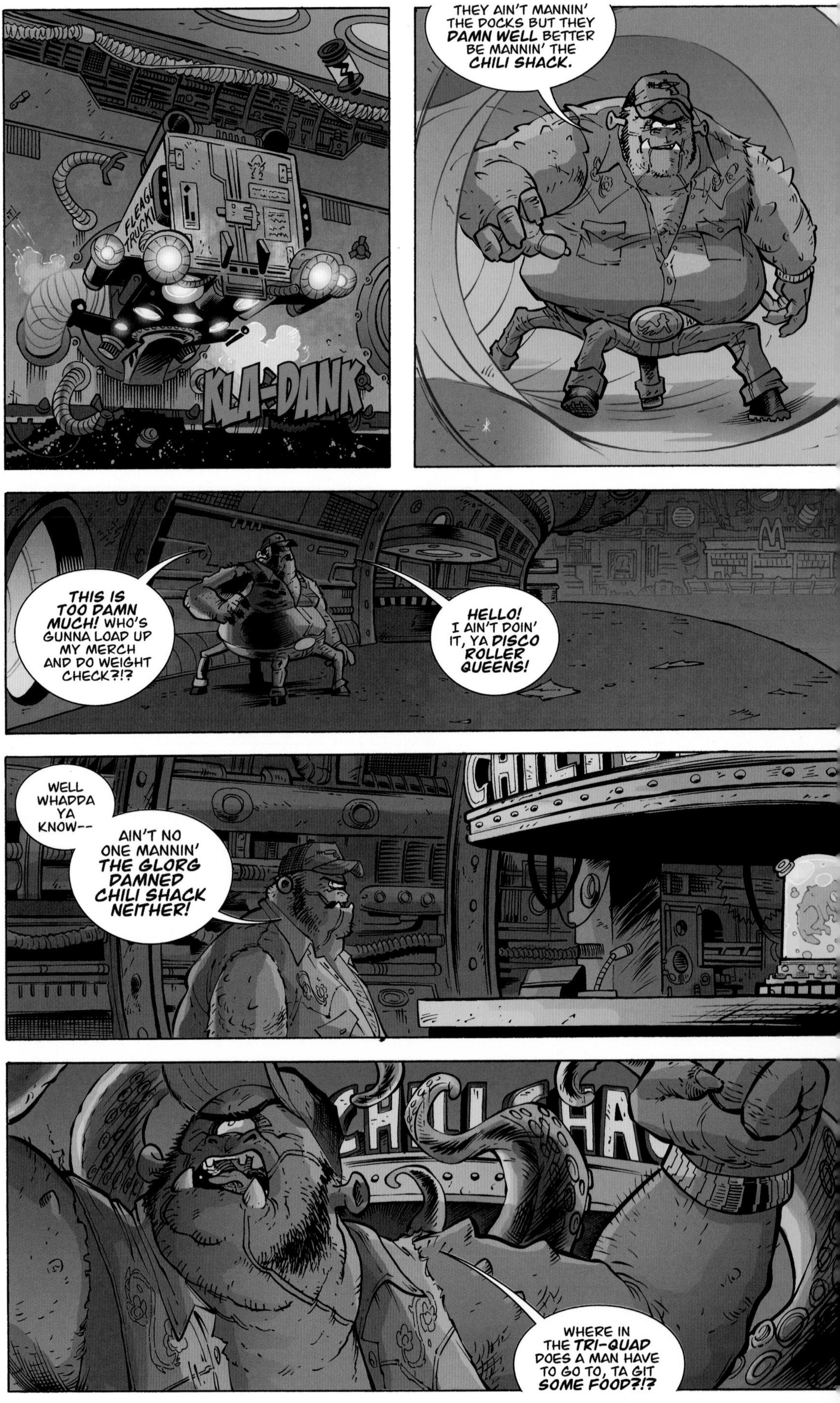
KLA-DANK
THEY AIN'T MANNIN' THE DOCKS BUT THEY DAMN WELL BETTER BE MANNIN' THE CHILI SHACK.
THIS IS TOO DAMN MUCH! WHO'S GUNNA LOAD UP MY MERCH AND DO WEIGHT CHECK?!?
HELLO! I AIN'T DOIN' IT, YA DISCO ROLLER QUEENS!
WELL WHADDA YA KNOW--
AIN'T NO ONE MANNIN' THE GLORG DAMNED CHILI SHACK NEITHER!
WHERE IN THE TRI-QUAD DOES A MAN HAVE TO GO TO, TA GIT SOME FOOD?!?

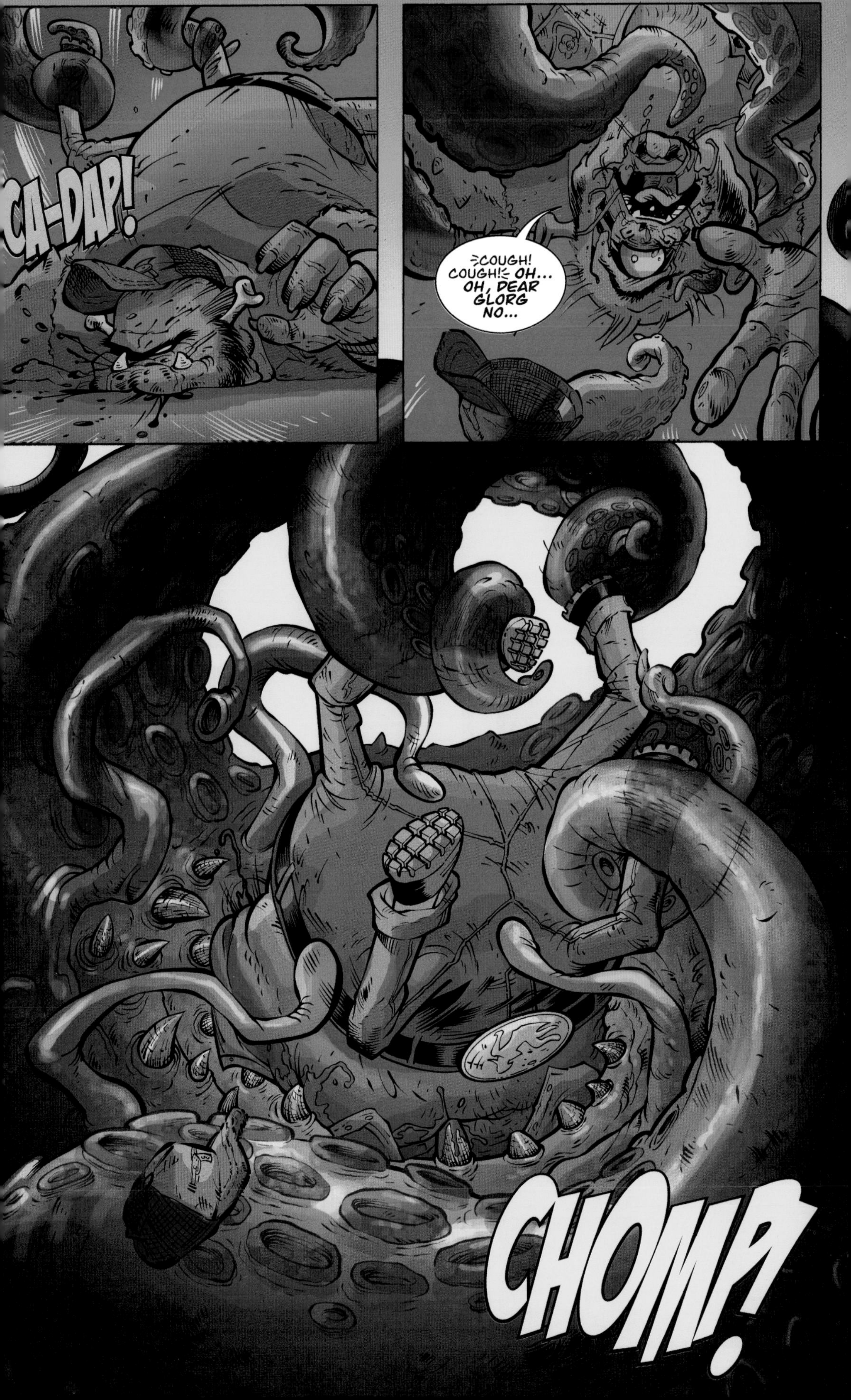
CA-DAP!
COUGH! COUGH! OH... OH, DEAR GLORG NO...
CHOMP!

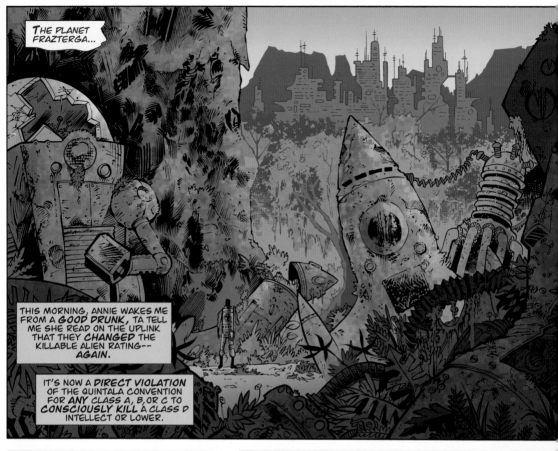

THE PLANET FRAZTERGA...

THIS MORNING, ANNIE WAKES ME FROM A *GOOD DRUNK*, TA TELL ME SHE READ ON THE UPLINK THAT THEY *CHANGED* THE KILLABLE ALIEN RATING-- *AGAIN.*

IT'S NOW A *DIRECT VIOLATION* OF THE QUINTALA CONVENTION FOR *ANY* CLASS A, B, OR C TO *CONSCIOUSLY KILL* A CLASS D INTELLECT OR LOWER.

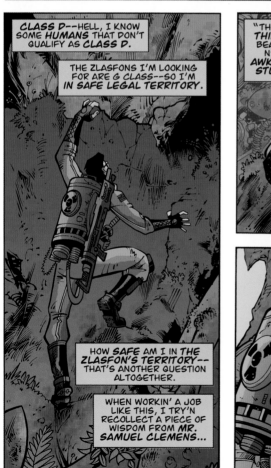

CLASS D--HELL, I KNOW SOME *HUMANS* THAT DON'T QUALIFY AS *CLASS D.*

THE ZLASFONS I'M LOOKING FOR ARE G CLASS--SO I'M *IN SAFE LEGAL TERRITORY.*

HOW *SAFE* AM I IN *THE ZLASFON'S* TERRITORY-- THAT'S ANOTHER QUESTION ALTOGETHER.

WHEN WORKIN' A JOB LIKE THIS, I TRY'N RECOLLECT A PIECE OF WISDOM FROM *MR. SAMUEL CLEMENS...*

"THERE'RE *SOME THINGS* THAT CAN BEAT SMARTNESS N' FORESIGHT. AWKWARDNESS N' STUPIDITY CAN."

"THE *BEST SWORDSMAN* IN THE WORLD DOESN'T NEED TO FEAR THE *SECOND BEST SWORDSMAN* IN THE WORLD...

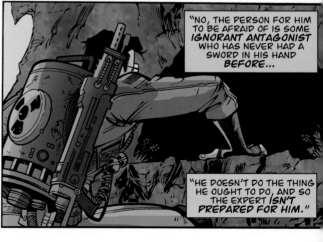

"NO, THE PERSON FOR HIM TO BE AFRAID OF IS SOME *IGNORANT ANTAGONIST* WHO HAS NEVER HAD A SWORD IN HIS HAND *BEFORE...*

"HE DOESN'T DO THE THING HE OUGHT TO DO, AND SO THE EXPERT *ISN'T* PREPARED FOR HIM."

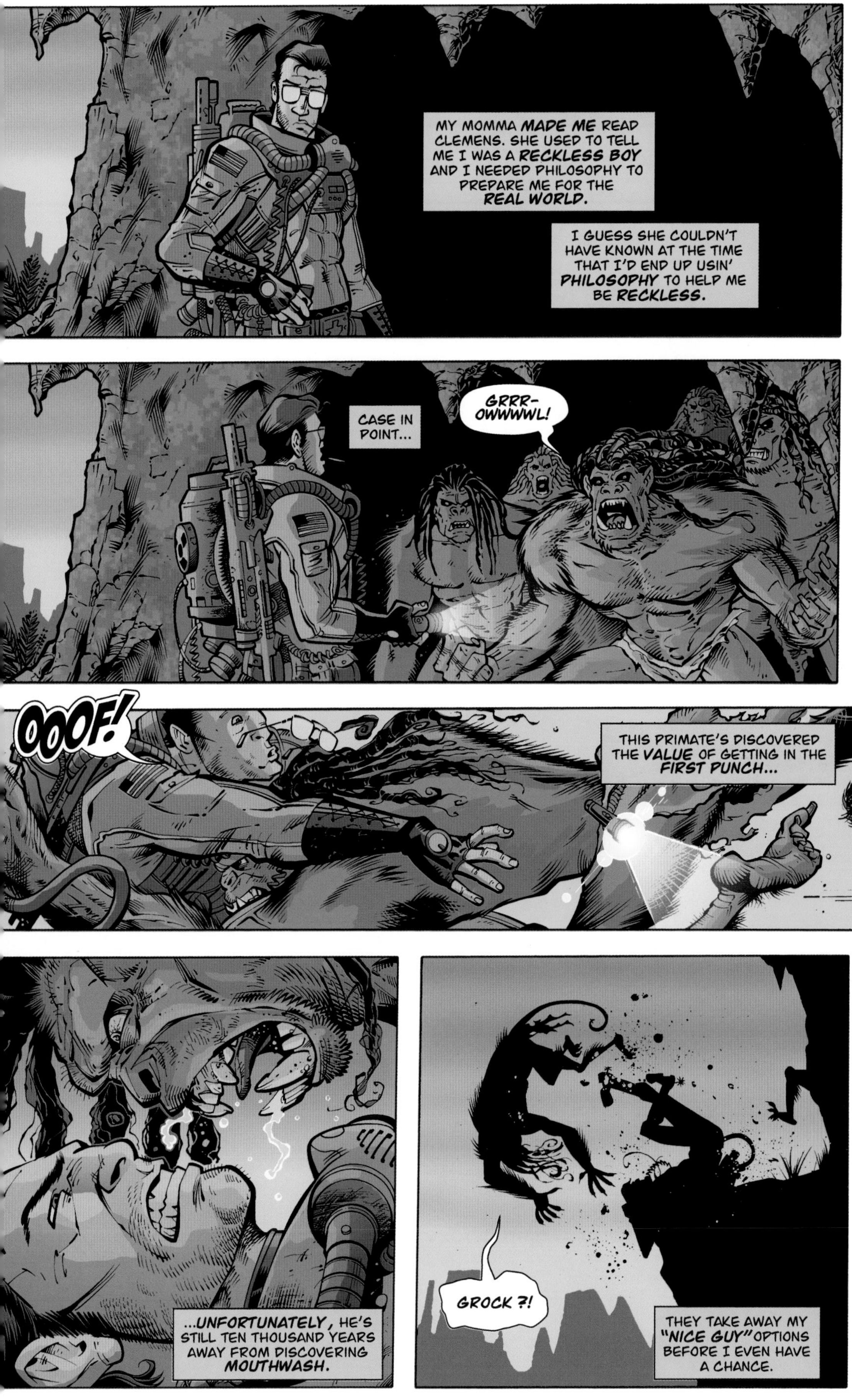
MY MOMMA MADE ME READ CLEMENS. SHE USED TO TELL ME I WAS A RECKLESS BOY AND I NEEDED PHILOSOPHY TO PREPARE ME FOR THE REAL WORLD.
I GUESS SHE COULDN'T HAVE KNOWN AT THE TIME THAT I'D END UP USIN' PHILOSOPHY TO HELP ME BE RECKLESS.
CASE IN POINT...
GRRR-OWWWWL!
OOOF!
THIS PRIMATE'S DISCOVERED THE VALUE OF GETTING IN THE FIRST PUNCH...
...UNFORTUNATELY, HE'S STILL TEN THOUSAND YEARS AWAY FROM DISCOVERING MOUTHWASH.
GROCK ?!
THEY TAKE AWAY MY "NICE GUY" OPTIONS BEFORE I EVEN HAVE A CHANCE.

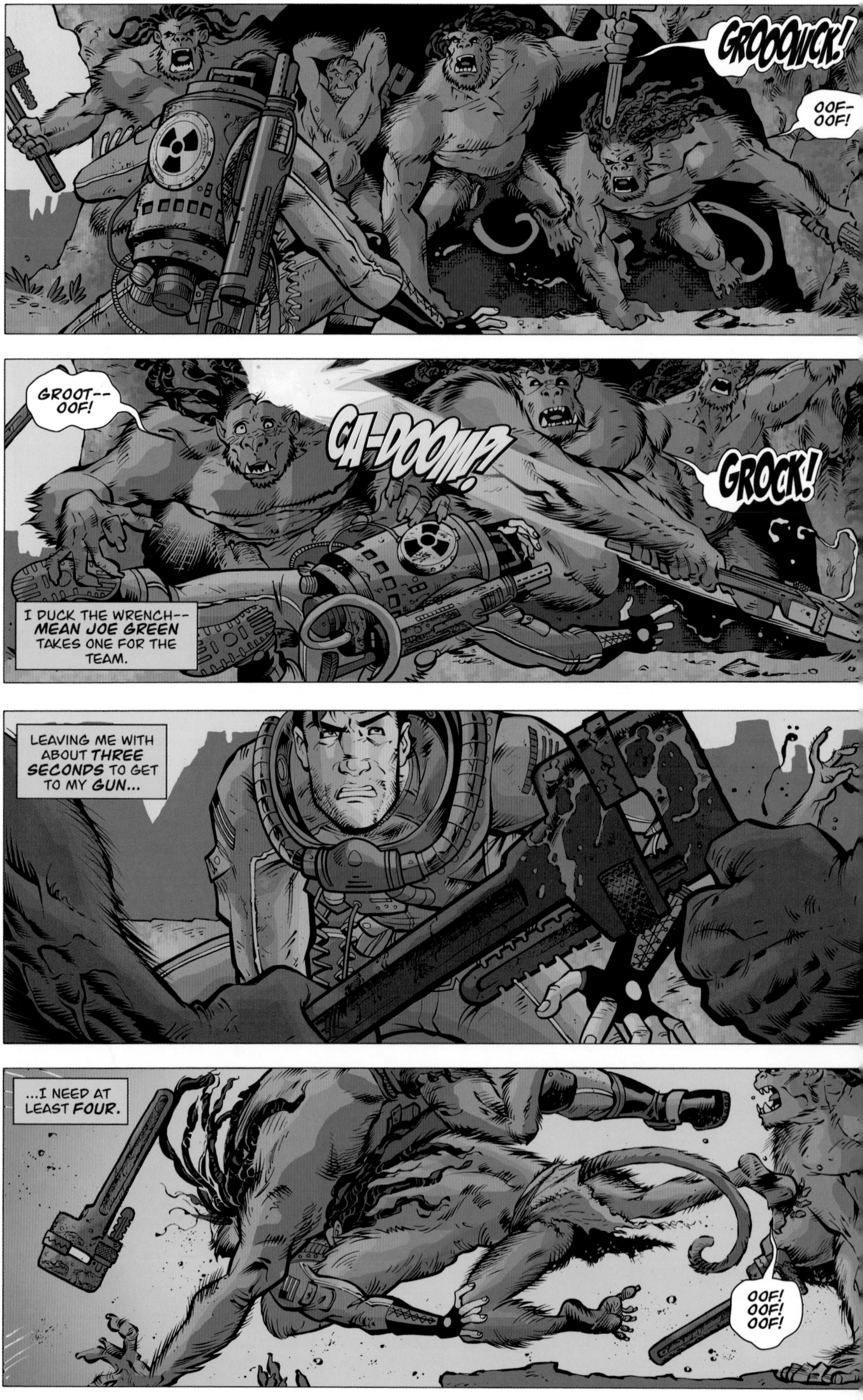
GROOOWCK!
OOF-OOF!
GROOT--OOF!
CA-DOOMP!
GROCK!
I DUCK THE WRENCH--MEAN JOE GREEN TAKES ONE FOR THE TEAM.
LEAVING ME WITH ABOUT THREE SECONDS TO GET TO MY GUN...
...I NEED AT LEAST FOUR.
OOF! OOF! OOF!

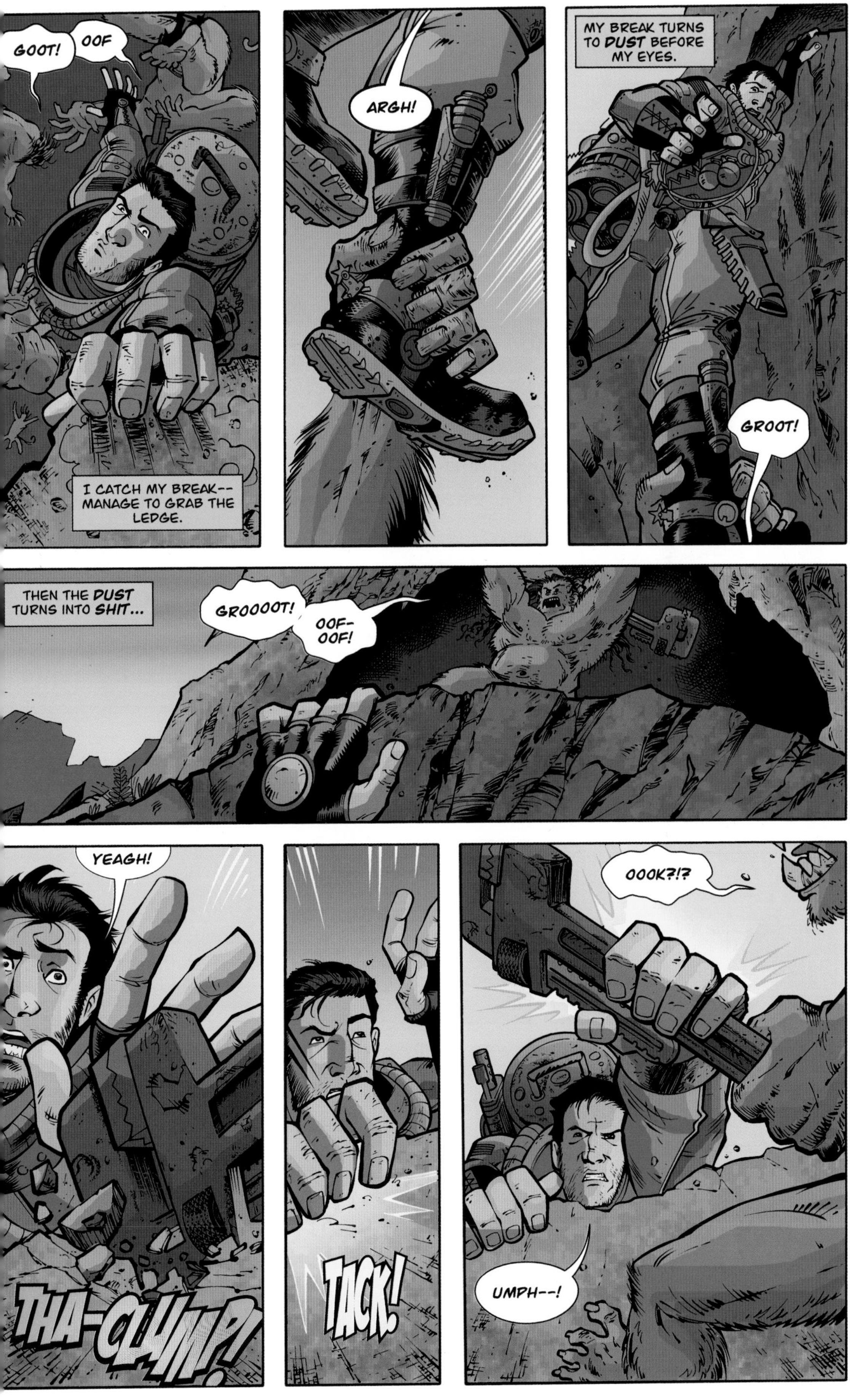
GOOT!
OOF
I CATCH MY BREAK-- MANAGE TO GRAB THE LEDGE.
ARGH!
MY BREAK TURNS TO DUST BEFORE MY EYES.
GROOT!
THEN THE DUST TURNS INTO SHIT...
GROOOOT!
OOF-OOF!
YEAGH!
THA-CLUNP!
TACK!
OOOK?!?
UMPH--!

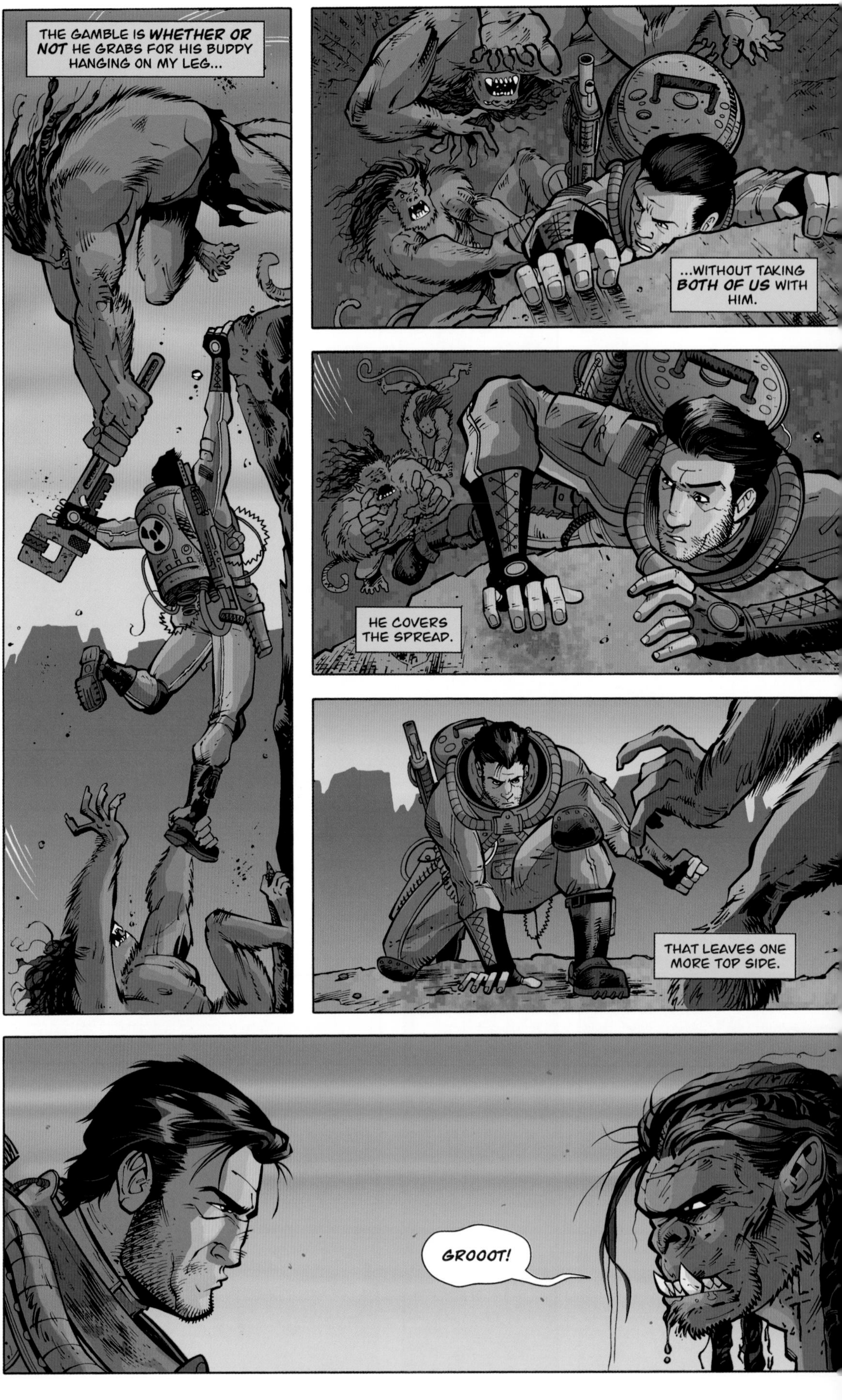
THE GAMBLE IS *WHETHER OR NOT* HE GRABS FOR HIS BUDDY HANGING ON MY LEG...
...WITHOUT TAKING *BOTH OF US* WITH HIM.
HE COVERS THE SPREAD.
THAT LEAVES ONE MORE TOP SIDE.
GROOOT!

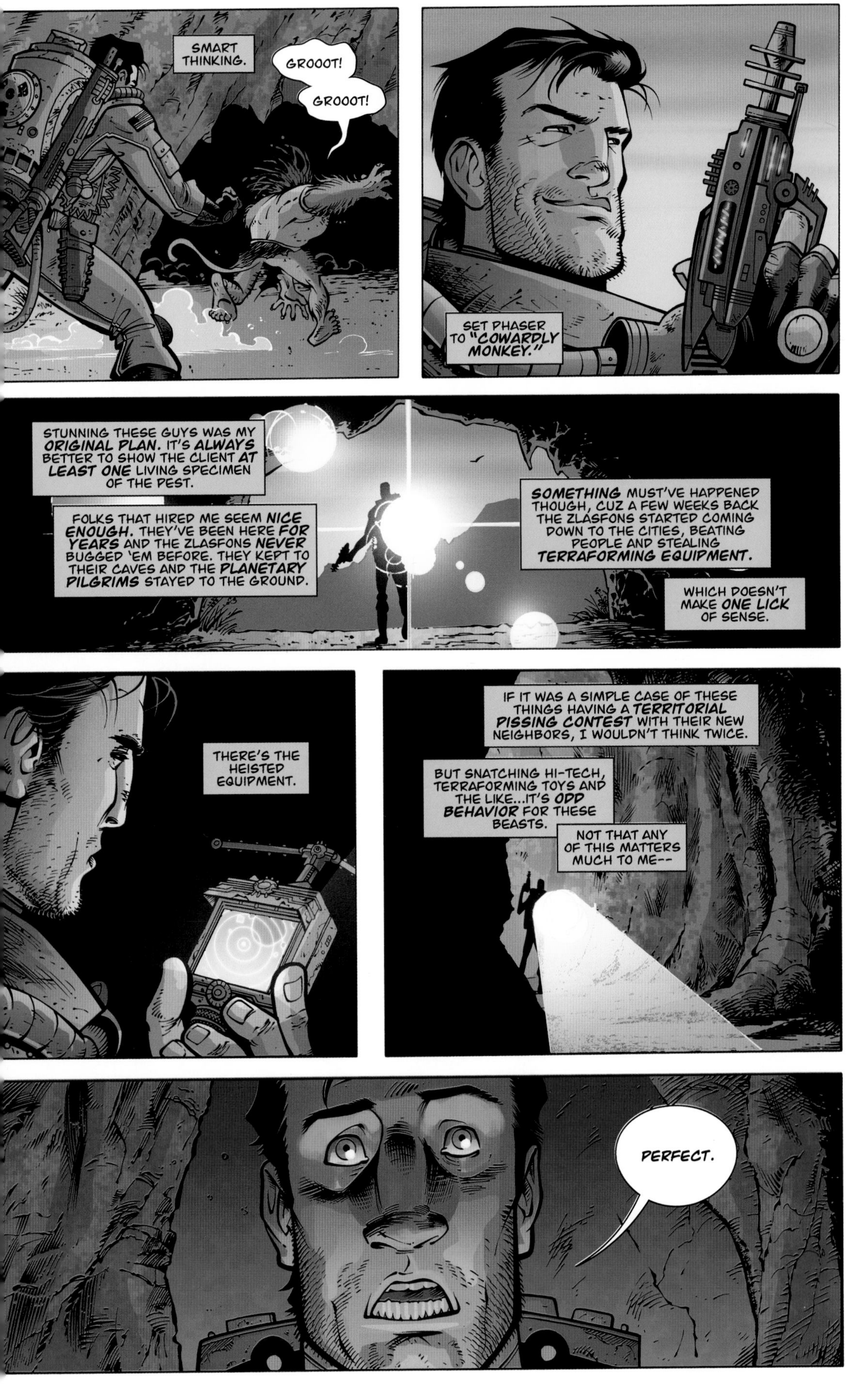
SMART THINKING.
GROOOT!
GROOOT!
SET PHASER TO "COWARDLY MONKEY."
STUNNING THESE GUYS WAS MY ORIGINAL PLAN. IT'S ALWAYS BETTER TO SHOW THE CLIENT AT LEAST ONE LIVING SPECIMEN OF THE PEST.
FOLKS THAT HIRED ME SEEM NICE ENOUGH. THEY'VE BEEN HERE FOR YEARS AND THE ZLASFONS NEVER BUGGED 'EM BEFORE. THEY KEPT TO THEIR CAVES AND THE PLANETARY PILGRIMS STAYED TO THE GROUND.
SOMETHING MUST'VE HAPPENED THOUGH, CUZ A FEW WEEKS BACK THE ZLASFONS STARTED COMING DOWN TO THE CITIES, BEATING PEOPLE AND STEALING TERRAFORMING EQUIPMENT.
WHICH DOESN'T MAKE ONE LICK OF SENSE.
THERE'S THE HEISTED EQUIPMENT.
IF IT WAS A SIMPLE CASE OF THESE THINGS HAVING A TERRITORIAL PISSING CONTEST WITH THEIR NEW NEIGHBORS, I WOULDN'T THINK TWICE.
BUT SNATCHING HI-TECH, TERRAFORMING TOYS AND THE LIKE...IT'S ODD BEHAVIOR FOR THESE BEASTS.
NOT THAT ANY OF THIS MATTERS MUCH TO ME--
PERFECT.

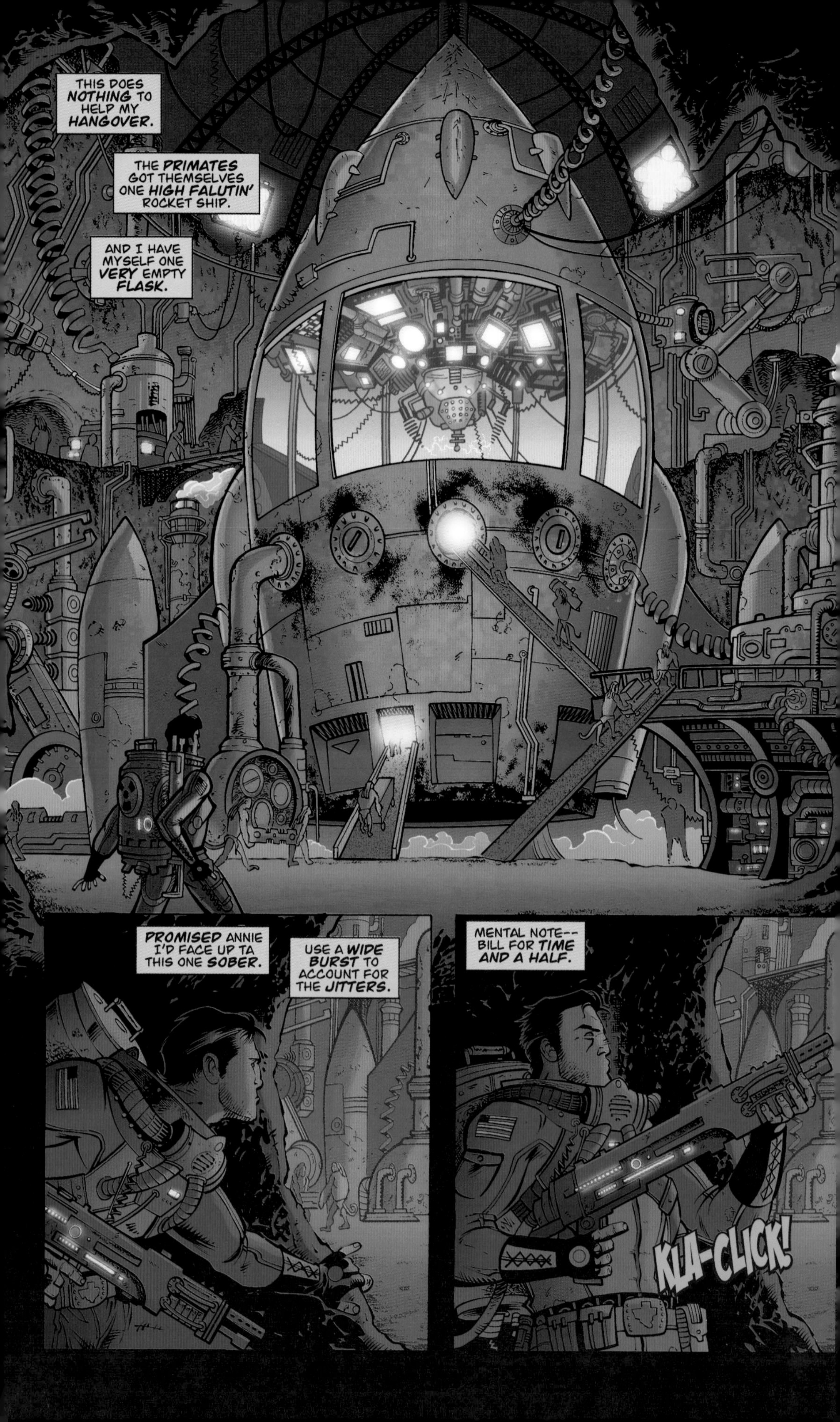
THIS DOES NOTHING TO HELP MY HANGOVER.
THE PRIMATES GOT THEMSELVES ONE HIGH FALUTIN' ROCKET SHIP.
AND I HAVE MYSELF ONE VERY EMPTY FLASK.
PROMISED ANNIE I'D FACE UP TA THIS ONE SOBER.
USE A WIDE BURST TO ACCOUNT FOR THE JITTERS.
MENTAL NOTE-- BILL FOR TIME AND A HALF.
KLA-CLICK!

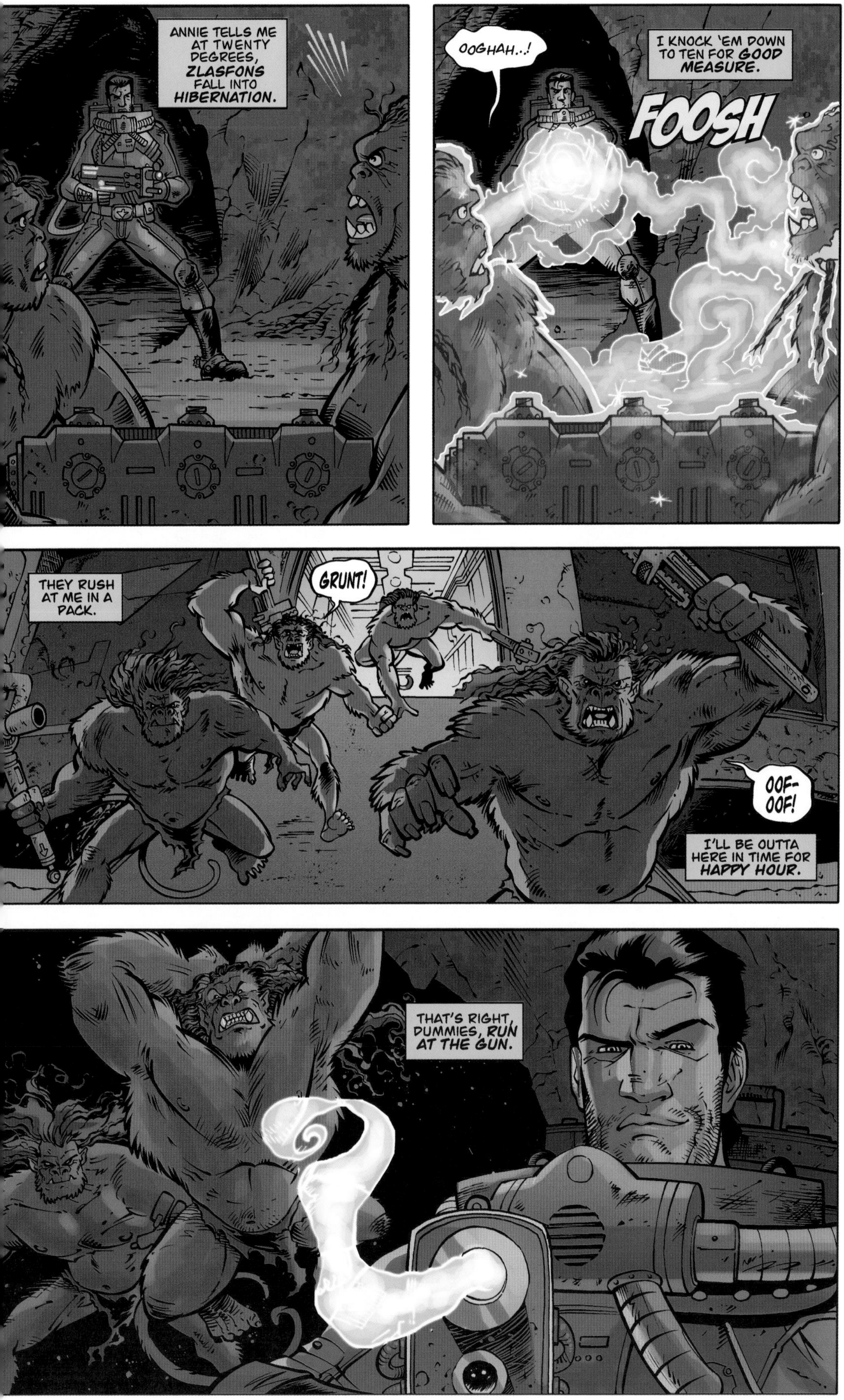

ANNIE TELLS ME AT TWENTY DEGREES, ZLASFONS FALL INTO HIBERNATION.
OOGHAH..!
I KNOCK 'EM DOWN TO TEN FOR GOOD MEASURE.
FOOSH
THEY RUSH AT ME IN A PACK.
GRUNT!
OOF-OOF!
I'LL BE OUTTA HERE IN TIME FOR HAPPY HOUR.
THAT'S RIGHT, DUMMIES, RUN AT THE GUN.

OOF!

CLOMP

GRAWK!

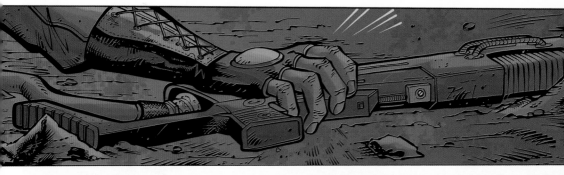

PHFFFFSSSST!

YEARGH!

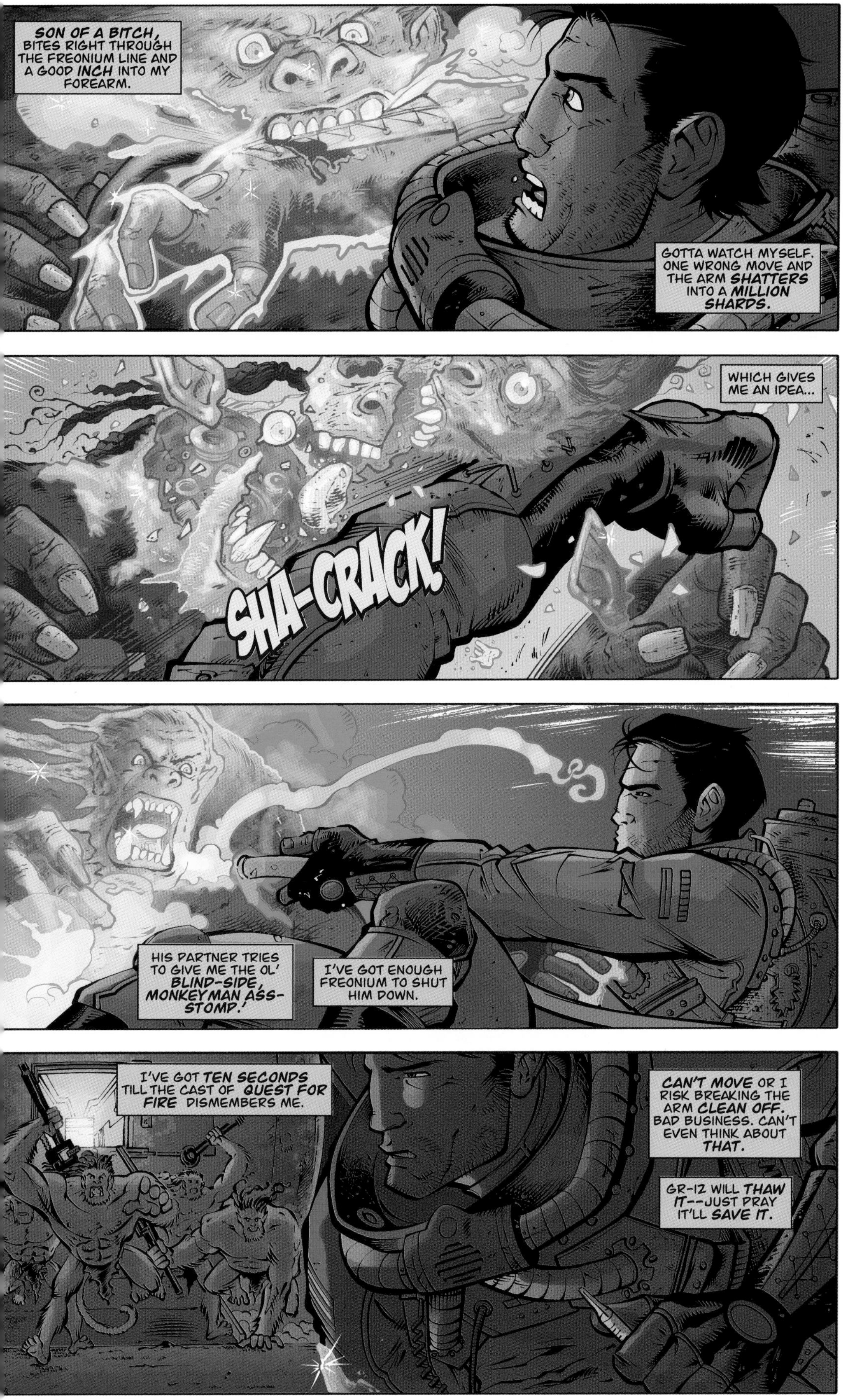
SON OF A BITCH, BITES RIGHT THROUGH THE FREONIUM LINE AND A GOOD INCH INTO MY FOREARM.
GOTTA WATCH MYSELF. ONE WRONG MOVE AND THE ARM SHATTERS INTO A MILLION SHARDS.
WHICH GIVES ME AN IDEA...
SHA-CRACK!
HIS PARTNER TRIES TO GIVE ME THE OL' BLIND-SIDE, MONKEYMAN ASS-STOMP.'
I'VE GOT ENOUGH FREONIUM TO SHUT HIM DOWN.
I'VE GOT TEN SECONDS TILL THE CAST OF QUEST FOR FIRE DISMEMBERS ME.
CAN'T MOVE OR I RISK BREAKING THE ARM CLEAN OFF. BAD BUSINESS. CAN'T EVEN THINK ABOUT THAT.
GR-12 WILL THAW IT--JUST PRAY IT'LL SAVE IT.

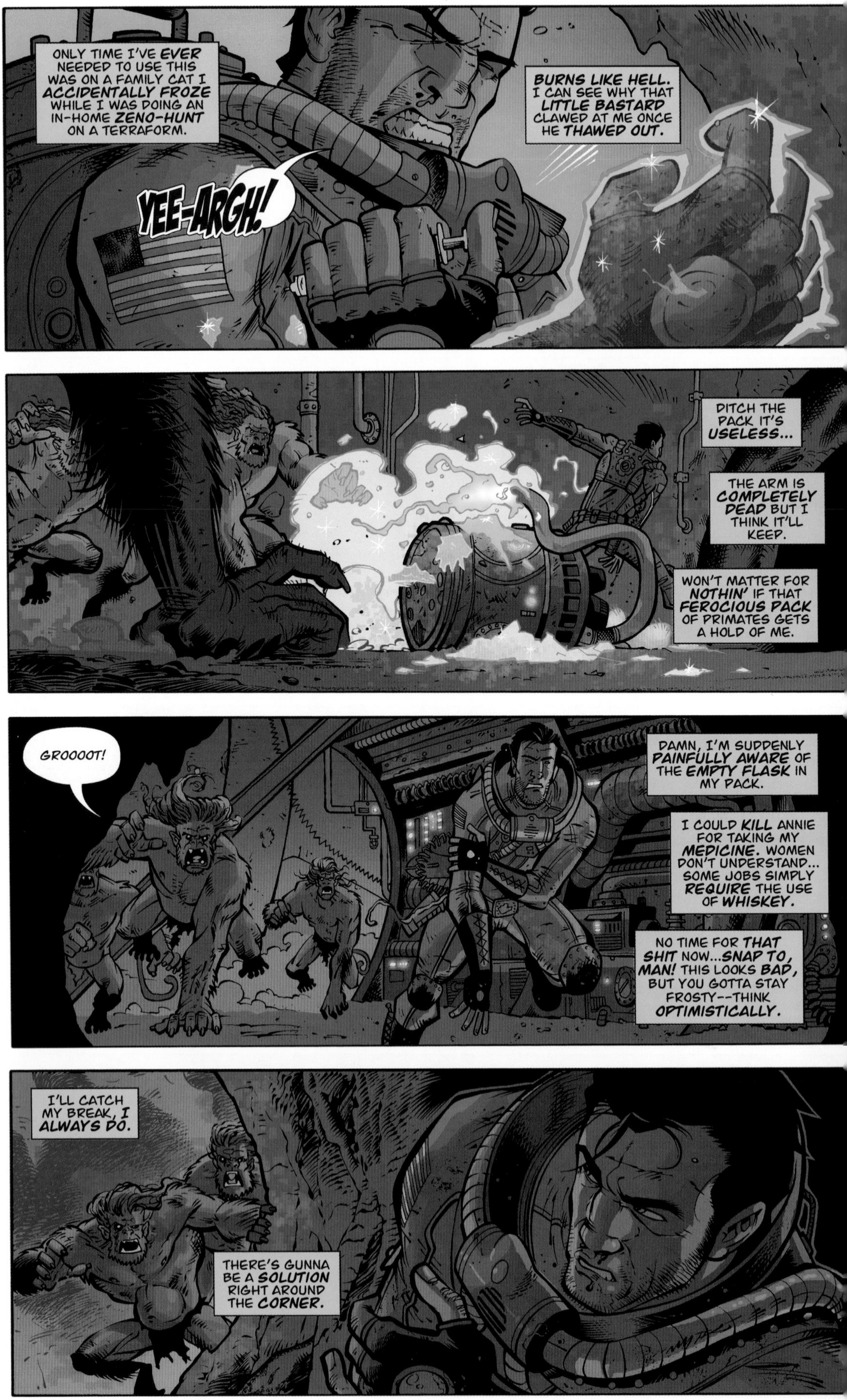
ONLY TIME I'VE EVER NEEDED TO USE THIS WAS ON A FAMILY CAT I ACCIDENTALLY FROZE WHILE I WAS DOING AN IN-HOME ZENO-HUNT ON A TERRAFORM.
YEE-ARGH!
BURNS LIKE HELL. I CAN SEE WHY THAT LITTLE BASTARD CLAWED AT ME ONCE HE THAWED OUT.
DITCH THE PACK IT'S USELESS...
THE ARM IS COMPLETELY DEAD BUT I THINK IT'LL KEEP.
WON'T MATTER FOR NOTHIN' IF THAT FEROCIOUS PACK OF PRIMATES GETS A HOLD OF ME.
GROOOOT!
DAMN, I'M SUDDENLY PAINFULLY AWARE OF THE EMPTY FLASK IN MY PACK.
I COULD KILL ANNIE FOR TAKING MY MEDICINE. WOMEN DON'T UNDERSTAND... SOME JOBS SIMPLY REQUIRE THE USE OF WHISKEY.
NO TIME FOR THAT SHIT NOW...SNAP TO, MAN! THIS LOOKS BAD, BUT YOU GOTTA STAY FROSTY--THINK OPTIMISTICALLY.
I'LL CATCH MY BREAK, I ALWAYS DO.
THERE'S GUNNA BE A SOLUTION RIGHT AROUND THE CORNER.

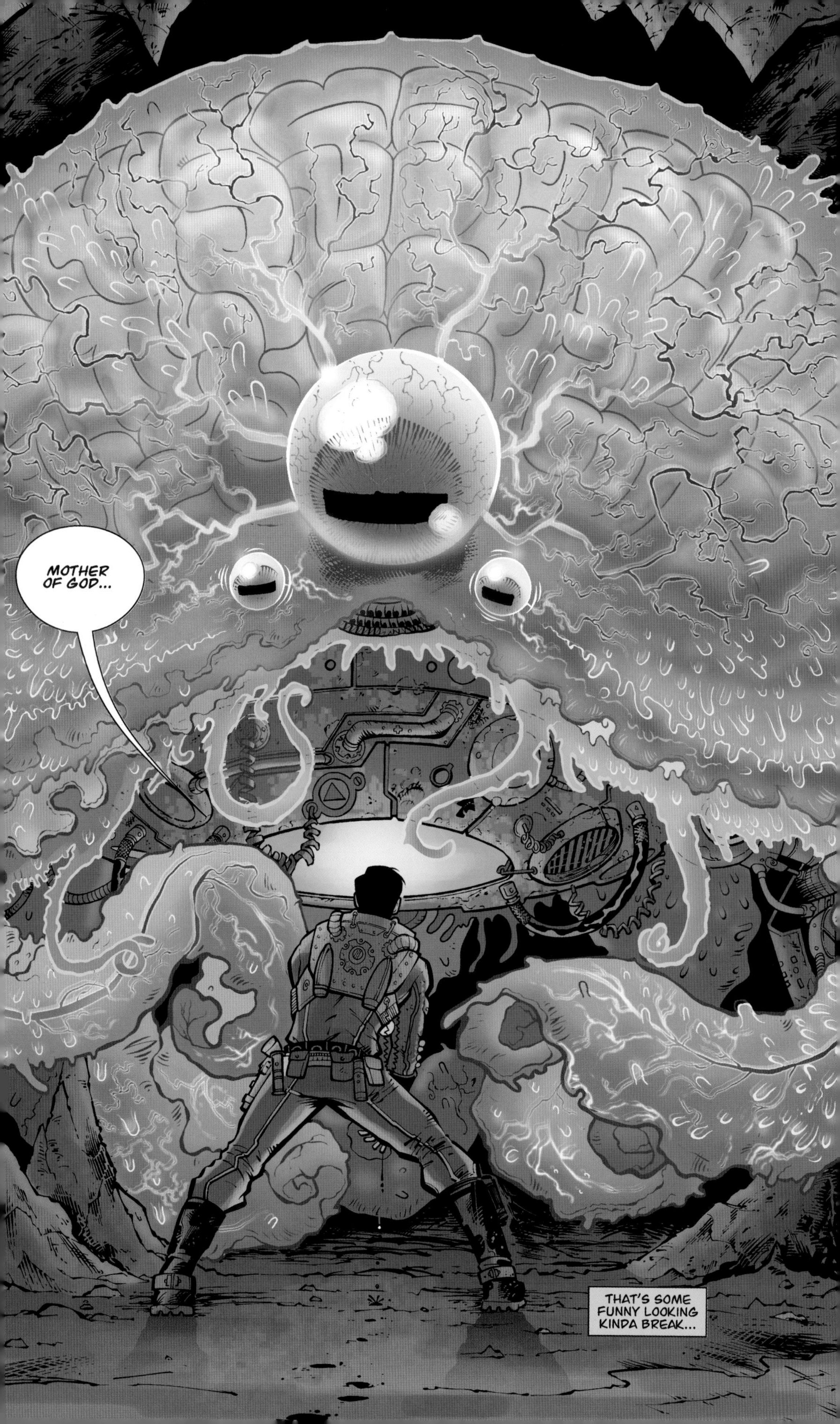
MOTHER OF GOD...
THAT'S SOME FUNNY LOOKING KINDA BREAK...

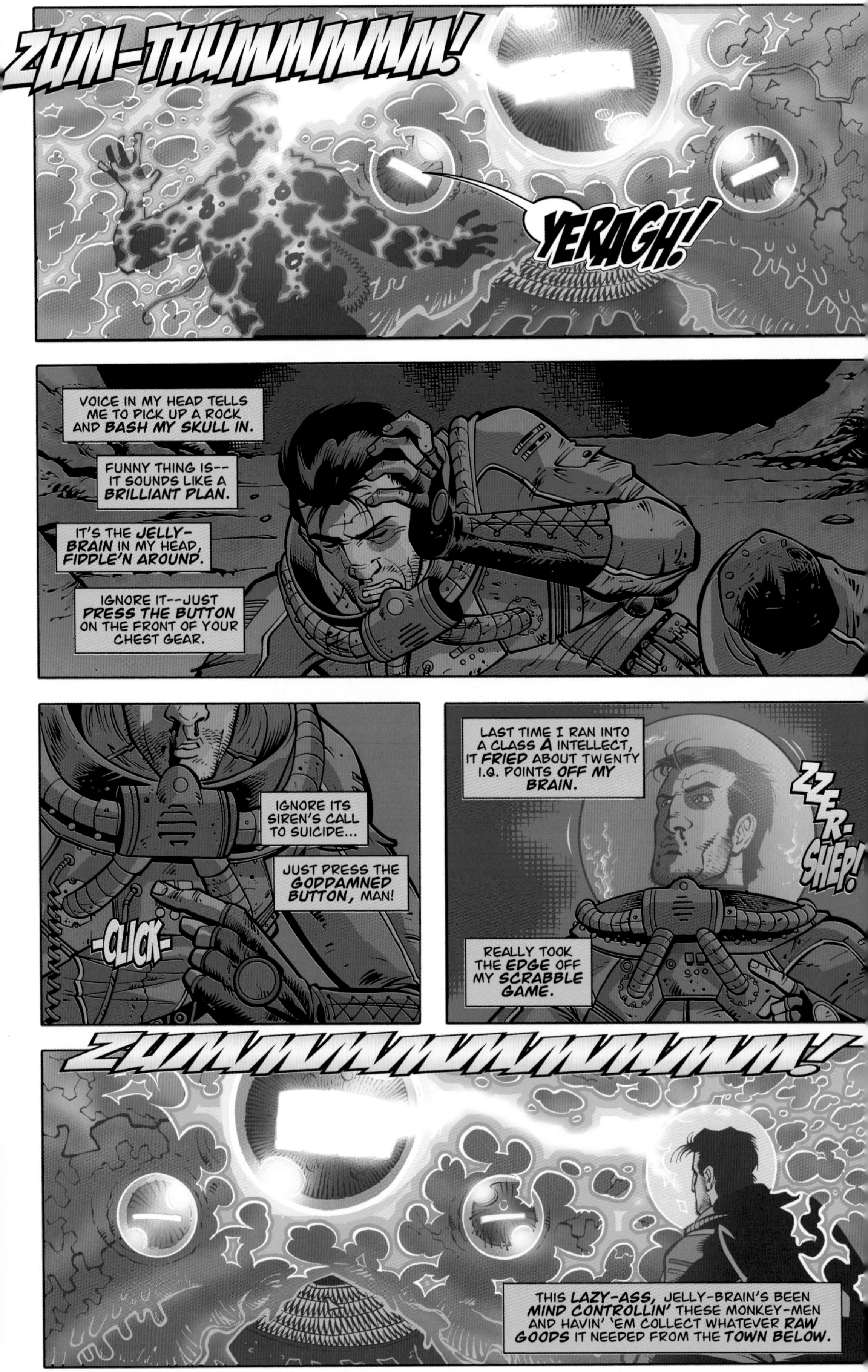
ZUM-THUMMMMMM!
YERAGH!
VOICE IN MY HEAD TELLS ME TO PICK UP A ROCK AND BASH MY SKULL IN.
FUNNY THING IS-- IT SOUNDS LIKE A BRILLIANT PLAN.
IT'S THE JELLY-BRAIN IN MY HEAD, FIDDLE'N AROUND.
IGNORE IT--JUST PRESS THE BUTTON ON THE FRONT OF YOUR CHEST GEAR.
IGNORE ITS SIREN'S CALL TO SUICIDE...
JUST PRESS THE GODDAMNED BUTTON, MAN!
-CLICK-
LAST TIME I RAN INTO A CLASS A INTELLECT, IT FRIED ABOUT TWENTY I.Q. POINTS OFF MY BRAIN.
ZZER-SHEP!
REALLY TOOK THE EDGE OFF MY SCRABBLE GAME.
ZUMMMMMMMMMMM!
THIS LAZY-ASS, JELLY-BRAIN'S BEEN MIND CONTROLLIN' THESE MONKEY-MEN AND HAVIN' 'EM COLLECT WHATEVER RAW GOODS IT NEEDED FROM THE TOWN BELOW.

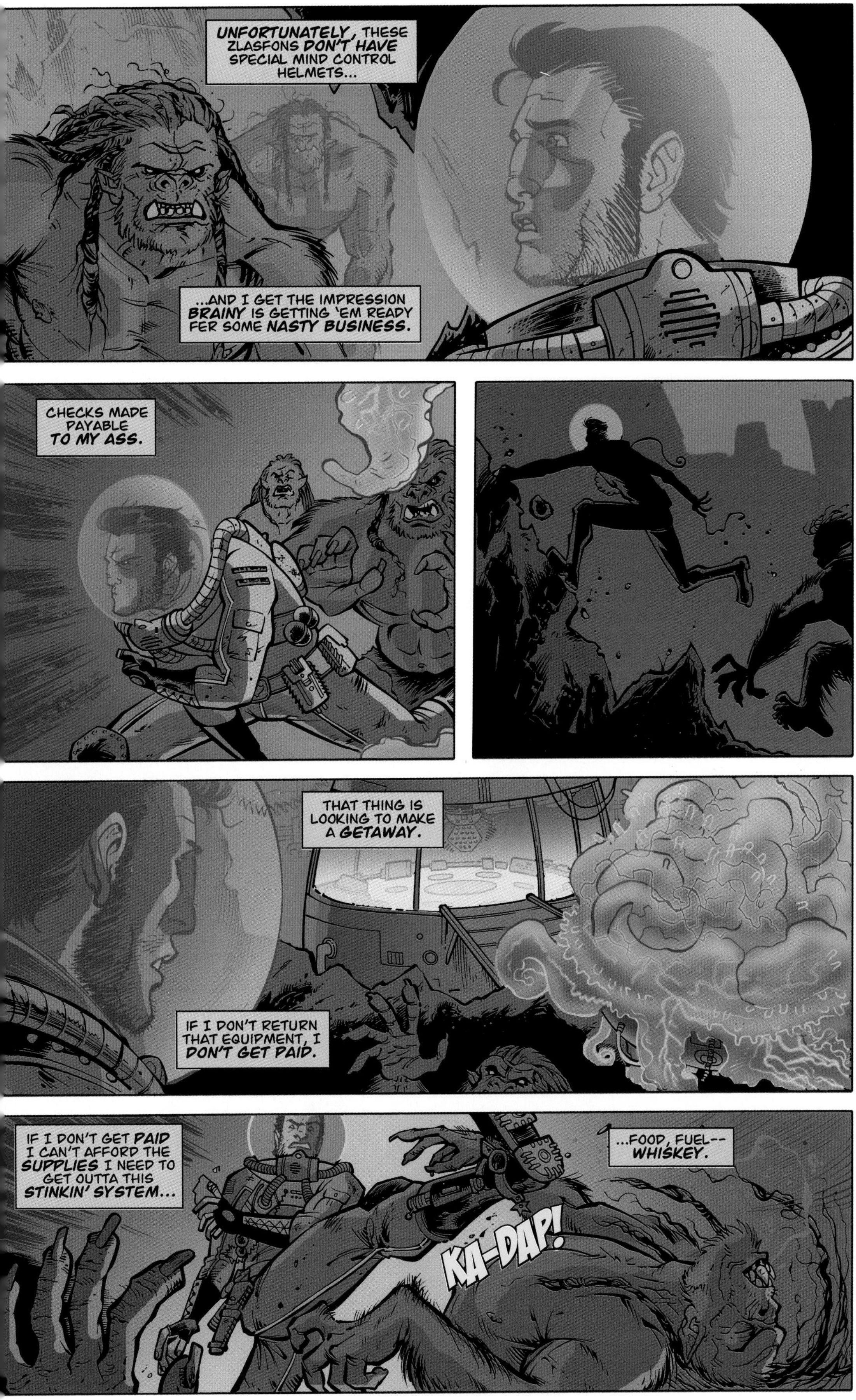
UNFORTUNATELY, THESE ZLASFONS DON'T HAVE SPECIAL MIND CONTROL HELMETS...
...AND I GET THE IMPRESSION BRAINY IS GETTING 'EM READY FER SOME NASTY BUSINESS.
CHECKS MADE PAYABLE TO MY ASS.
THAT THING IS LOOKING TO MAKE A GETAWAY.
IF I DON'T RETURN THAT EQUIPMENT, I DON'T GET PAID.
IF I DON'T GET PAID I CAN'T AFFORD THE SUPPLIES I NEED TO GET OUTTA THIS STINKIN' SYSTEM...
...FOOD, FUEL-- WHISKEY.
KA-DAP!

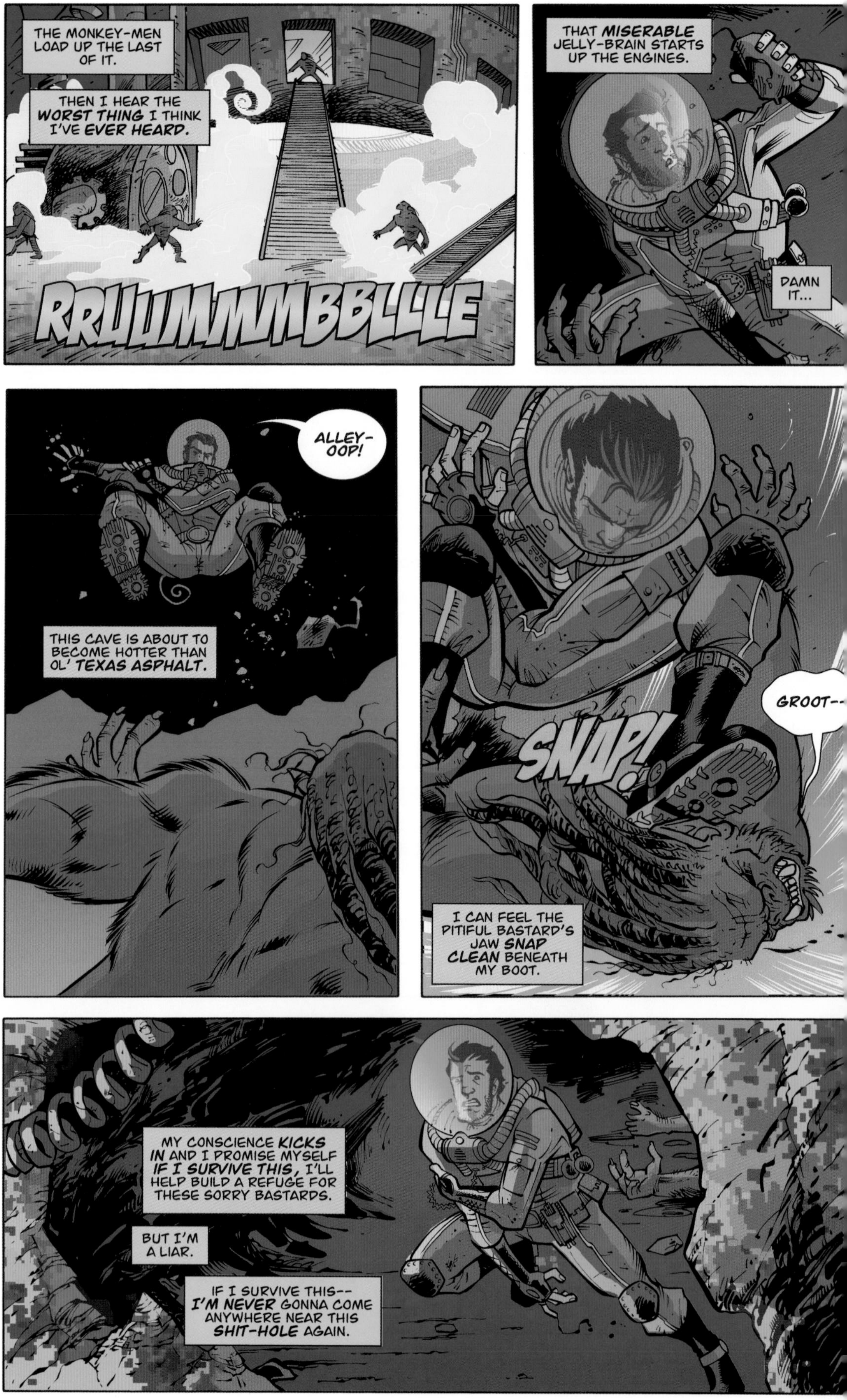
THE MONKEY-MEN LOAD UP THE LAST OF IT.
THEN I HEAR THE WORST THING I THINK I'VE EVER HEARD.
RRUUMMMMBBLLLE
THAT MISERABLE JELLY-BRAIN STARTS UP THE ENGINES.
DAMN IT...
ALLEY-OOP!
THIS CAVE IS ABOUT TO BECOME HOTTER THAN OL' TEXAS ASPHALT.
GROOT--
SNAP!
I CAN FEEL THE PITIFUL BASTARD'S JAW SNAP CLEAN BENEATH MY BOOT.
MY CONSCIENCE KICKS IN AND I PROMISE MYSELF IF I SURVIVE THIS, I'LL HELP BUILD A REFUGE FOR THESE SORRY BASTARDS.
BUT I'M A LIAR.
IF I SURVIVE THIS-- I'M NEVER GONNA COME ANYWHERE NEAR THIS SHIT-HOLE AGAIN.

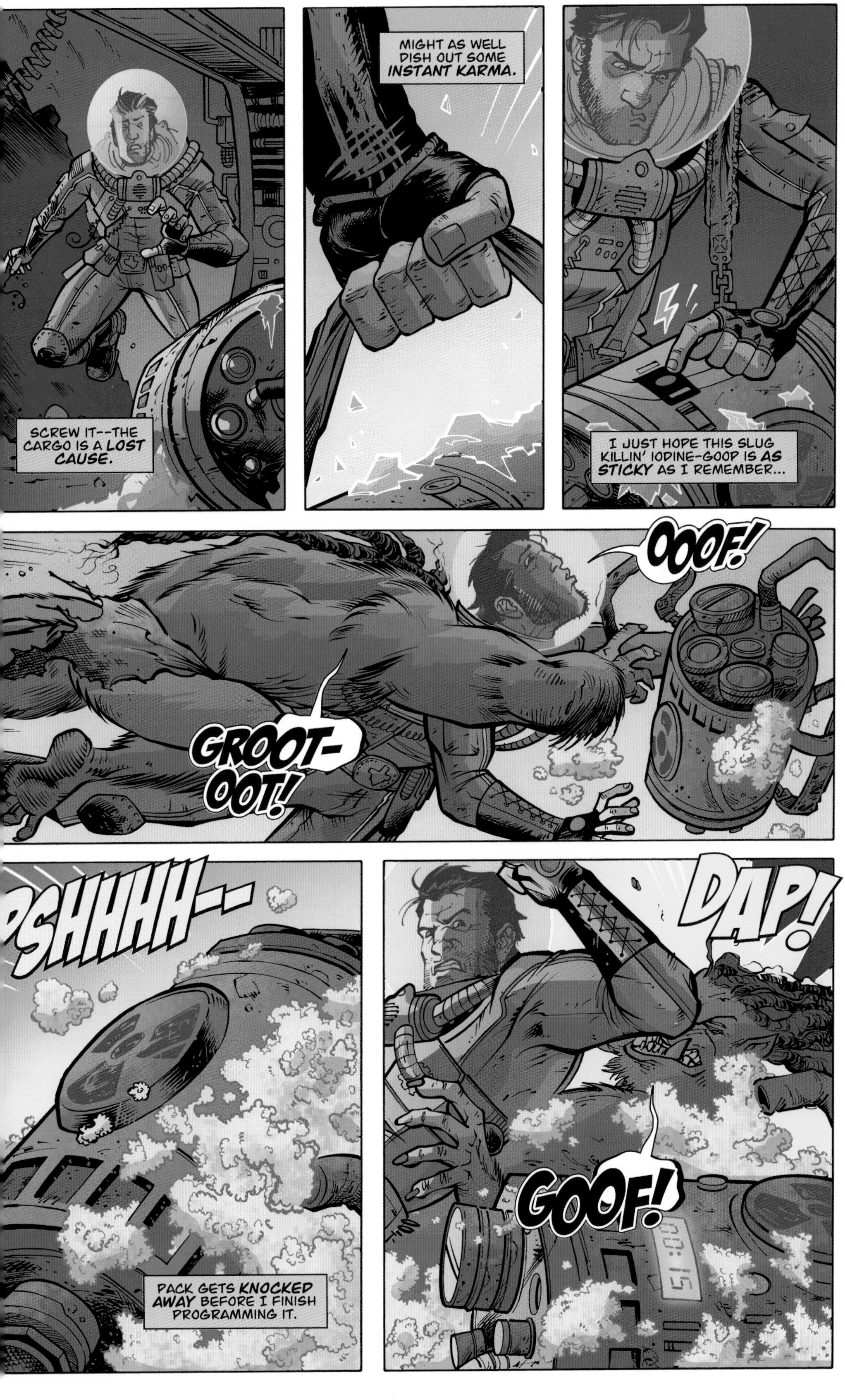
SCREW IT--THE CARGO IS A LOST CAUSE.
MIGHT AS WELL DISH OUT SOME INSTANT KARMA.
I JUST HOPE THIS SLUG KILLIN' IODINE-GOOP IS AS STICKY AS I REMEMBER...
OOOF!
GROOT-OOT!
PSHHHH--
PACK GETS KNOCKED AWAY BEFORE I FINISH PROGRAMMING IT.
DAP!
GOOF!
00:15

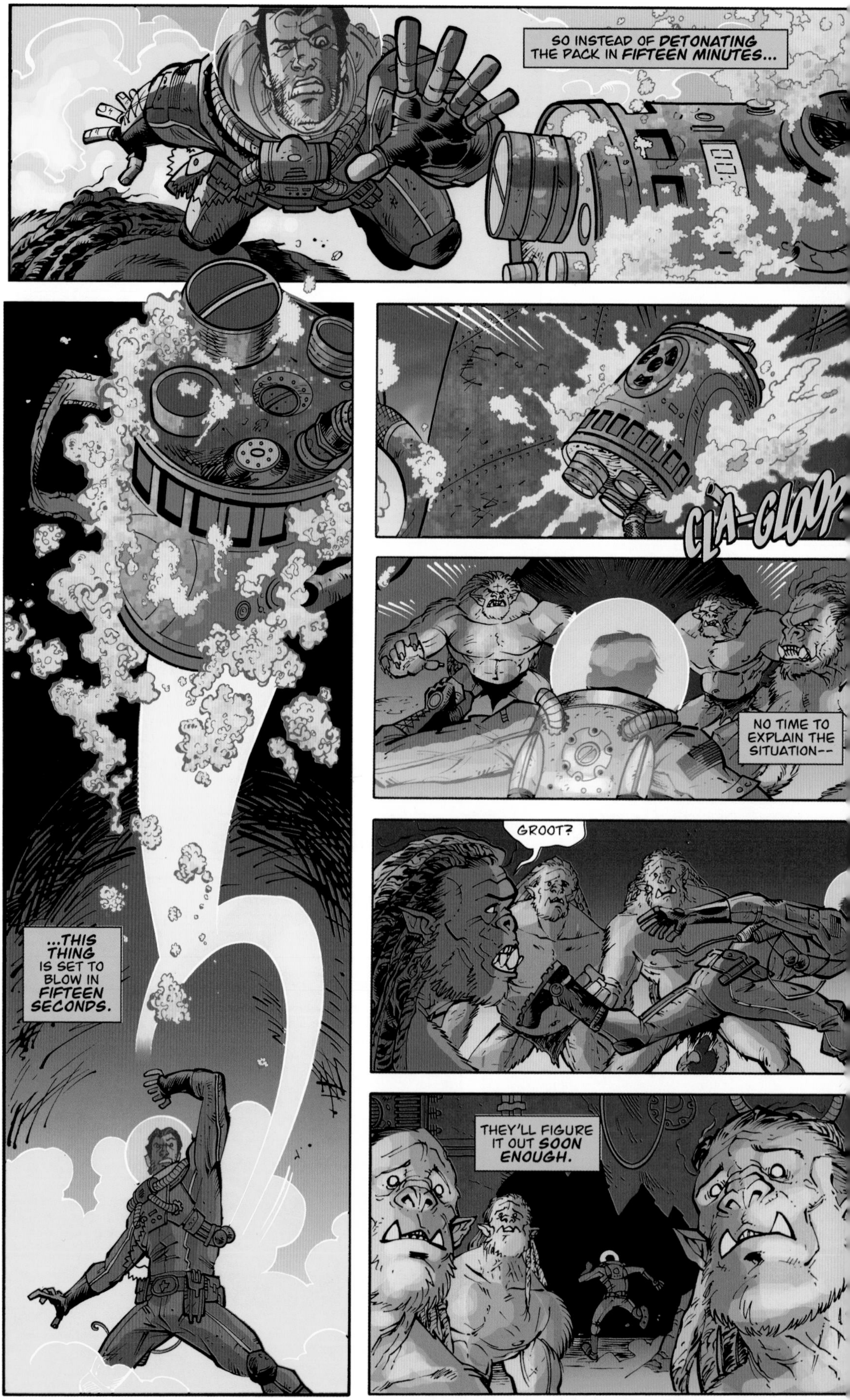
SO INSTEAD OF DETONATING THE PACK IN FIFTEEN MINUTES...
...THIS THING IS SET TO BLOW IN FIFTEEN SECONDS.
CLA-GLOOP
NO TIME TO EXPLAIN THE SITUATION--
GROOT?
THEY'LL FIGURE IT OUT SOON ENOUGH.

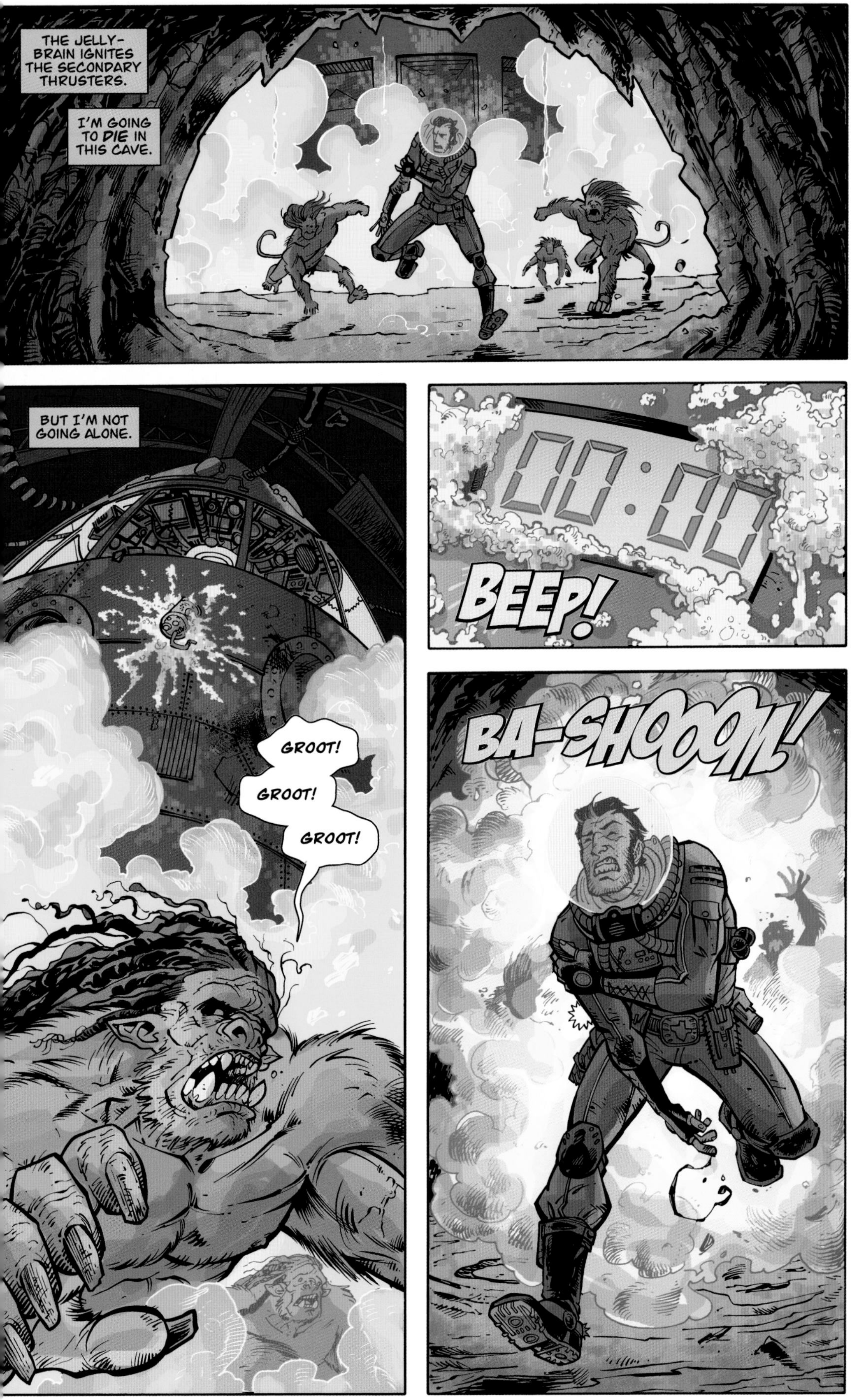
THE JELLY-BRAIN IGNITES THE SECONDARY THRUSTERS.
I'M GOING TO DIE IN THIS CAVE.
BUT I'M NOT GOING ALONE.
GROOT!
GROOT!
GROOT!
00:00
BEEP!
BA-SHOOOM!

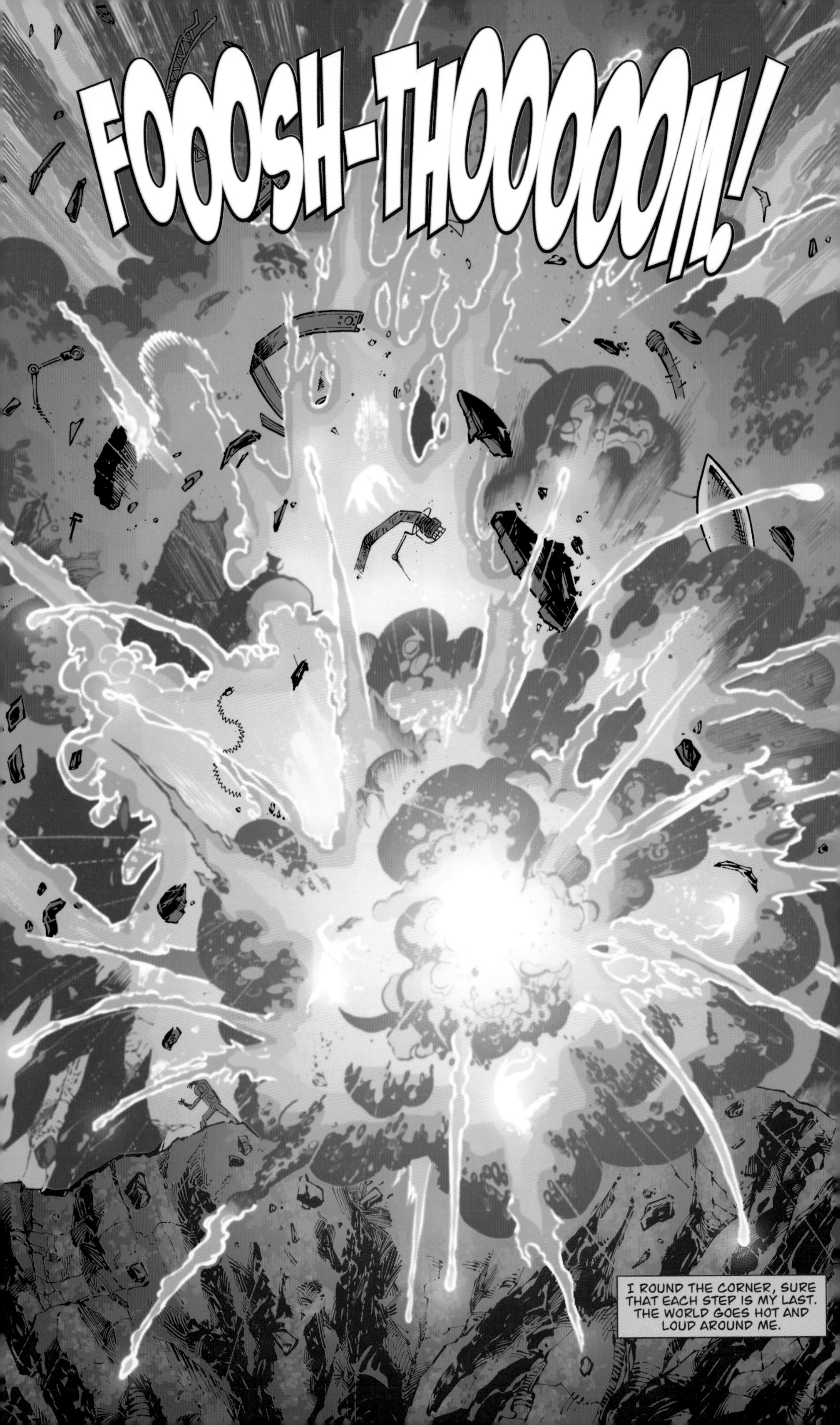
FOOOSH-THOOOOOM!
I ROUND THE CORNER, SURE THAT EACH STEP IS MY LAST. THE WORLD GOES HOT AND LOUD AROUND ME.

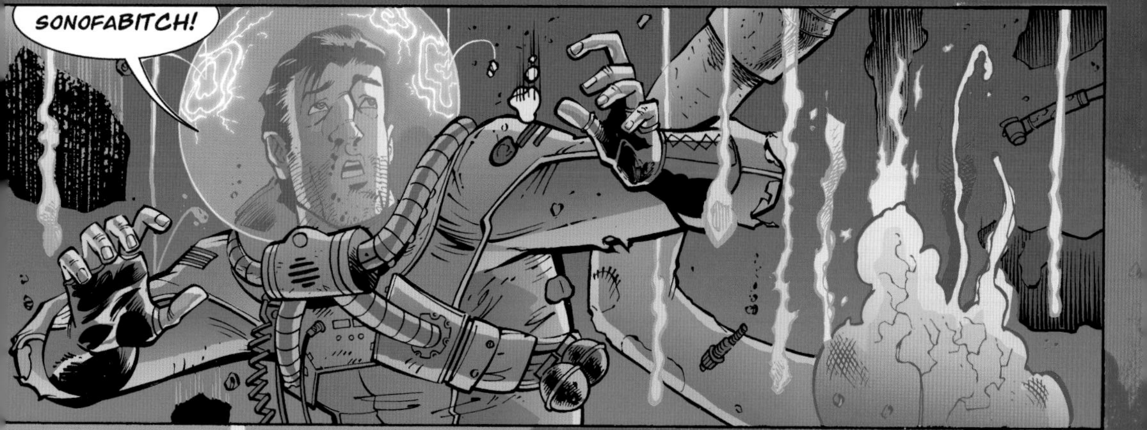
SONOFABITCH!

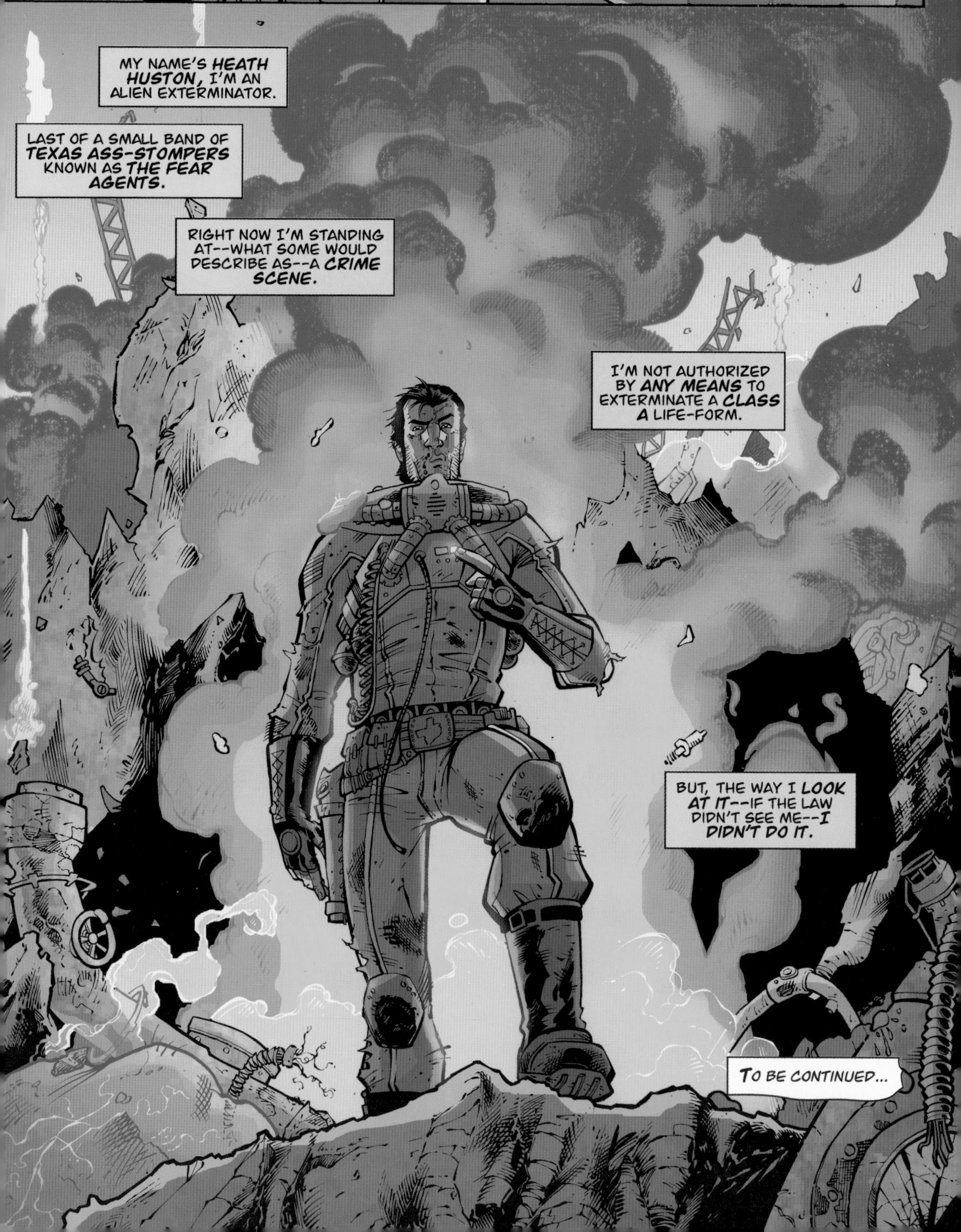
MY NAME'S HEATH HUSTON, I'M AN ALIEN EXTERMINATOR.
LAST OF A SMALL BAND OF TEXAS ASS-STOMPERS KNOWN AS THE FEAR AGENTS.
RIGHT NOW I'M STANDING AT--WHAT SOME WOULD DESCRIBE AS--A CRIME SCENE.
I'M NOT AUTHORIZED BY ANY MEANS TO EXTERMINATE A CLASS A LIFE-FORM.
BUT, THE WAY I LOOK AT IT--IF THE LAW DIDN'T SEE ME--I DIDN'T DO IT.
TO BE CONTINUED...

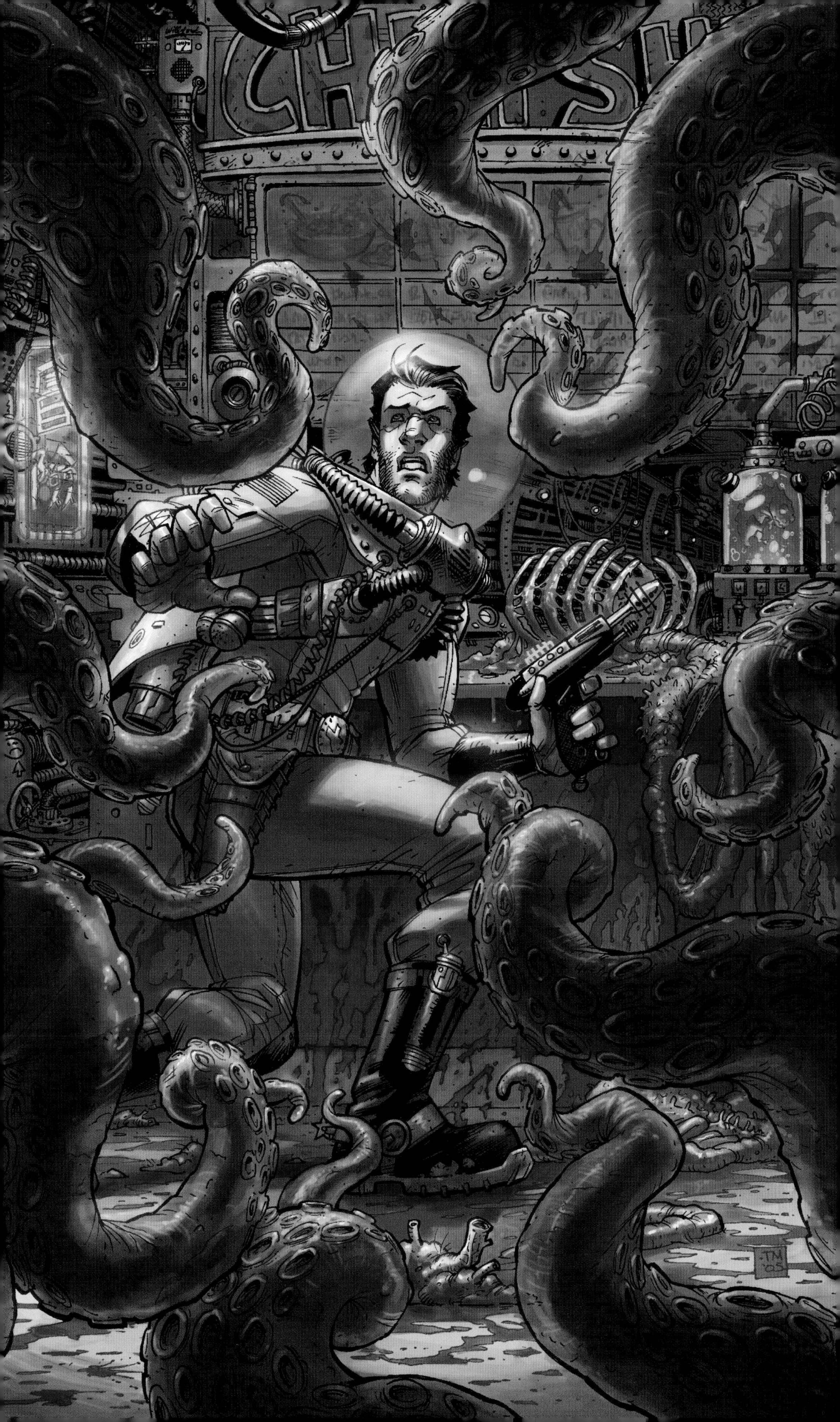

RE-IGNITION CHAPTER 2

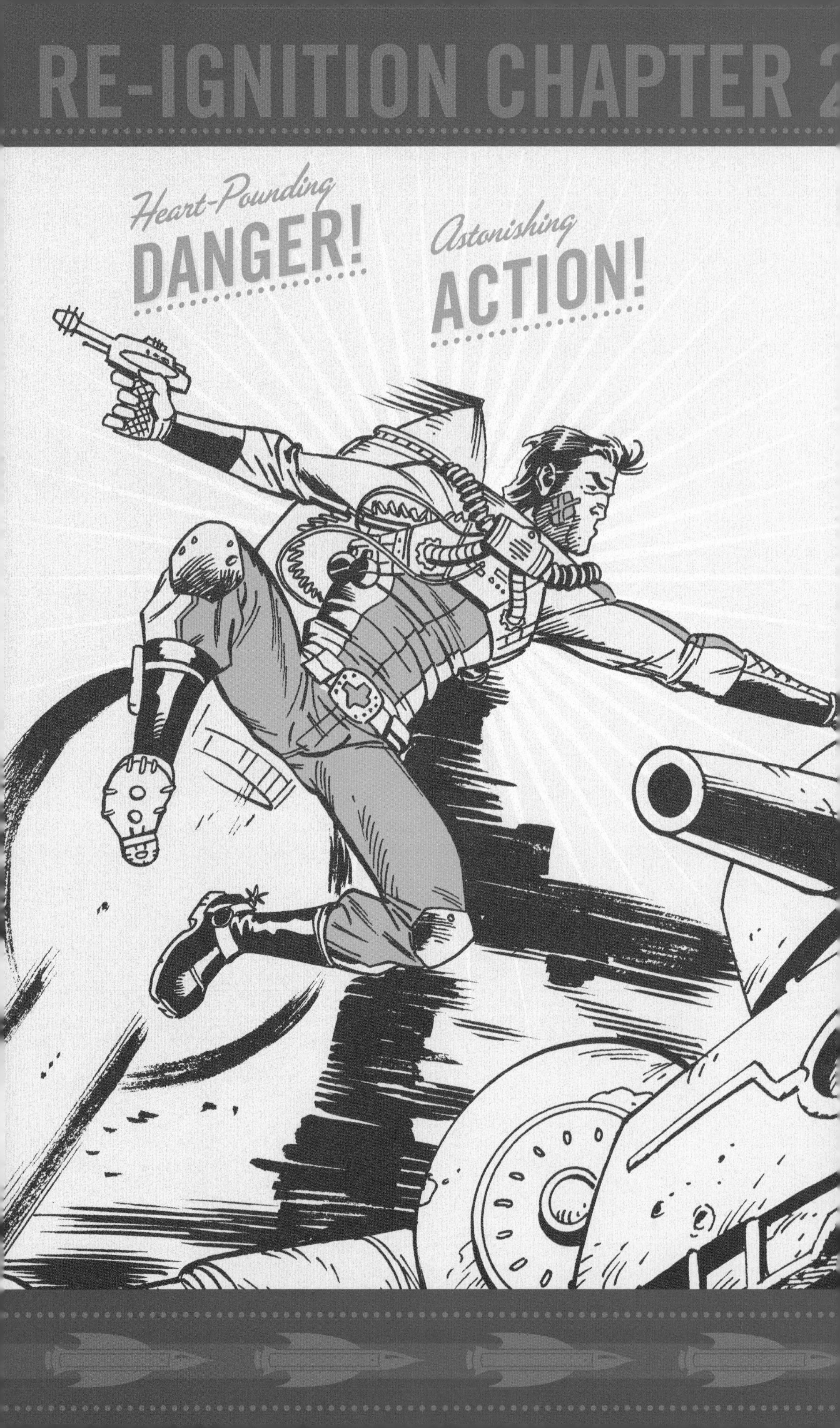
Heart-Pounding
DANGER!
Astonishing
ACTION!

Huston Extermination
000-238775-93429 on the zelta line

Have alien pests invaded your settlement or space craft?
Heath Huston is a veteran of the annubius conflict and has over twenty years' experience with thermal pest eradication

What we do for you:

- ☒ Send a highly trained Service Technician
- ☒ Stay up-to-date in entomology and pest control science
- ☒ Inspect thoroughly to identify the pest and the source of infestation
- ☒ Respond promptly with customized treatment and prevention recommendations
- ☒ Provide related extra service at no extra charge
- ☒ Guarantee results
- ☒ Zlasfon taraform job
- ☒ Canister of Freonium
- ☒ Supply pack
- ☒ Other worldly lifeform extermination
- ☒ Time 4½ hours
- ☒ Time and a half for full infe...

LET'S SEE HERE... FOUR HOURS LABOR, A FULL CANISTER OF MULTI-PURPOSE PESTICIDE, TIME AND A HALF FOR THE JELLYBRAIN I FOUND UP THERE...

YOU'RE INTO ME FOR ABOUT FORTY-THREE HUNDRED UNI-CREDS.

YOU BLOW UP THESE MONKEYS' NESTING CAVERN, SENDING THEM FLOODING INTO OUR CITY ON A *PANICKED RAMPAGE*...

...AND YOU WANT ME-- *TO PAY YOU?!?*

HMMM...

TELL YA WHAT-- I'M GUNNA TAKE *THIRTY PERCENT* OFF THAT FREONIUM.

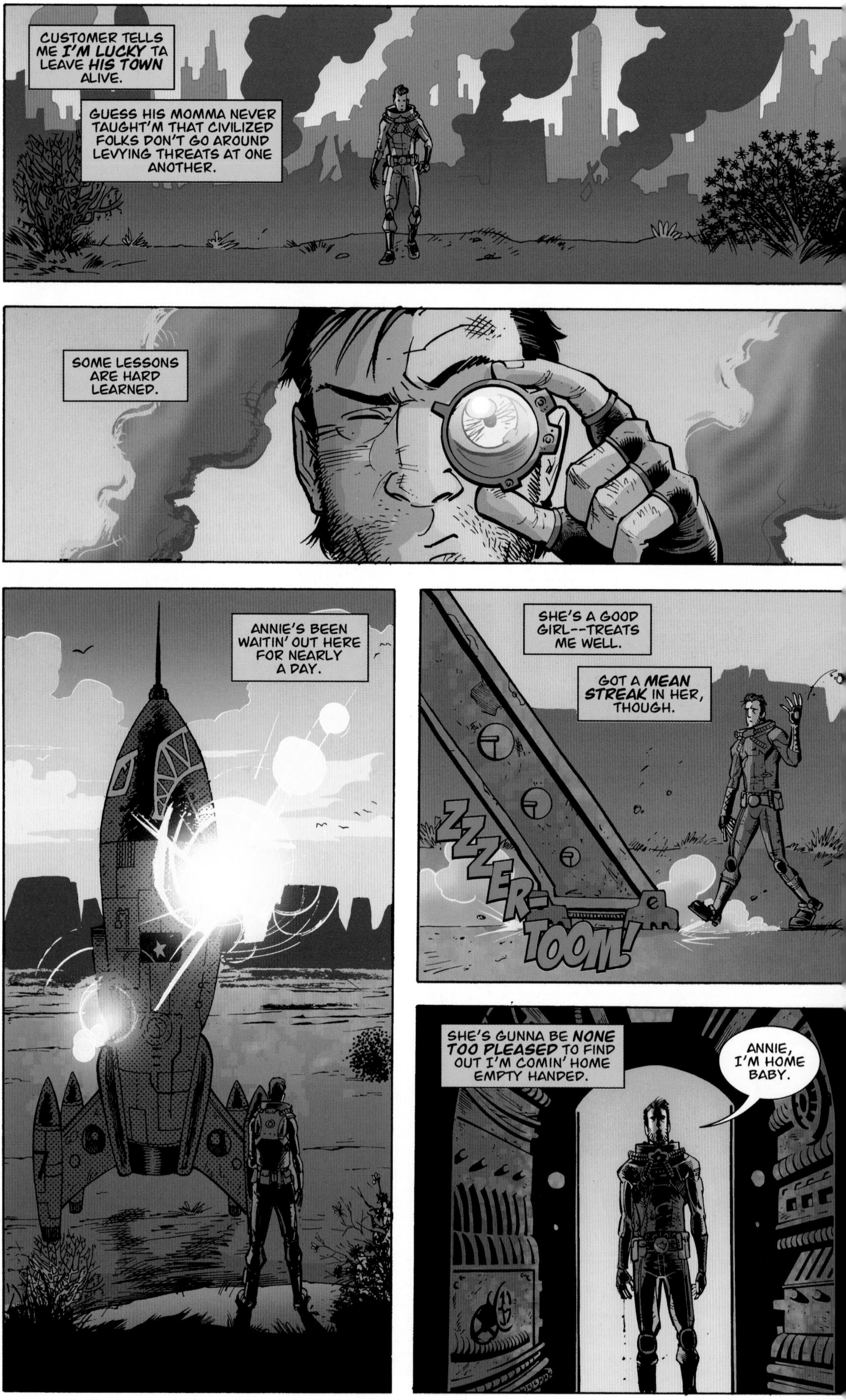
CUSTOMER TELLS ME I'M LUCKY TA LEAVE HIS TOWN ALIVE.
GUESS HIS MOMMA NEVER TAUGHT'M THAT CIVILIZED FOLKS DON'T GO AROUND LEVYING THREATS AT ONE ANOTHER.
SOME LESSONS ARE HARD LEARNED.
ANNIE'S BEEN WAITIN' OUT HERE FOR NEARLY A DAY.
SHE'S A GOOD GIRL--TREATS ME WELL.
GOT A MEAN STREAK IN HER, THOUGH.
ZZZER-TOOM!
SHE'S GUNNA BE NONE TOO PLEASED TO FIND OUT I'M COMIN' HOME EMPTY HANDED.
ANNIE, I'M HOME BABY.

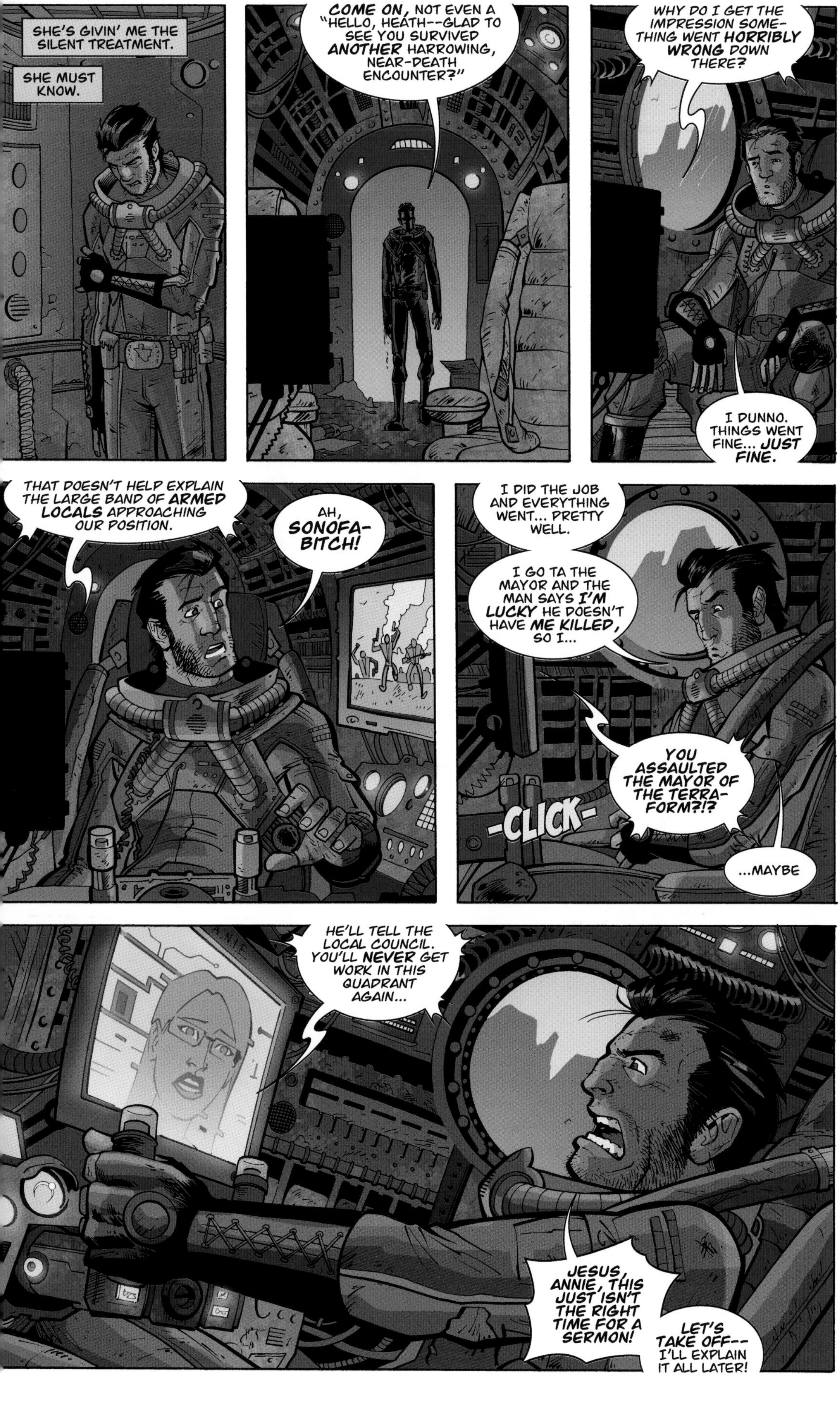
SHE'S GIVIN' ME THE SILENT TREATMENT.
SHE MUST KNOW.
COME ON, NOT EVEN A "HELLO, HEATH--GLAD TO SEE YOU SURVIVED ANOTHER HARROWING, NEAR-DEATH ENCOUNTER?"
WHY DO I GET THE IMPRESSION SOMETHING WENT HORRIBLY WRONG DOWN THERE?
I DUNNO. THINGS WENT FINE... JUST FINE.
THAT DOESN'T HELP EXPLAIN THE LARGE BAND OF ARMED LOCALS APPROACHING OUR POSITION.
AH, SONOFA-BITCH!
I DID THE JOB AND EVERYTHING WENT... PRETTY WELL.
I GO TA THE MAYOR AND THE MAN SAYS I'M LUCKY HE DOESN'T HAVE ME KILLED, SO I...
-CLICK-
YOU ASSAULTED THE MAYOR OF THE TERRA-FORM?!?
...MAYBE
HE'LL TELL THE LOCAL COUNCIL. YOU'LL NEVER GET WORK IN THIS QUADRANT AGAIN...
JESUS, ANNIE, THIS JUST ISN'T THE RIGHT TIME FOR A SERMON!
LET'S TAKE OFF-- I'LL EXPLAIN IT ALL LATER!

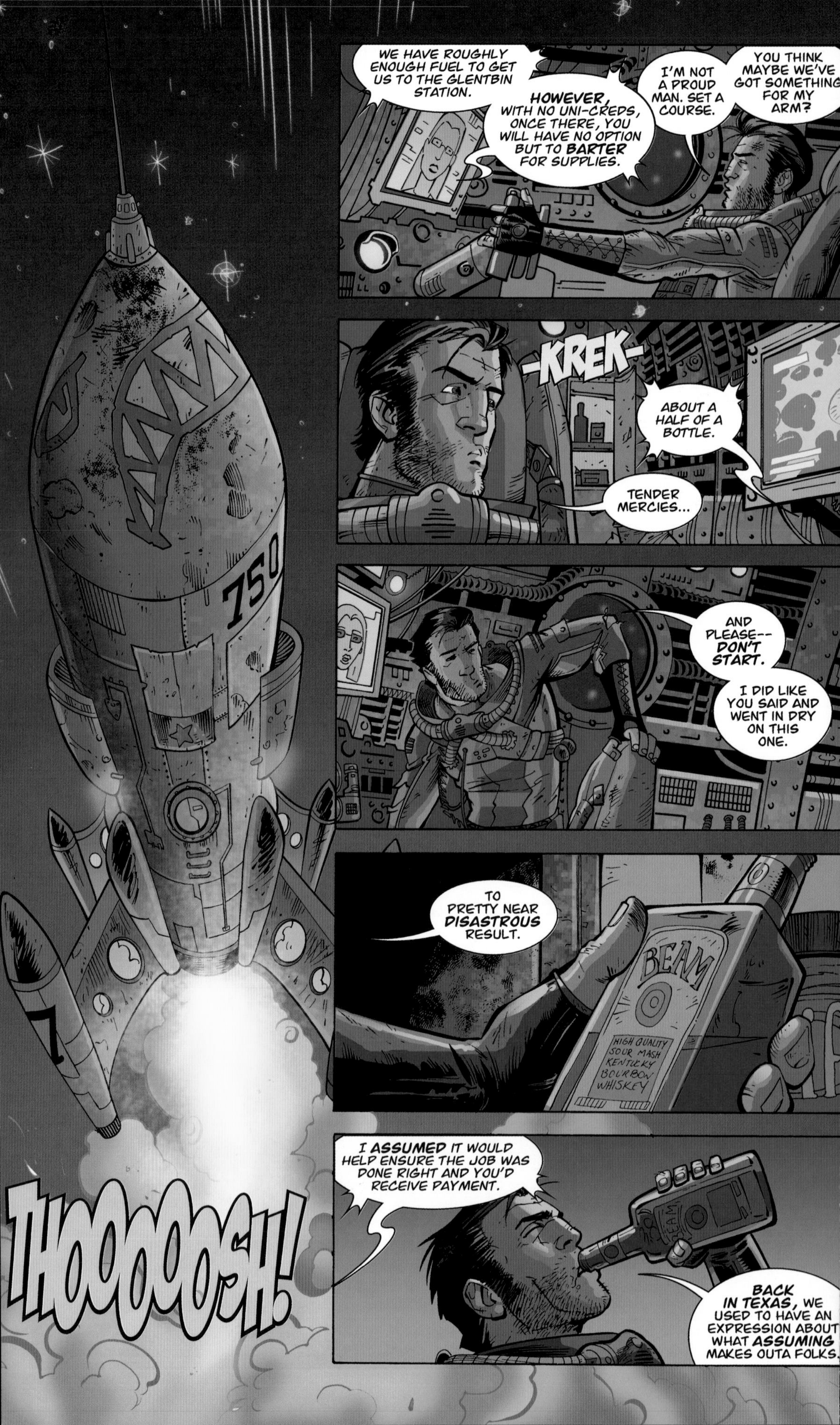
WE HAVE ROUGHLY ENOUGH FUEL TO GET US TO THE GLENTBIN STATION.
HOWEVER, WITH NO UNI-CREDS, ONCE THERE, YOU WILL HAVE NO OPTION BUT TO BARTER FOR SUPPLIES.
I'M NOT A PROUD MAN. SET A COURSE.
YOU THINK MAYBE WE'VE GOT SOMETHING FOR MY ARM?
-KREK-
ABOUT A HALF OF A BOTTLE.
TENDER MERCIES...
AND PLEASE-- DON'T START.
I DID LIKE YOU SAID AND WENT IN DRY ON THIS ONE.
TO PRETTY NEAR DISASTROUS RESULT.
BEAM
HIGH QUALITY SOUR MASH KENTUCKY BOURBON WHISKEY
I ASSUMED IT WOULD HELP ENSURE THE JOB WAS DONE RIGHT AND YOU'D RECEIVE PAYMENT.
BACK IN TEXAS, WE USED TO HAVE AN EXPRESSION ABOUT WHAT ASSUMING MAKES OUTA FOLKS.
750
THOOOOOSH!

THIS GIG DIDN'T GO AWRY ON ACOUNT OF ANY SCREW-UP BY ME, ANYHOW.

THERE WAS A *JELLY-BRAIN* DOWN THERE CONTROL-LING THOSE ZLASFONS.

AWWW? *WHAT THE DEUCE!*

WHERE'D ALL MY PEANUT BUT-TER GET TO?

YOU ATE IT.

WHEN I WAS A BOY, THE SCI-FI SHOWS WERE MY FAVORITE.

I REMEMBER IN ONE SHOW THEY HAD THESE MACHINES THAT WOULD SYNTHESIZE ANY OL' FOOD A MAN ASKED FOR.

WELL, HERE IN REALITY THAT'S ALL *MINDLESS BULLSHIT.*

THERE AIN'T NO SUCH THING AS A *MAGIC FOOD MACHINE.*

FOOD, *ESPECIALLY HUMAN FOOD,* IS NEAR IMPOSSIBLE TO COME BY IN THE OUTER QUADS.

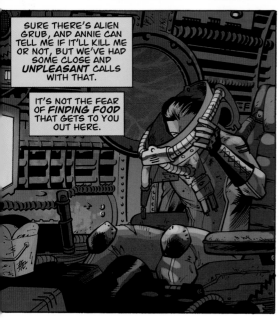

SURE THERE'S ALIEN GRUB, AND ANNIE CAN TELL ME IF IT'LL KILL ME OR NOT, BUT WE'VE HAD SOME CLOSE AND *UNPLEASANT* CALLS WITH THAT.

IT'S NOT THE FEAR OF *FINDING FOOD* THAT GETS TO YOU OUT HERE.

IT'S THE *FEAR ITSELF* THAT TURNS ON YA OUT HERE--IT TENDS TO GET *BURIED IN* LIKE A TICK.

OUT IN THE DEEP IT'S WORSE THAN *ANY* SOLITARY CONFINEMENT.

NO ONE'S GUNNA SHOW WITH A KEY OUT HERE.

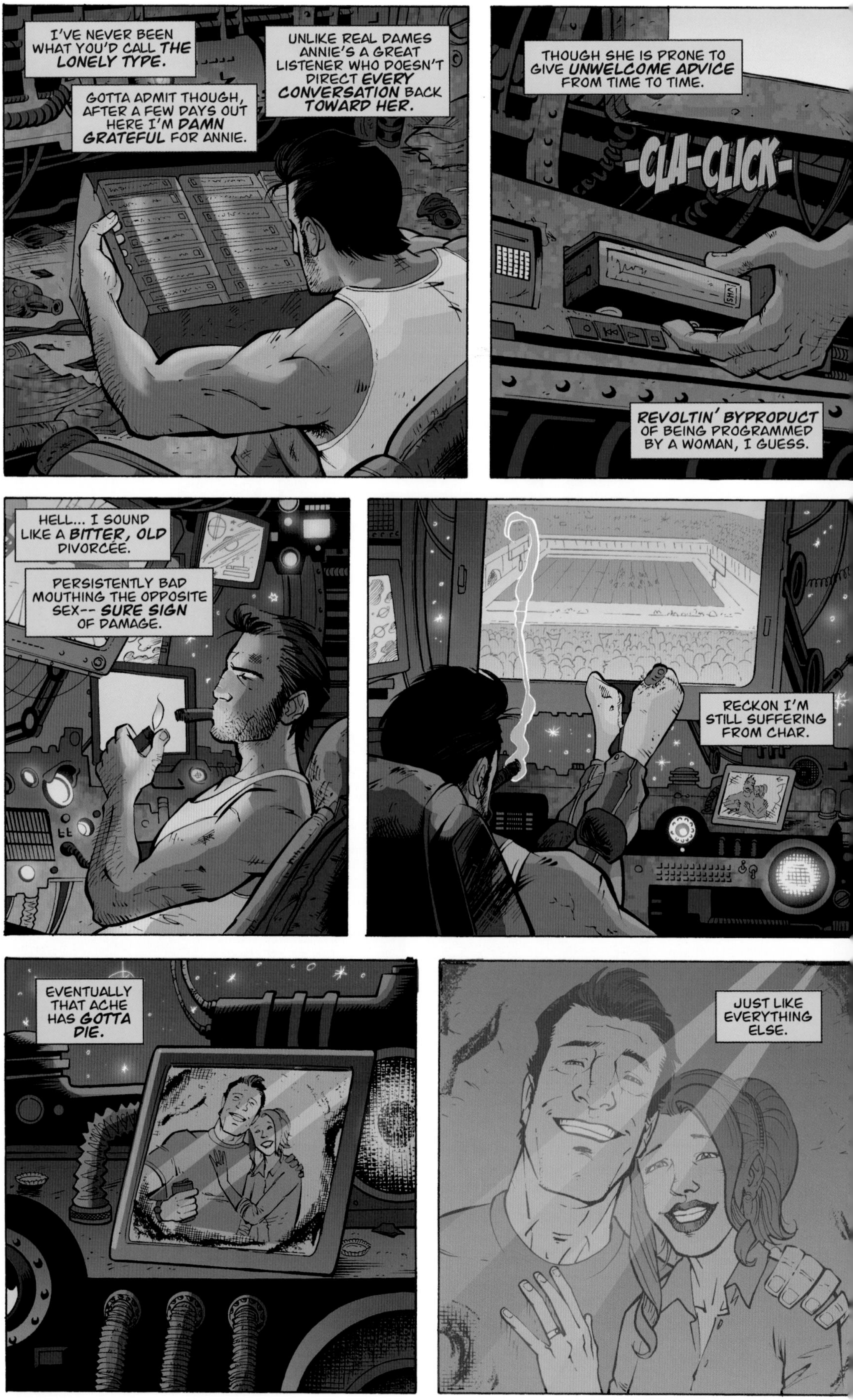
I'VE NEVER BEEN WHAT YOU'D CALL THE LONELY TYPE.
GOTTA ADMIT THOUGH, AFTER A FEW DAYS OUT HERE I'M DAMN GRATEFUL FOR ANNIE.
UNLIKE REAL DAMES ANNIE'S A GREAT LISTENER WHO DOESN'T DIRECT EVERY CONVERSATION BACK TOWARD HER.
THOUGH SHE IS PRONE TO GIVE UNWELCOME ADVICE FROM TIME TO TIME.
-CLA-CLICK-
REVOLTIN' BYPRODUCT OF BEING PROGRAMMED BY A WOMAN, I GUESS.
HELL... I SOUND LIKE A BITTER, OLD DIVORCÉE.
PERSISTENTLY BAD MOUTHING THE OPPOSITE SEX-- SURE SIGN OF DAMAGE.
RECKON I'M STILL SUFFERING FROM CHAR.
EVENTUALLY THAT ACHE HAS GOTTA DIE.
JUST LIKE EVERYTHING ELSE.

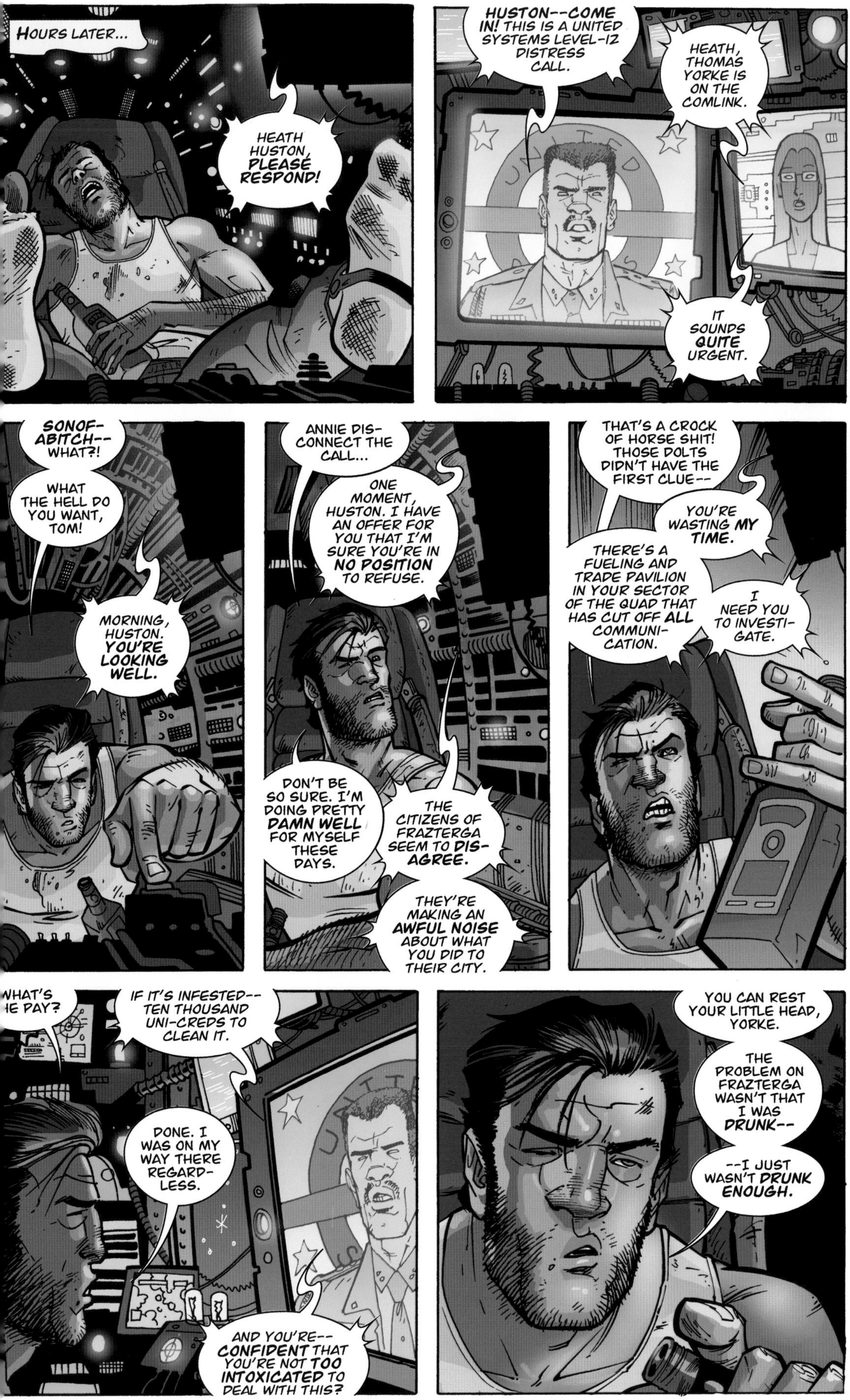
HOURS LATER...
HEATH HUSTON, PLEASE RESPOND!
HUSTON--COME IN! THIS IS A UNITED SYSTEMS LEVEL-12 DISTRESS CALL.
HEATH, THOMAS YORKE IS ON THE COMLINK.
IT SOUNDS QUITE URGENT.
SONOFABITCH--WHAT?!
WHAT THE HELL DO YOU WANT, TOM!
MORNING, HUSTON. YOU'RE LOOKING WELL.
ANNIE DISCONNECT THE CALL...
ONE MOMENT, HUSTON. I HAVE AN OFFER FOR YOU THAT I'M SURE YOU'RE IN NO POSITION TO REFUSE.
DON'T BE SO SURE. I'M DOING PRETTY DAMN WELL FOR MYSELF THESE DAYS.
THE CITIZENS OF FRAZTERGA SEEM TO DISAGREE.
THEY'RE MAKING AN AWFUL NOISE ABOUT WHAT YOU DID TO THEIR CITY.
THAT'S A CROCK OF HORSE SHIT! THOSE DOLTS DIDN'T HAVE THE FIRST CLUE--
YOU'RE WASTING MY TIME.
THERE'S A FUELING AND TRADE PAVILION IN YOUR SECTOR OF THE QUAD THAT HAS CUT OFF ALL COMMUNICATION.
I NEED YOU TO INVESTIGATE.
WHAT'S THE PAY?
IF IT'S INFESTED--TEN THOUSAND UNI-CREDS TO CLEAN IT.
DONE. I WAS ON MY WAY THERE REGARDLESS.
AND YOU'RE--CONFIDENT THAT YOU'RE NOT TOO INTOXICATED TO DEAL WITH THIS?
YOU CAN REST YOUR LITTLE HEAD, YORKE.
THE PROBLEM ON FRAZTERGA WASN'T THAT I WAS DRUNK--
--I JUST WASN'T DRUNK ENOUGH.

LATER...

READOUTS SHOW THERE TO BE ACTIVITY INSIDE BUT NO RADIO COMMUNI-CATIONS.

PERHAPS THIS IS A SYS-TEM-WIDE COM CRASH?

PERHAPS...

ONCE WE DOCK, STRAP INTO THE FUELING LINES AND LOAD UP.

-PSHHHHT-
CLANK!

I'M NOT TWO FEET FROM THE LINK TUBE--

--WHEN THE SMELL HITS ME.

BLORRGHA!

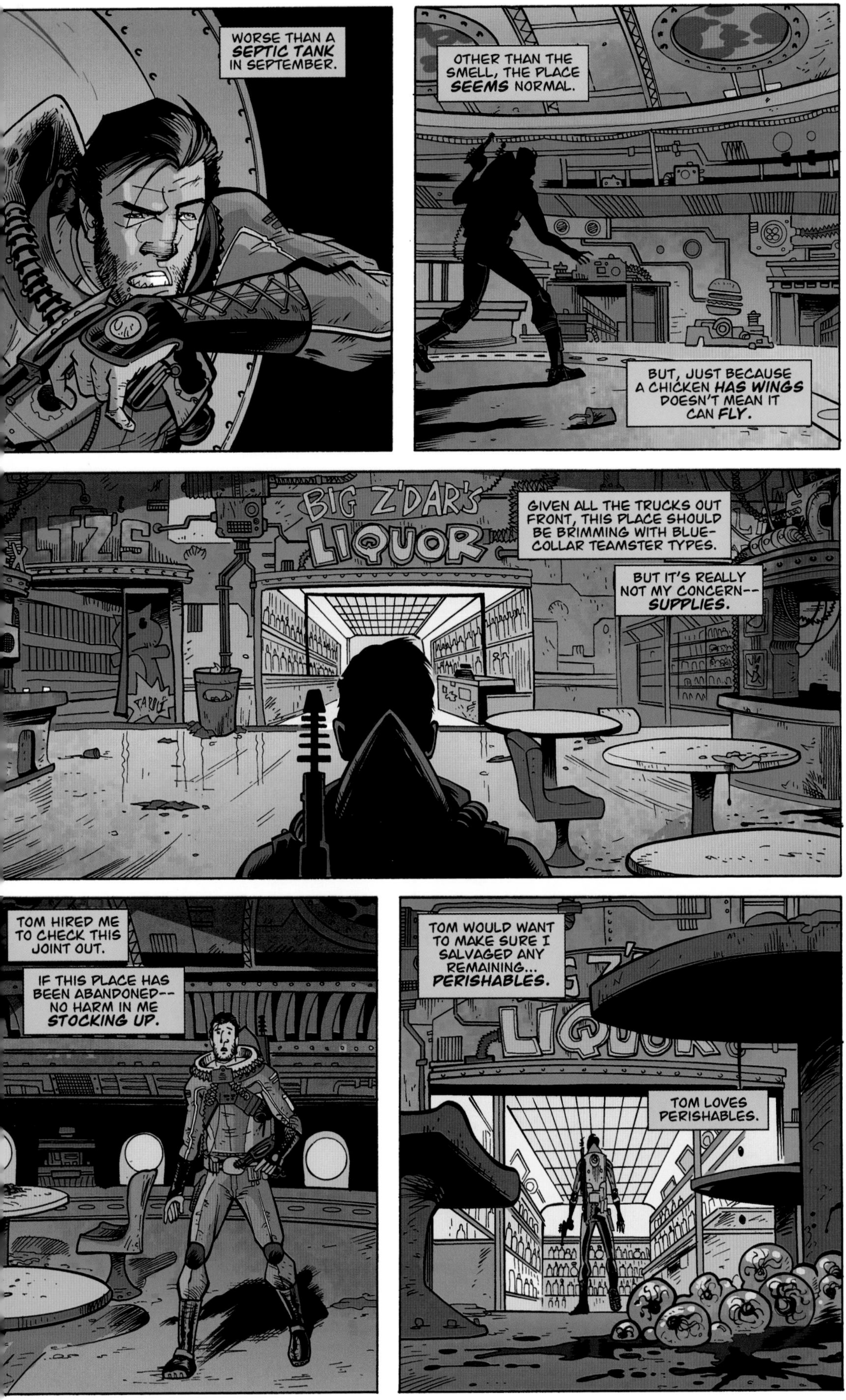
WORSE THAN A SEPTIC TANK IN SEPTEMBER.
OTHER THAN THE SMELL, THE PLACE SEEMS NORMAL.
BUT, JUST BECAUSE A CHICKEN HAS WINGS DOESN'T MEAN IT CAN FLY.
BIG Z'DAR'S LIQUOR
GIVEN ALL THE TRUCKS OUT FRONT, THIS PLACE SHOULD BE BRIMMING WITH BLUE-COLLAR TEAMSTER TYPES.
BUT IT'S REALLY NOT MY CONCERN-- SUPPLIES.
TOM HIRED ME TO CHECK THIS JOINT OUT.
IF THIS PLACE HAS BEEN ABANDONED-- NO HARM IN ME STOCKING UP.
TOM WOULD WANT TO MAKE SURE I SALVAGED ANY REMAINING... PERISHABLES.
TOM LOVES PERISHABLES.

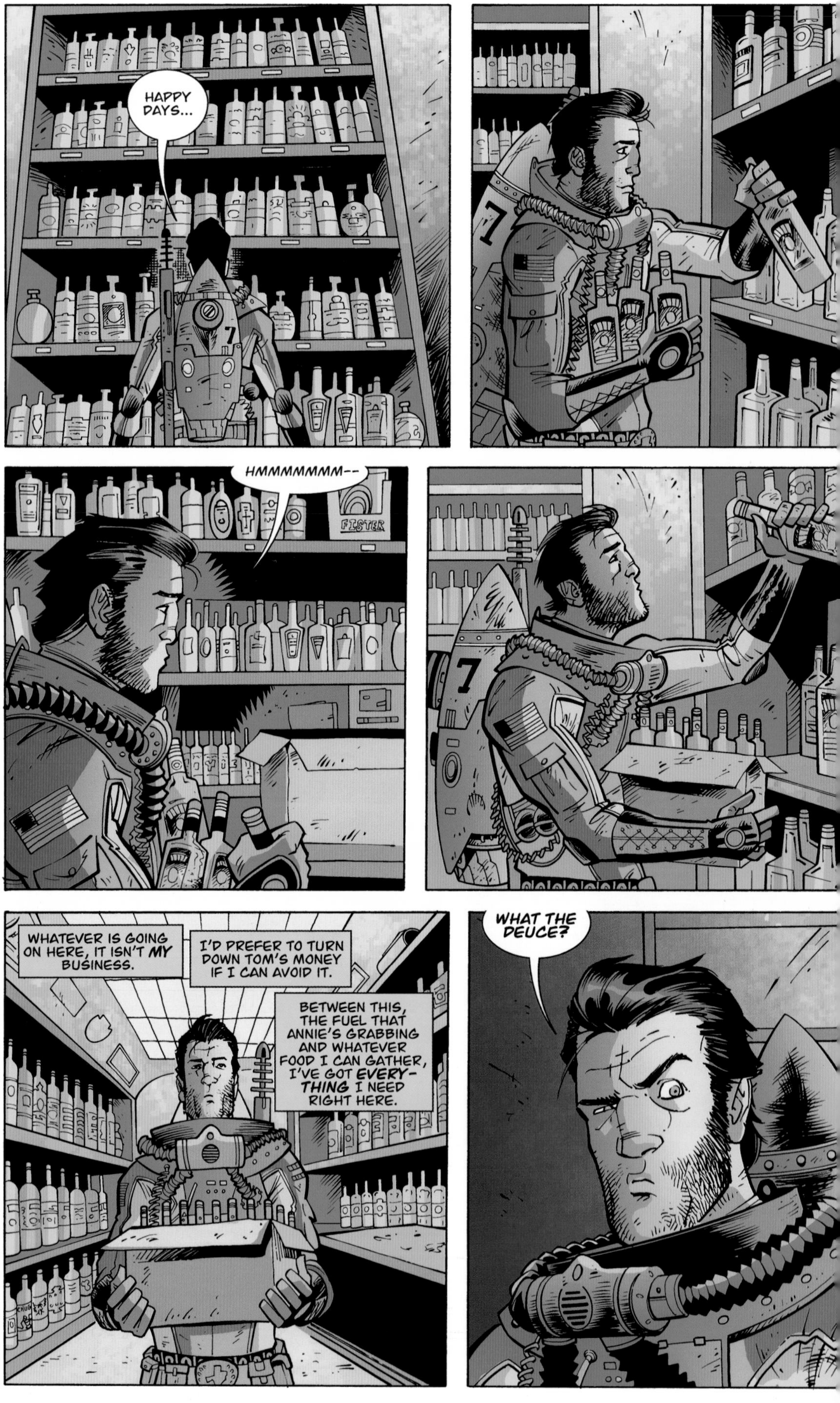
HAPPY DAYS...
HMMMMMMMM--
FISTER
WHATEVER IS GOING ON HERE, IT ISN'T MY BUSINESS.
I'D PREFER TO TURN DOWN TOM'S MONEY IF I CAN AVOID IT.
BETWEEN THIS, THE FUEL THAT ANNIE'S GRABBING AND WHATEVER FOOD I'VE GOT CAN GATHER, I'VE GOT EVERY-THING I NEED RIGHT HERE.
WHAT THE DEUCE?

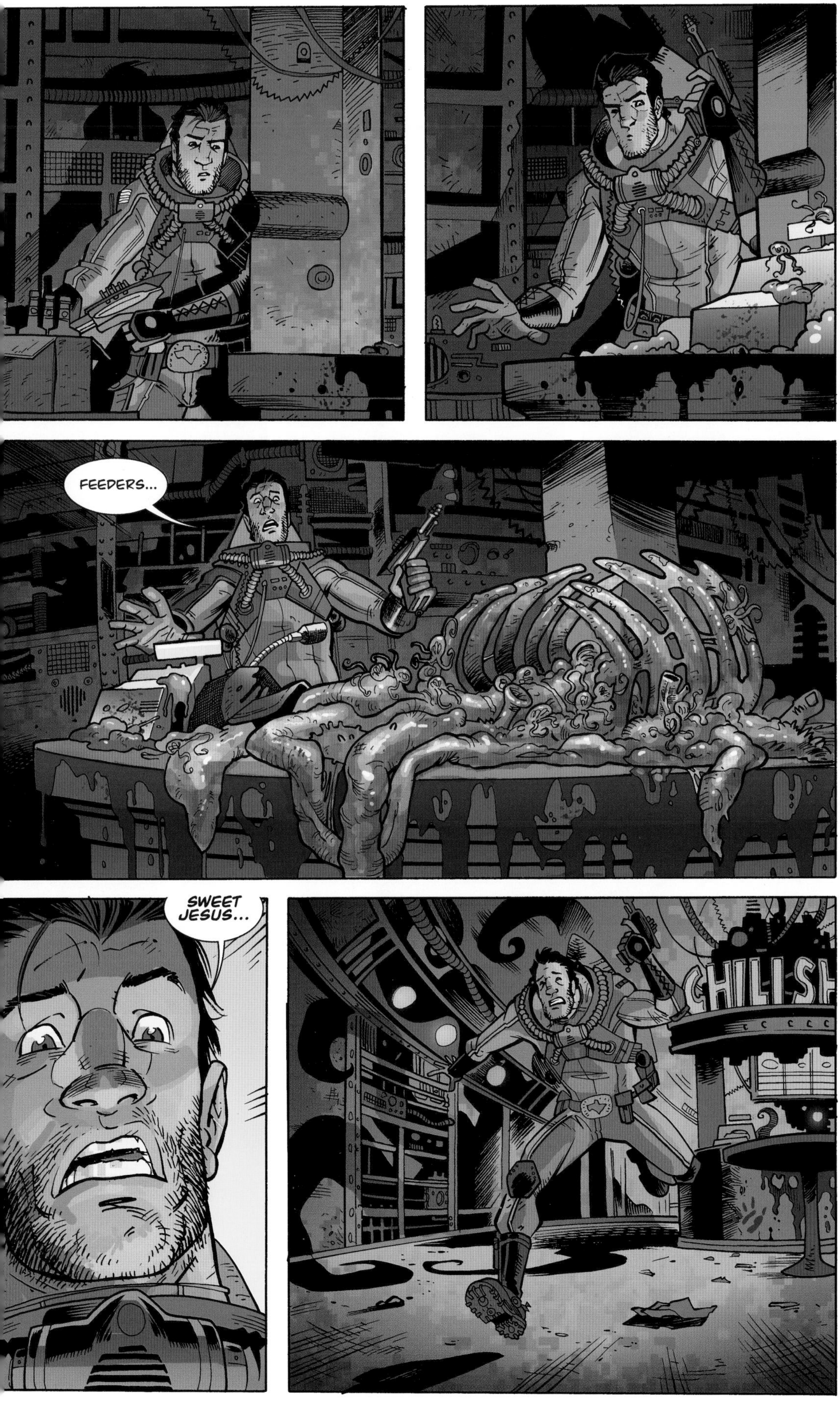
FEEDERS...
SWEET JESUS...
CHILI SH

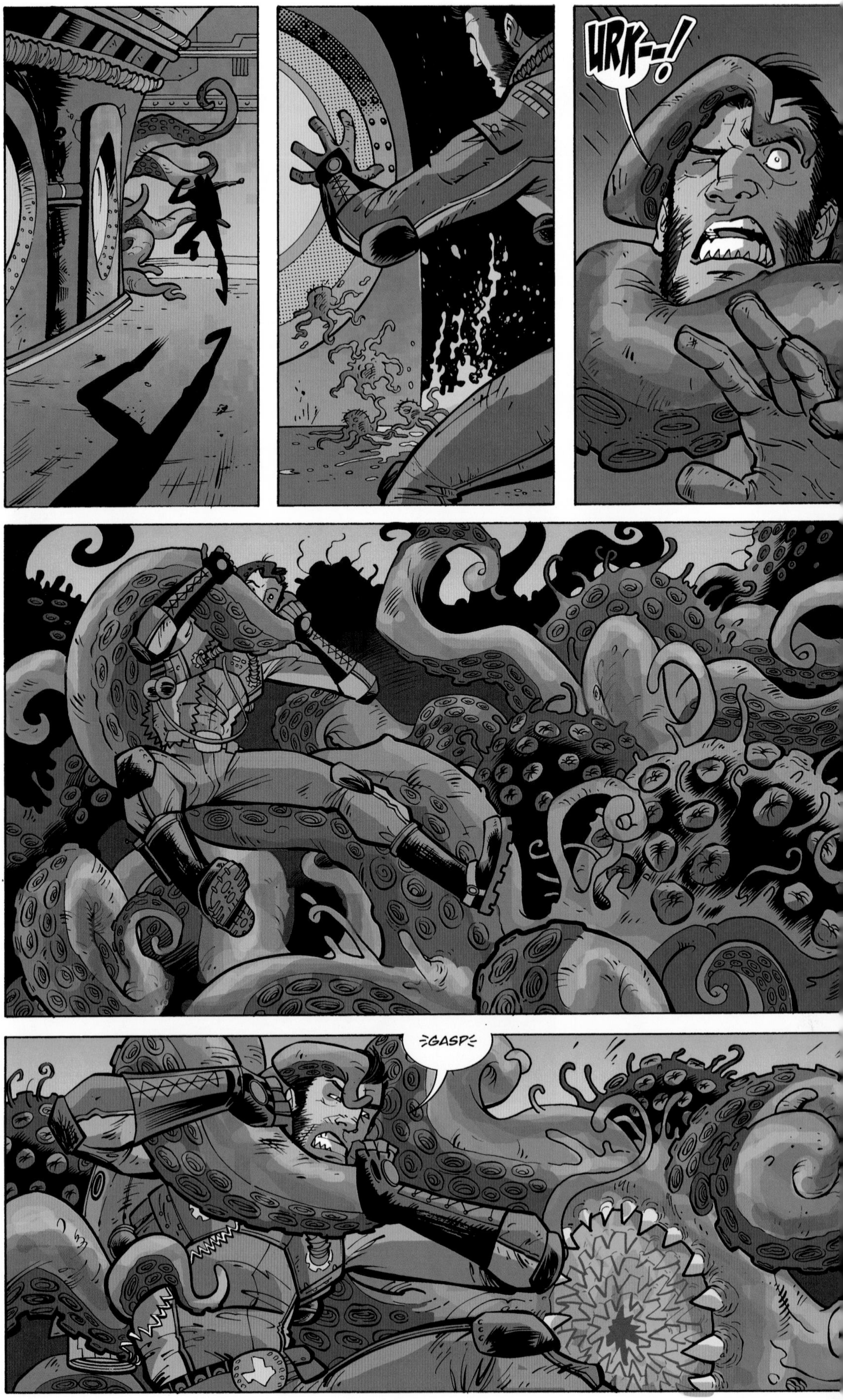
URK--!
GASP

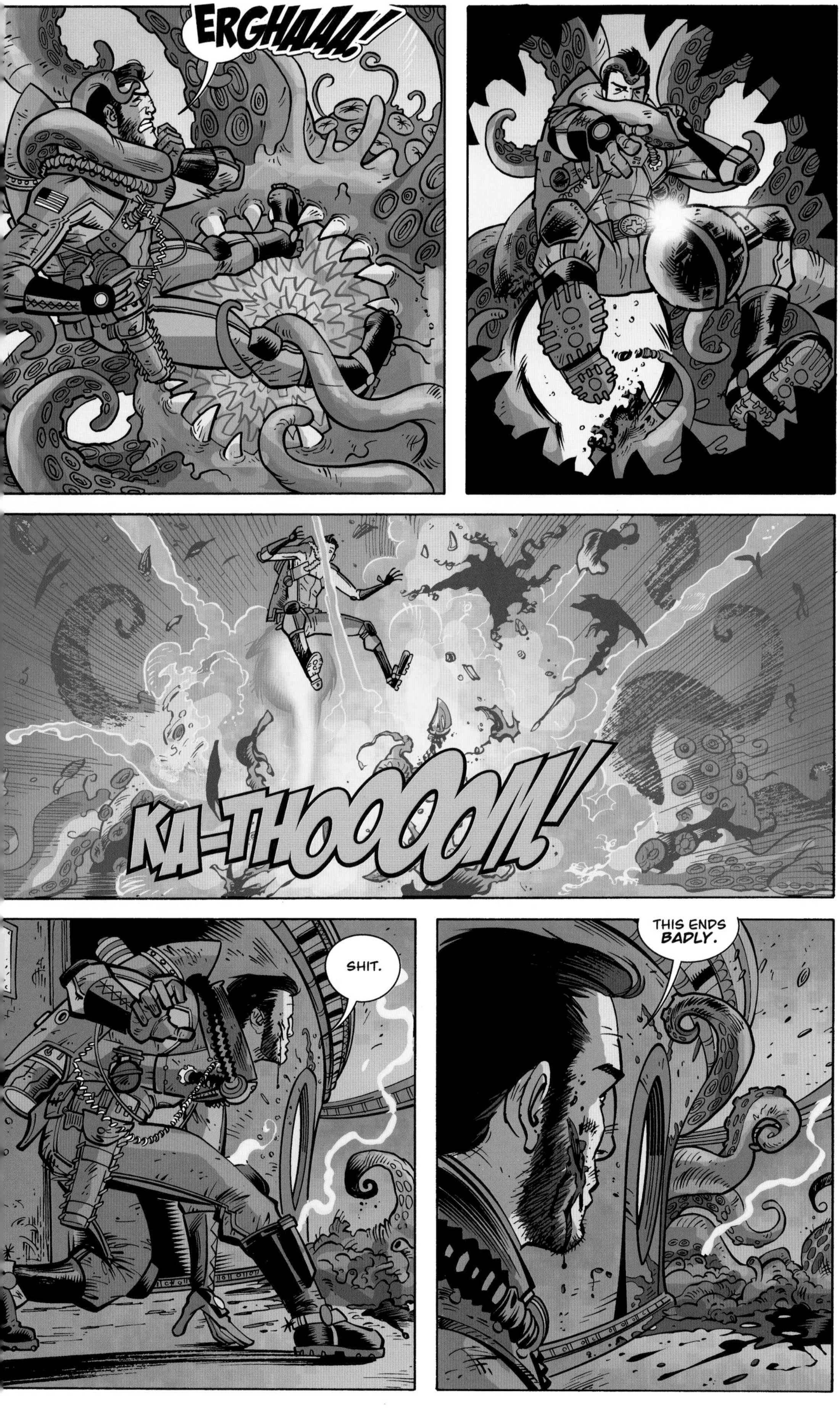
ERGHAAA!
KA-THOOOOM!
SHIT.
THIS ENDS BADLY.

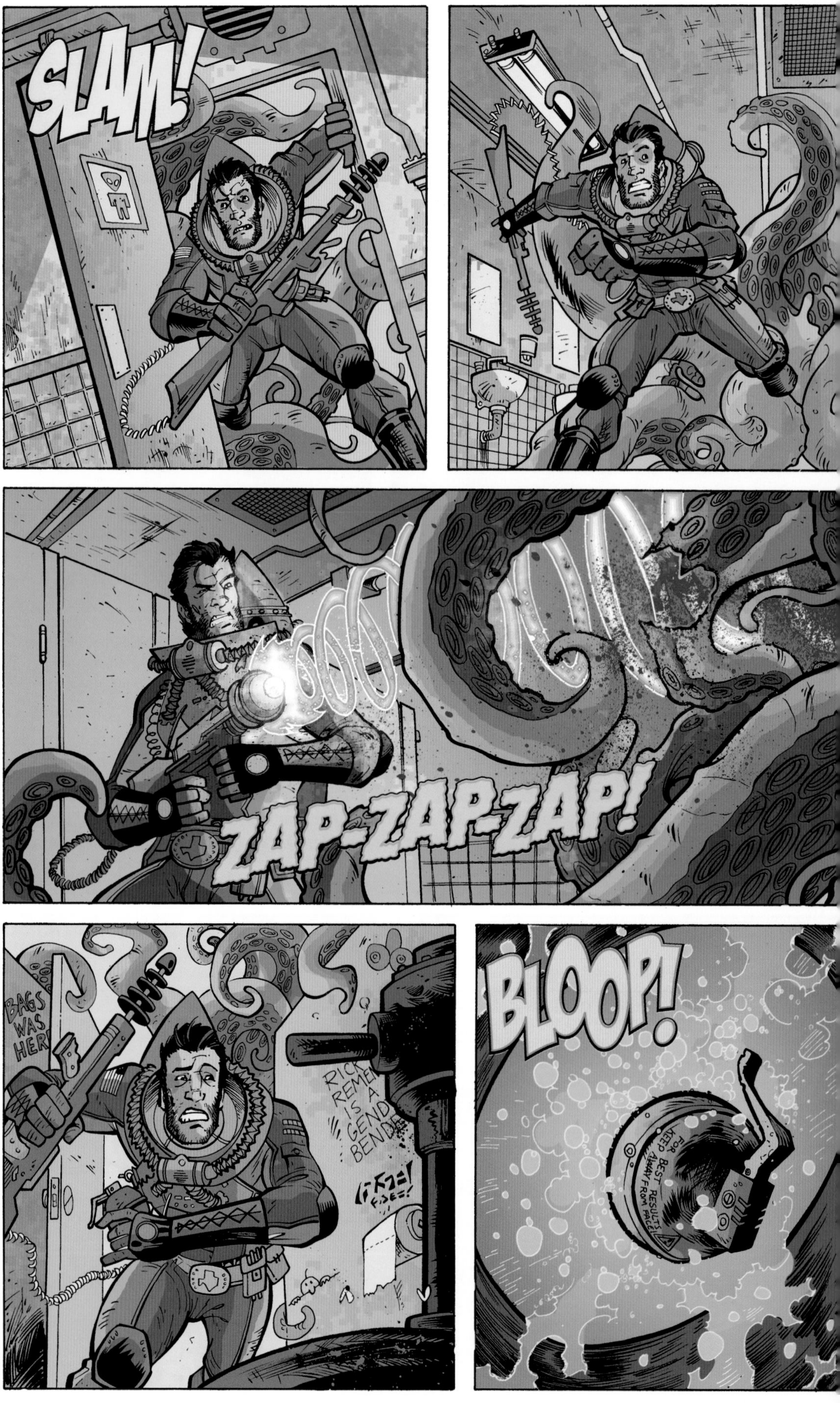
SLAM!
ZAP-ZAP-ZAP!
BAGS WAS HER
RICK REME IS A GEND BENDE
BLOOP!
FOR BEST RESULTS KEEP AWAY FROM FACE!

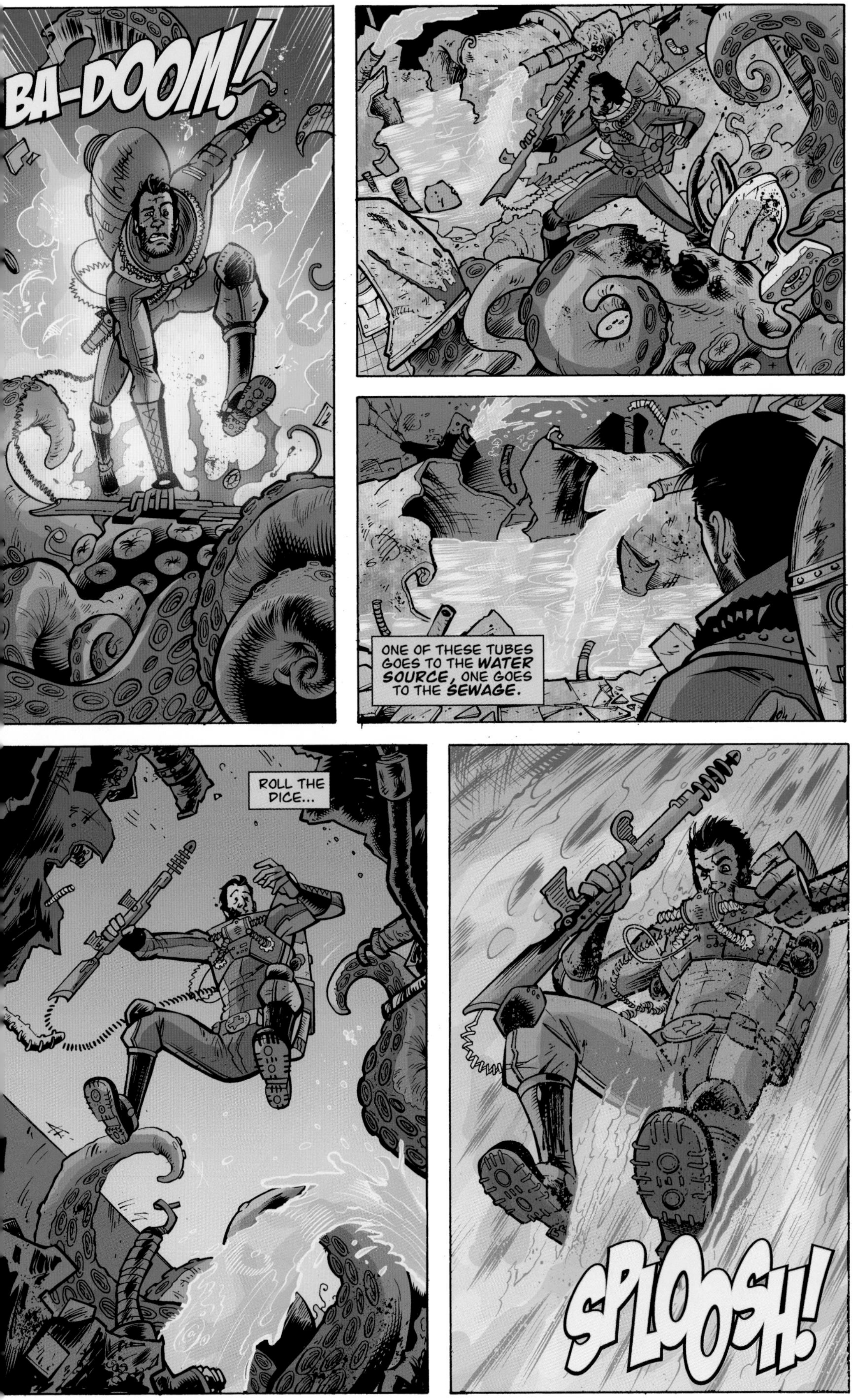
BA-DOOM!
ONE OF THESE TUBES GOES TO THE WATER SOURCE, ONE GOES TO THE SEWAGE.
ROLL THE DICE...
SPLOOSH!

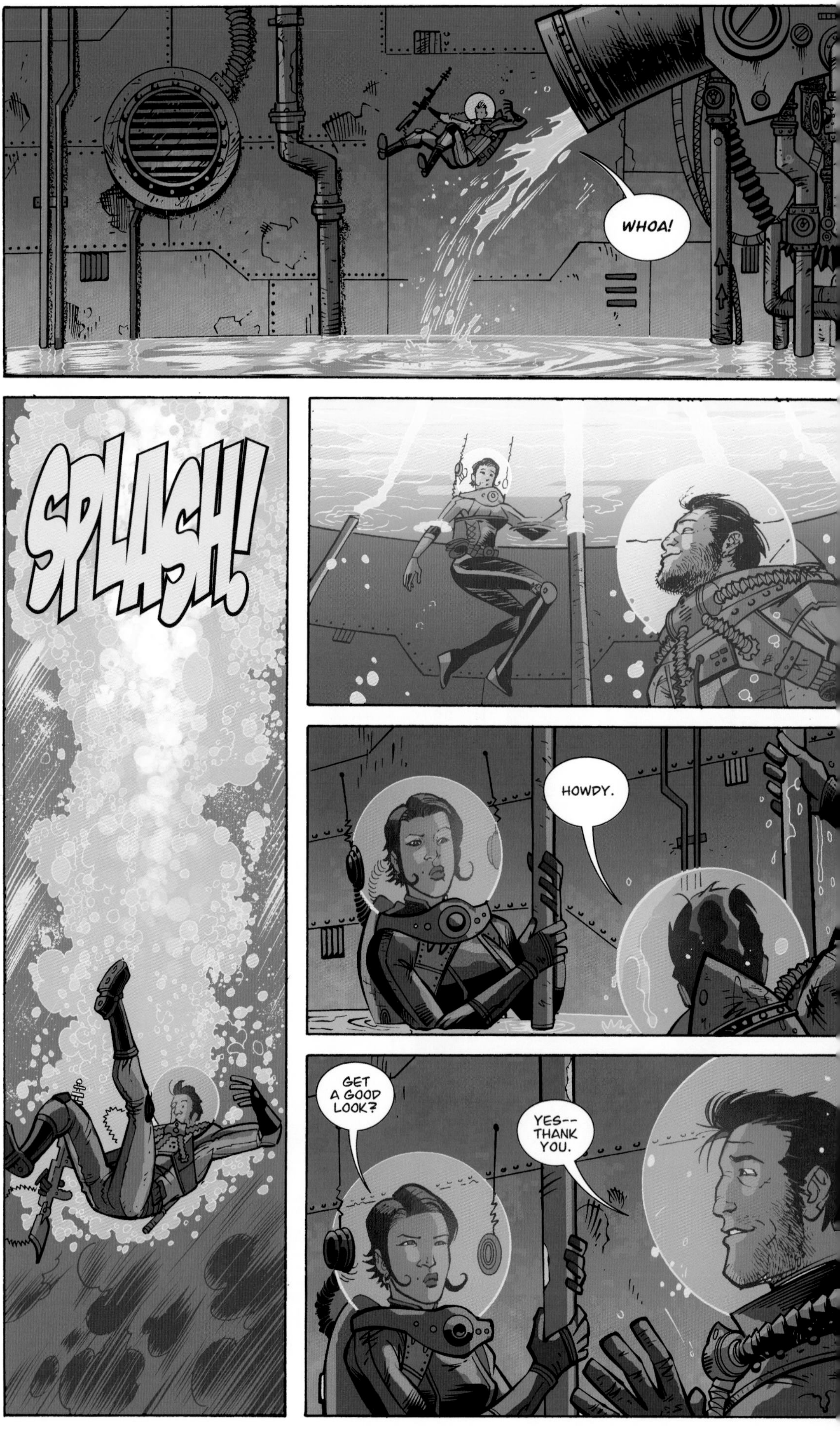
WHOA!
SPLASH!
HOWDY.
GET A GOOD LOOK?
YES-- THANK YOU.

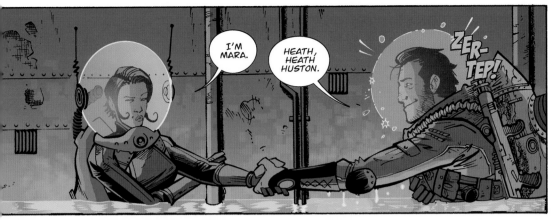

I'M. MARA.

HEATH, HEATH HUSTON.

ZER-TEP!

YOU'RE BLEEDING, HEATH HUSTON.

YEAH, THAT HAPPENS SOMETIMES.

I'M GUESSING YOU'RE DOWN HERE FOR THE SAME REASON I AM?

FLESH-EATING MONSTERS.

YOU GOT ANY IDEA WHAT THOSE THINGS ARE?

NO. I DO KNOW I WATCHED THEM CONSUME EVERY SOUL ON THE STATION.

WITHIN A DAY THEY HAD EXPONENTIALLY INCREASED TO IMPLAUSIBLE NUMBERS.

THEY'RE CALLED FEEDERS, THAT'S ALL THEY DO. MOST STREAMLINED LIFE-FORM IN EXISTENCE.

THEY CONSUME ANY FLESH AND THEY EXCRETE ONLY EGGS. NO WASTE, PURE REPRODUCTION.

THE COLONIES THAT FIRST TRIED TO SETTLE THE FEEDERS HOME WORLD WERE WIPED OUT IN A SINGLE CYCLE.

ONE POD ESCAPED TO CHARAMANTA AND... WELL I'M SURE YOU KNOW WHAT HAPPENED THERE.

THESE ARE THE THINGS THAT CAUSED THE ARMAGEDDON OF CHARAMANTA... JESUS.

UNITED SYSTEMS HAD TO ANNIHILATE ALL LIFE ON THE PLANET.

THESE THINGS ARE JUST PLAIN OL' UNSTOPPABLE.

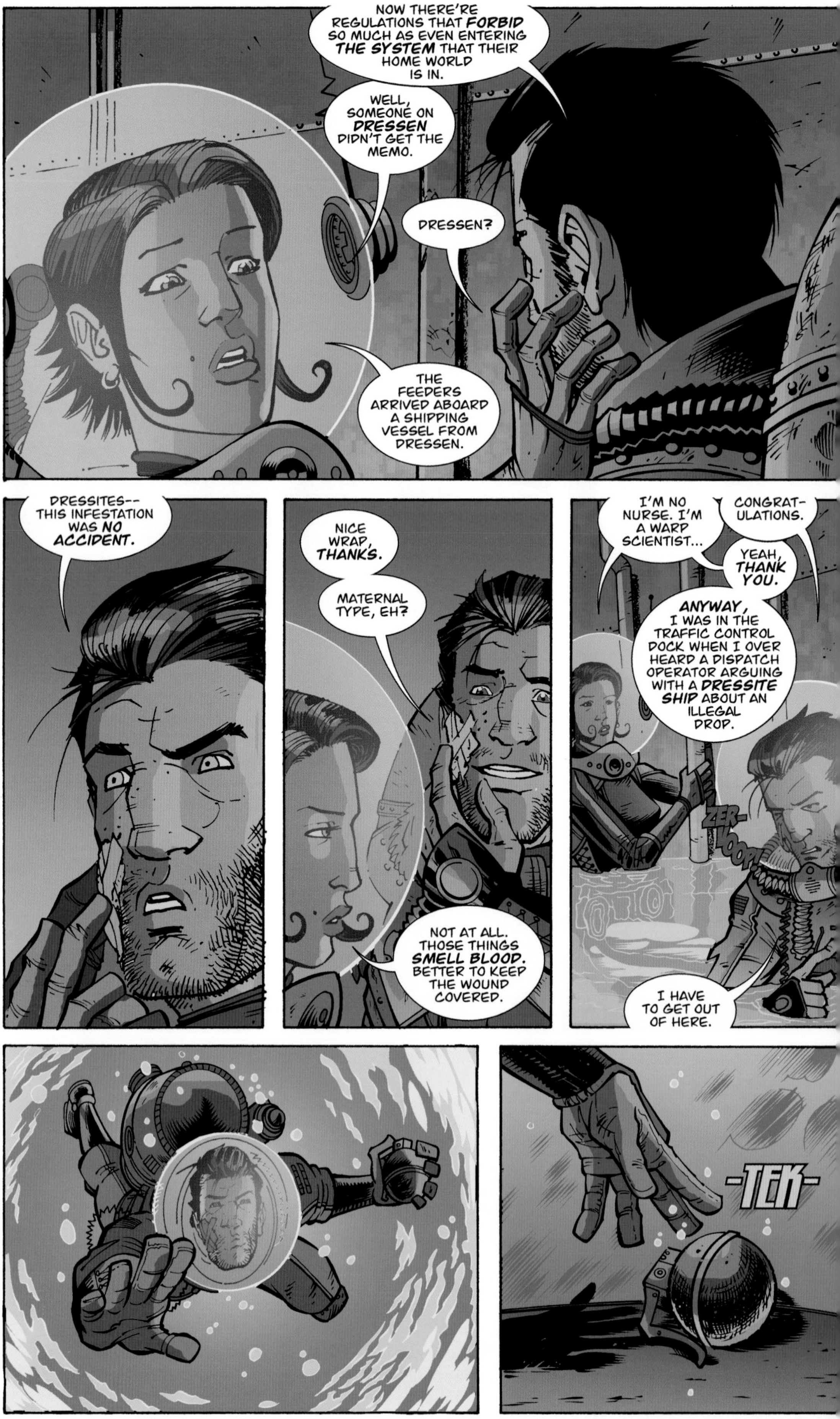

NOW THERE'RE REGULATIONS THAT **FORBID** SO MUCH AS EVEN ENTERING **THE SYSTEM** THAT THEIR HOME WORLD IS IN.
WELL, SOMEONE ON **DRESSEN** DIDN'T GET THE MEMO.
DRESSEN?
THE FEEDERS ARRIVED ABOARD A SHIPPING VESSEL FROM DRESSEN.
DRESSITES-- THIS INFESTATION WAS **NO ACCIDENT**.
NICE WRAP, **THANKS**.
MATERNAL TYPE, EH?
NOT AT ALL. THOSE THINGS **SMELL BLOOD**. BETTER TO KEEP THE WOUND COVERED.
I'M NO NURSE. I'M A WARP SCIENTIST...
CONGRAT- ULATIONS.
YEAH, **THANK YOU**.
ANYWAY, I WAS IN THE TRAFFIC CONTROL DOCK WHEN I OVER HEARD A DISPATCH OPERATOR ARGUING WITH A **DRESSITE SHIP** ABOUT AN ILLEGAL DROP.
ZER-WOOP!
I HAVE TO GET OUT OF HERE.
-TEK-

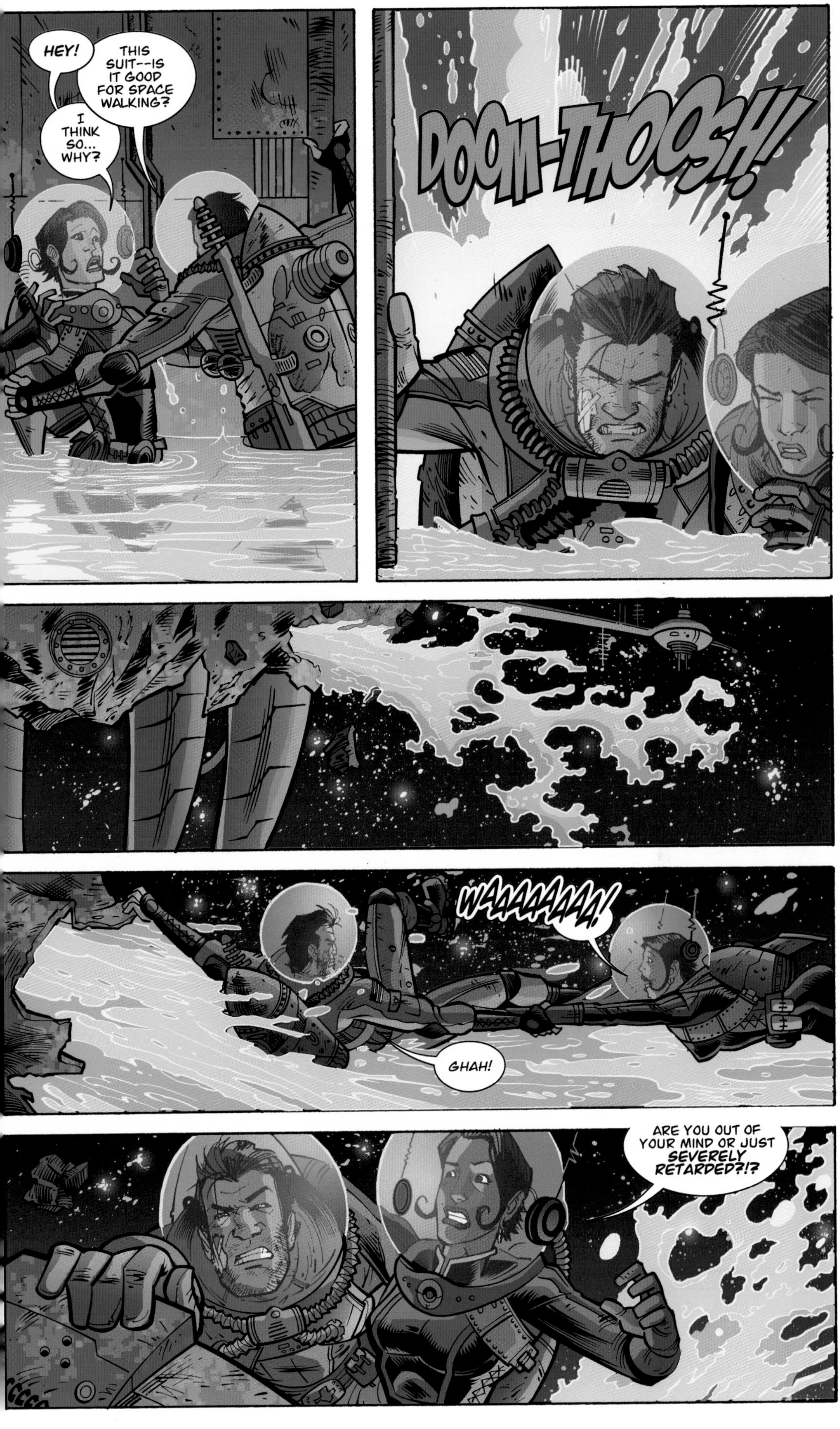
HEY!
THIS SUIT--IS IT GOOD FOR SPACE WALKING?
I THINK SO... WHY?
DOOM-THOOSH!
WAAAAAAA!
GHAH!
ARE YOU OUT OF YOUR MIND OR JUST SEVERELY RETARDED?!?

CATASTROPHE AVERTED. I THINK YOU CAN LET ME GO NOW.

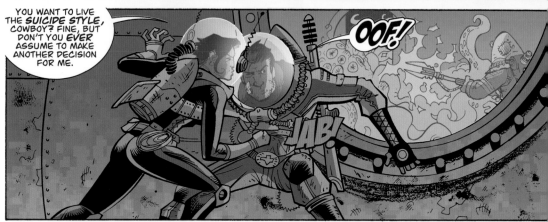

YOU WANT TO LIVE THE *SUICIDE STYLE*, COWBOY? FINE, BUT DON'T YOU *EVER* ASSUME TO MAKE ANOTHER DECISION FOR ME.

JAB!

OOF!

WHAT... ARE... *THOSE?*

DRESSITE SOLDIERS. THIS TAKES ME BACK.

WHAT ARE THEY DOING?

THEY'RE STUFFING THE TRUCKS FULL OF FEEDERS.

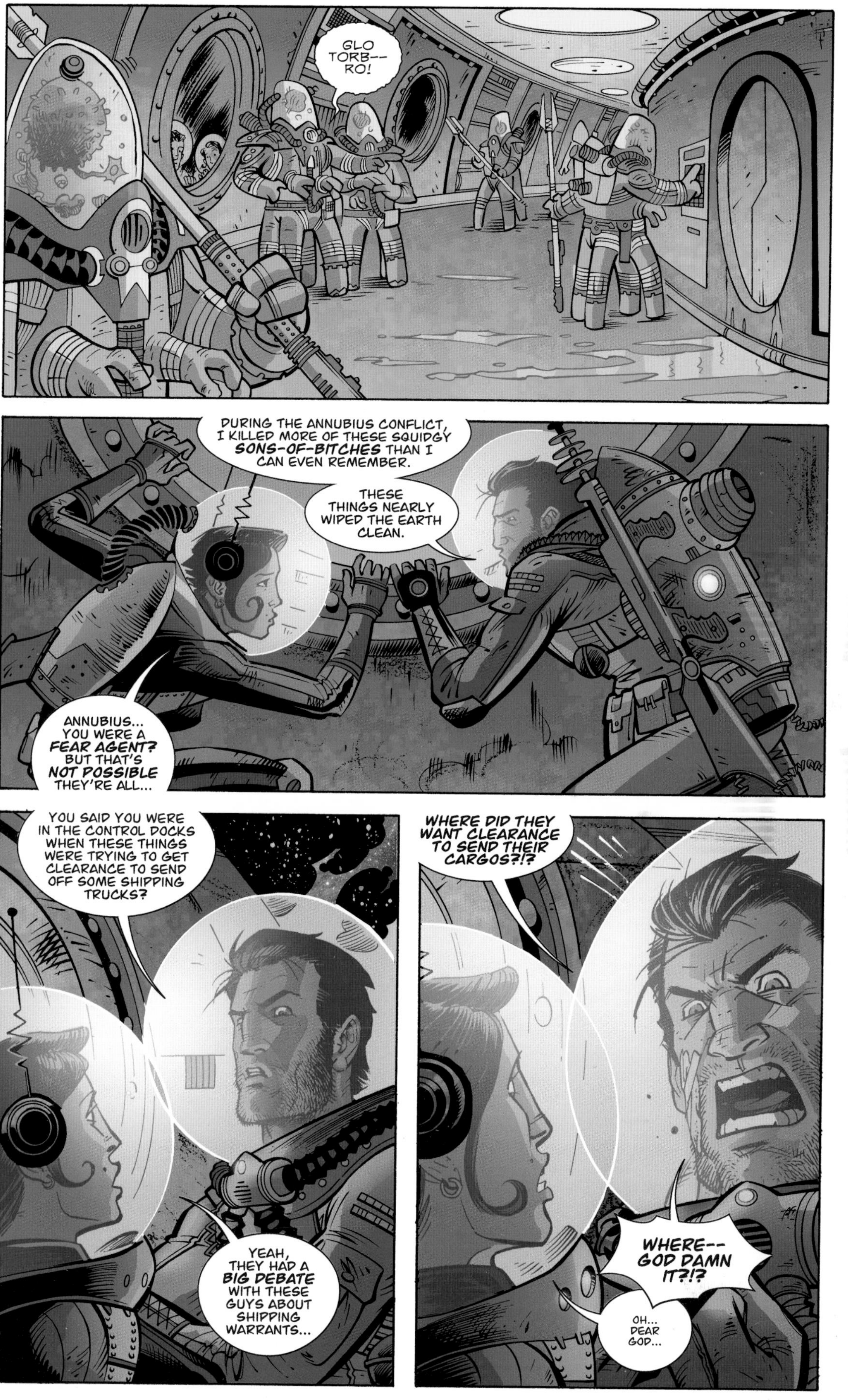
GLO TORB--RO!
DURING THE ANNUBIUS CONFLICT, I KILLED MORE OF THESE SQUIDGY **SONS-OF-BITCHES** THAN I CAN EVEN REMEMBER.
THESE THINGS NEARLY WIPED THE EARTH CLEAN.
ANNUBIUS... YOU WERE A **FEAR AGENT?** BUT THAT'S **NOT POSSIBLE** THEY'RE ALL...
YOU SAID YOU WERE IN THE CONTROL DOCKS WHEN THESE THINGS WERE TRYING TO GET CLEARANCE TO SEND OFF SOME SHIPPING TRUCKS?
YEAH, THEY HAD A **BIG DEBATE** WITH THESE GUYS ABOUT SHIPPING WARRANTS...
WHERE DID THEY WANT CLEARANCE TO SEND THEIR CARGOS?!?
WHERE--GOD DAMN IT?!?
OH... DEAR GOD...

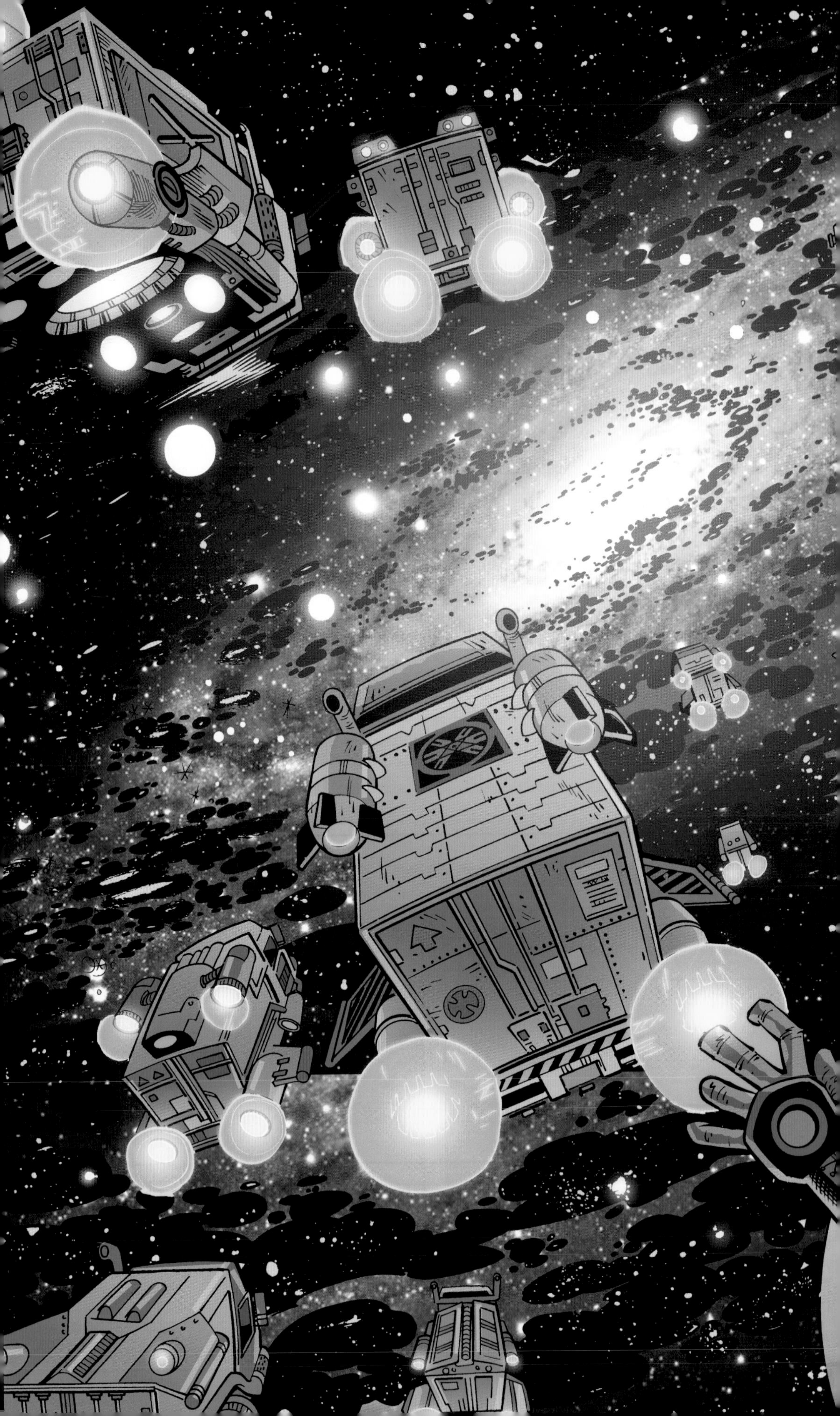

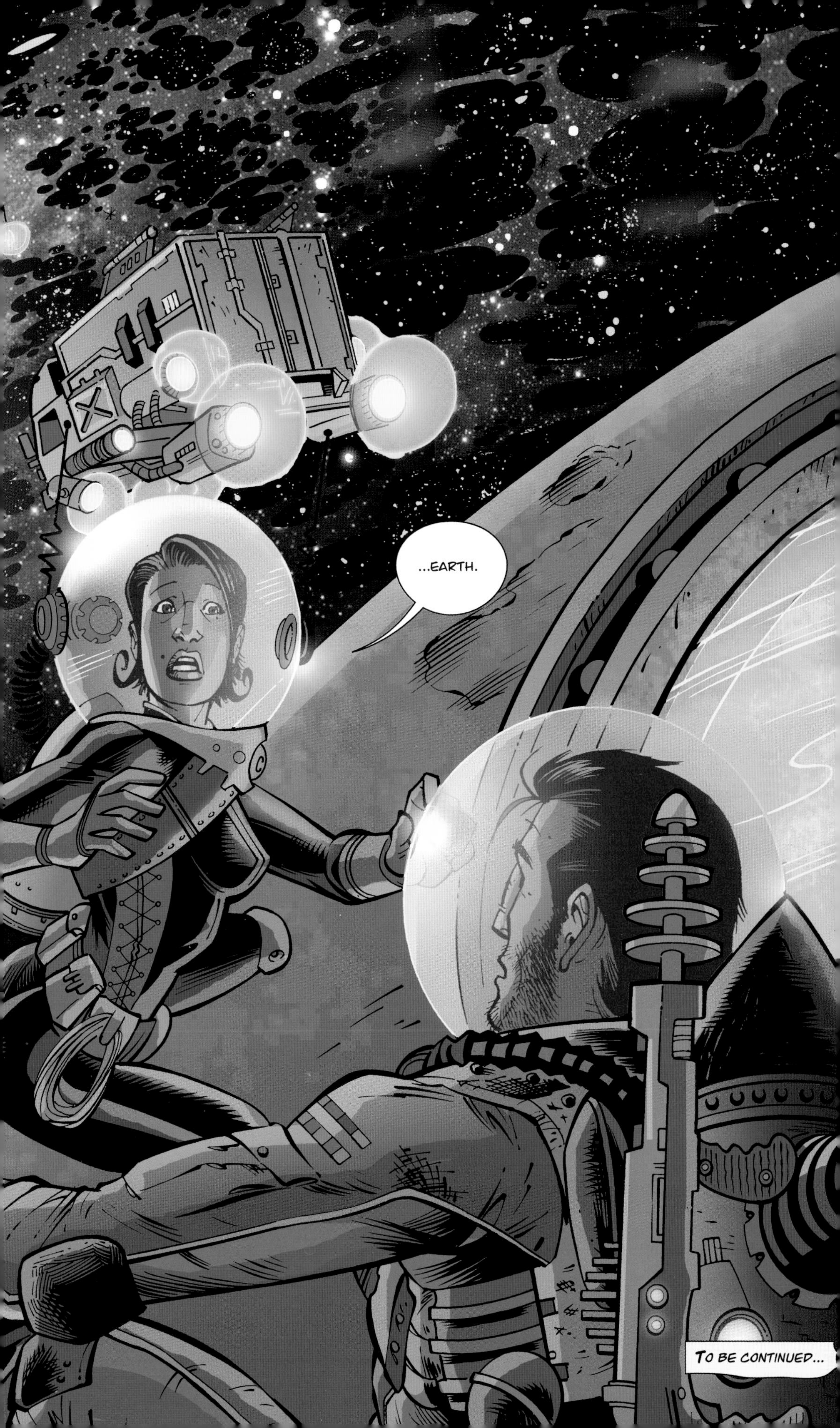
...EARTH.
TO BE CONTINUED...

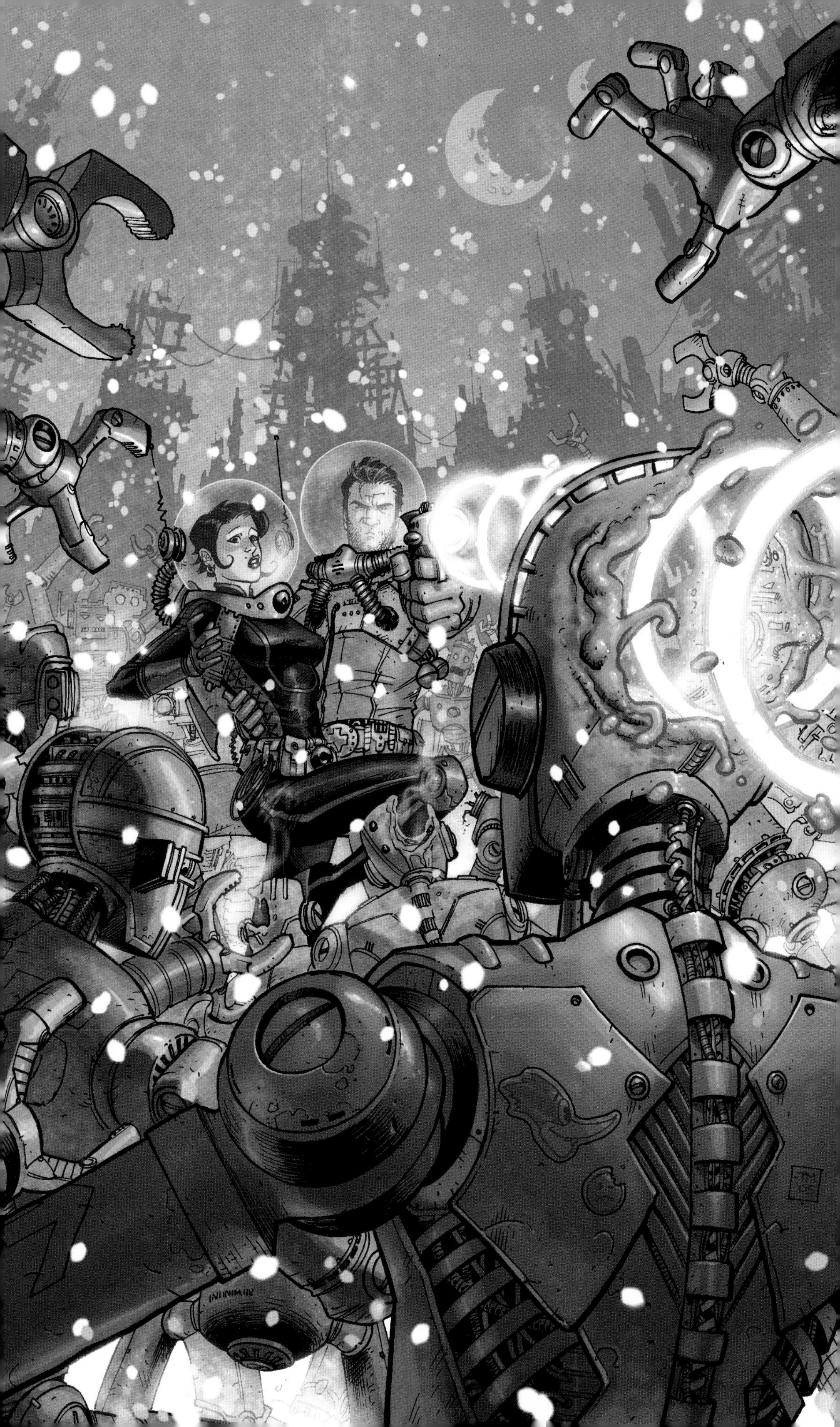

RE-IGNITION CHAPTER 3

Narrow
ESCAPES!

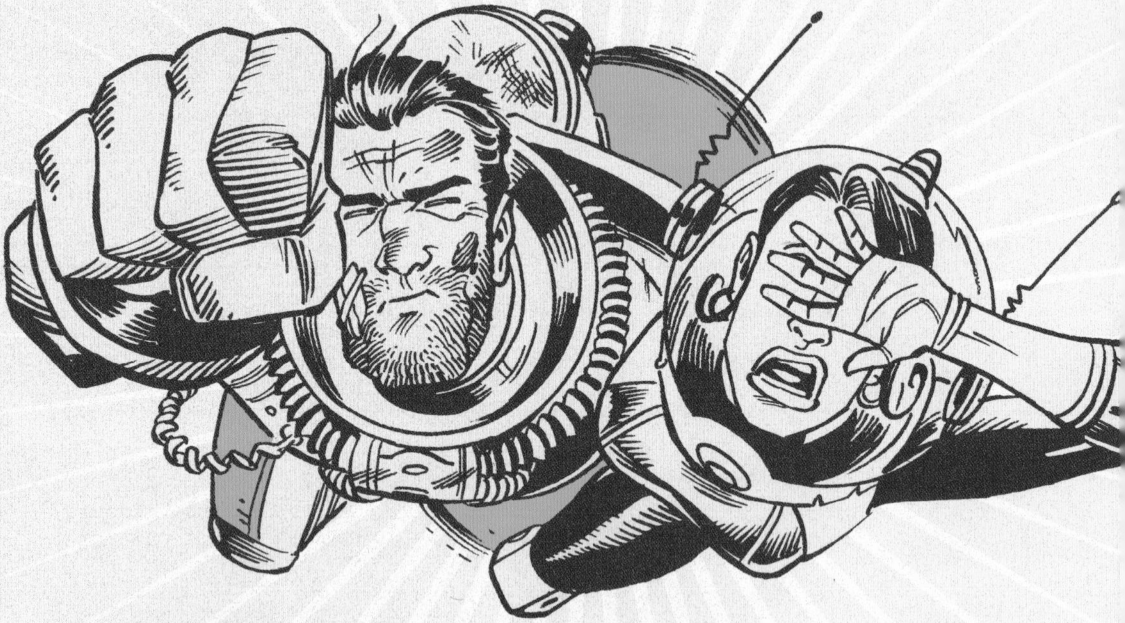

Terrifying
STUNTS!

Interplanetary
INTRIGUE!

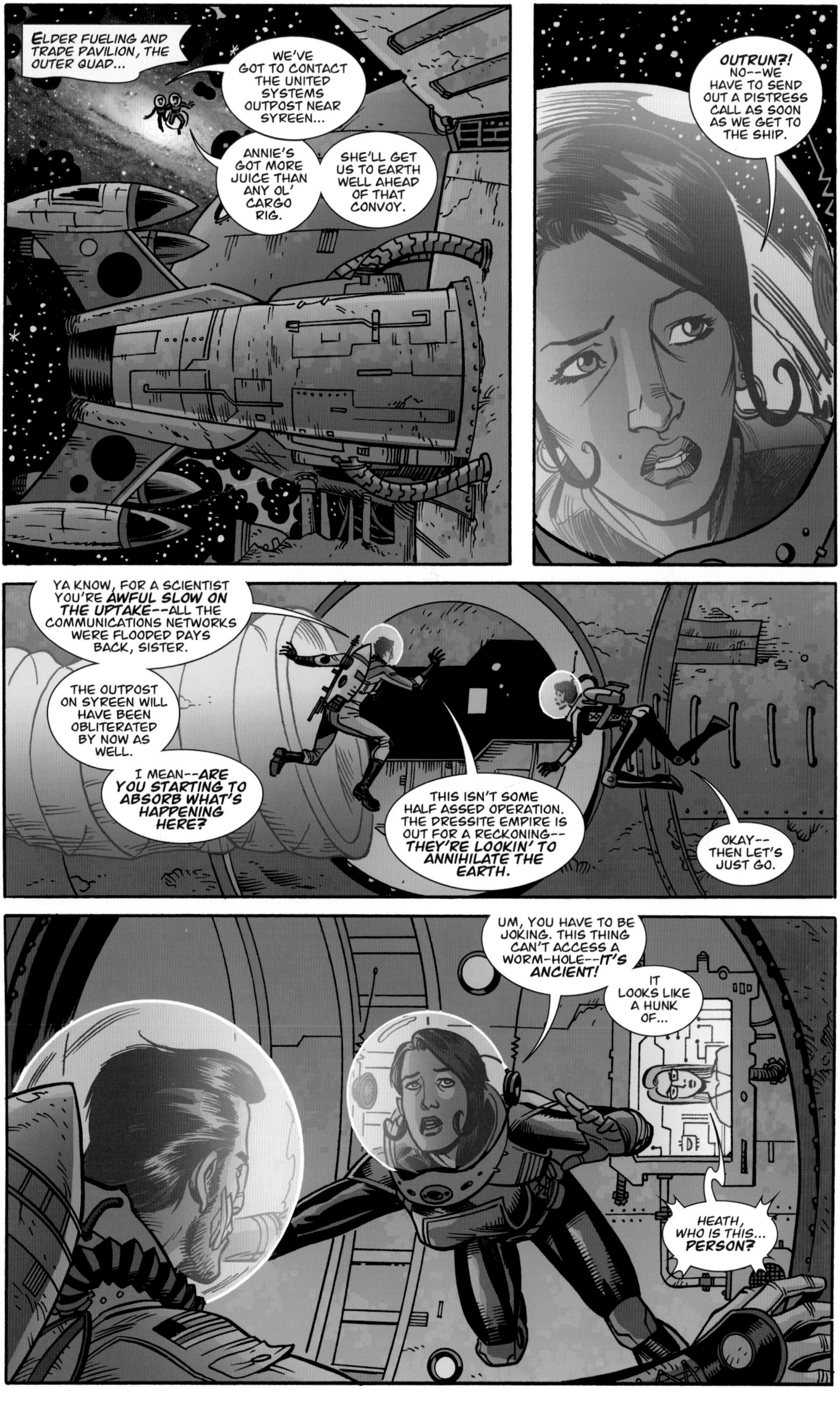

ELDER FUELING AND TRADE PAVILION, THE OUTER QUAD...
WE'VE GOT TO CONTACT THE UNITED SYSTEMS OUTPOST NEAR SYREEN...
ANNIE'S GOT MORE JUICE THAN ANY OL' CARGO RIG.
SHE'LL GET US TO EARTH WELL AHEAD OF THAT CONVOY.
OUTRUN?! NO--WE HAVE TO SEND OUT A DISTRESS CALL AS SOON AS WE GET TO THE SHIP.
YA KNOW, FOR A SCIENTIST YOU'RE AWFUL SLOW ON THE UPTAKE--ALL THE COMMUNICATIONS NETWORKS WERE FLOODED DAYS BACK, SISTER.
THE OUTPOST ON SYREEN WILL HAVE BEEN OBLITERATED BY NOW AS WELL.
I MEAN--ARE YOU STARTING TO ABSORB WHAT'S HAPPENING HERE?
THIS ISN'T SOME HALF ASSED OPERATION. THE DRESSITE EMPIRE IS OUT FOR A RECKONING--THEY'RE LOOKIN' TO ANNIHILATE THE EARTH.
OKAY--THEN LET'S JUST GO.
UM, YOU HAVE TO BE JOKING. THIS THING CAN'T ACCESS A WORM-HOLE--IT'S ANCIENT!
IT LOOKS LIKE A HUNK OF...
HEATH, WHO IS THIS... PERSON?

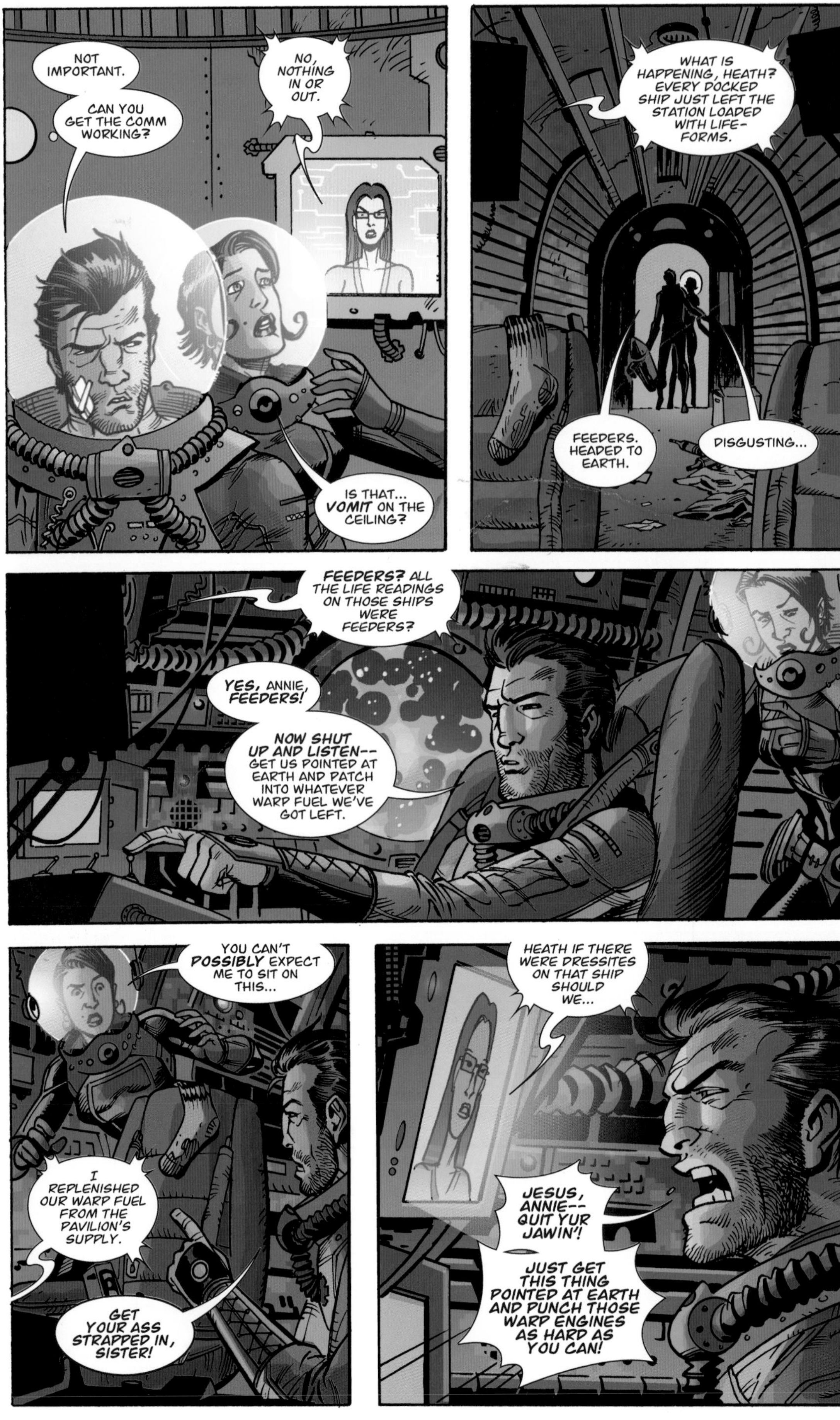
NOT IMPORTANT.
CAN YOU GET THE COMM WORKING?
NO, NOTHING IN OR OUT.
IS THAT... VOMIT ON THE CEILING?
WHAT IS HAPPENING, HEATH? EVERY DOCKED SHIP JUST LEFT THE STATION LOADED WITH LIFE-FORMS.
FEEDERS. HEADED TO EARTH.
DISGUSTING...
FEEDERS? ALL THE LIFE READINGS ON THOSE SHIPS WERE FEEDERS?
YES, ANNIE, FEEDERS!
NOW SHUT UP AND LISTEN-- GET US POINTED AT EARTH AND PATCH INTO WHATEVER WARP FUEL WE'VE GOT LEFT.
YOU CAN'T POSSIBLY EXPECT ME TO SIT ON THIS...
I REPLENISHED OUR WARP FUEL FROM THE PAVILION'S SUPPLY.
GET YOUR ASS STRAPPED IN, SISTER!
HEATH IF THERE WERE DRESSITES ON THAT SHIP SHOULD WE...
JESUS, ANNIE-- QUIT YUR JAWIN'!
JUST GET THIS THING POINTED AT EARTH AND PUNCH THOSE WARP ENGINES AS HARD AS YOU CAN!

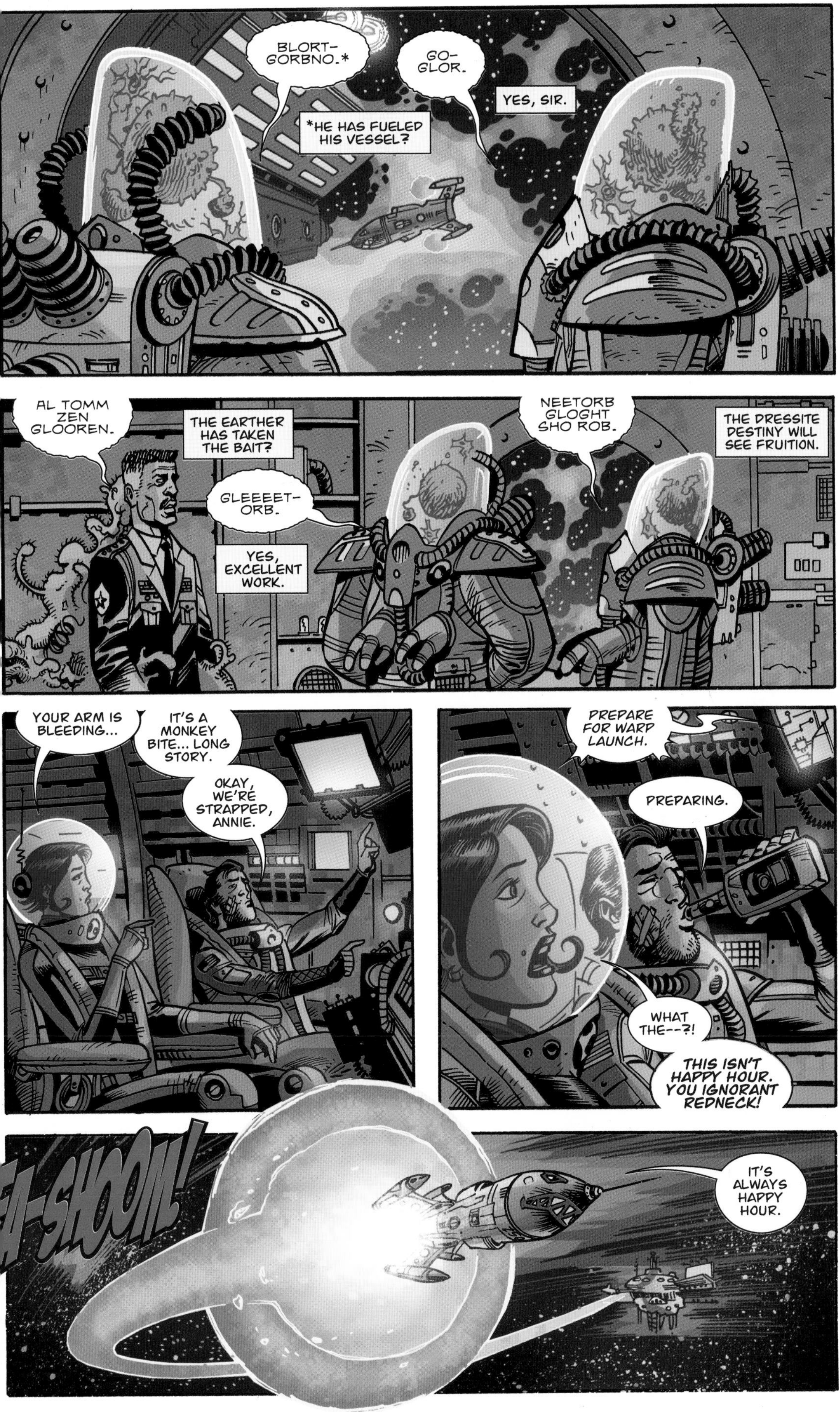
BLORT-GORBNO.*
*HE HAS FUELED HIS VESSEL?
GO-GLOR.
YES, SIR.
AL TOMM ZEN GLOOREN.
THE EARTHER HAS TAKEN THE BAIT?
GLEEEET-ORB.
YES, EXCELLENT WORK.
NEETORB GLOGHT SHO ROB.
THE DRESSITE DESTINY WILL SEE FRUITION.
YOUR ARM IS BLEEDING...
IT'S A MONKEY BITE... LONG STORY.
OKAY, WE'RE STRAPPED, ANNIE.
PREPARE FOR WARP LAUNCH.
PREPARING.
WHAT THE--?!
THIS ISN'T HAPPY HOUR. YOU IGNORANT REDNECK!
A-SHOOM!
IT'S ALWAYS HAPPY HOUR.

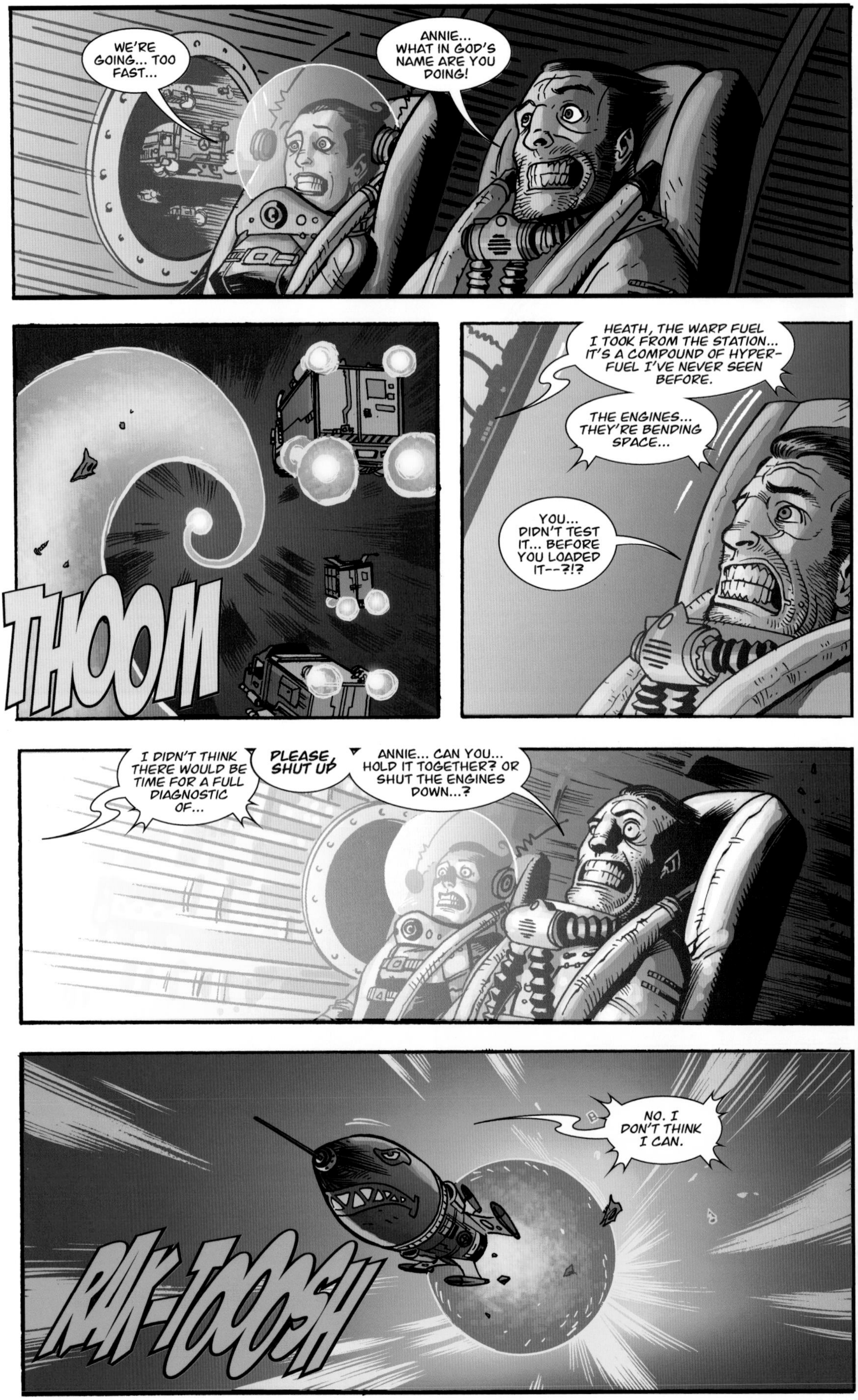
WE'RE GOING... TOO FAST...
ANNIE... WHAT IN GOD'S NAME ARE YOU DOING!
THOOM
HEATH, THE WARP FUEL I TOOK FROM THE STATION... IT'S A COMPOUND OF HYPER-FUEL I'VE NEVER SEEN BEFORE.
THE ENGINES... THEY'RE BENDING SPACE...
YOU... DIDN'T TEST IT... BEFORE YOU LOADED IT--?!?
I DIDN'T THINK THERE WOULD BE TIME FOR A FULL DIAGNOSTIC OF...
PLEASE, SHUT UP
ANNIE... CAN YOU... HOLD IT TOGETHER? OR SHUT THE ENGINES DOWN...?
NO. I DON'T THINK I CAN.
RAK-TOOOSH

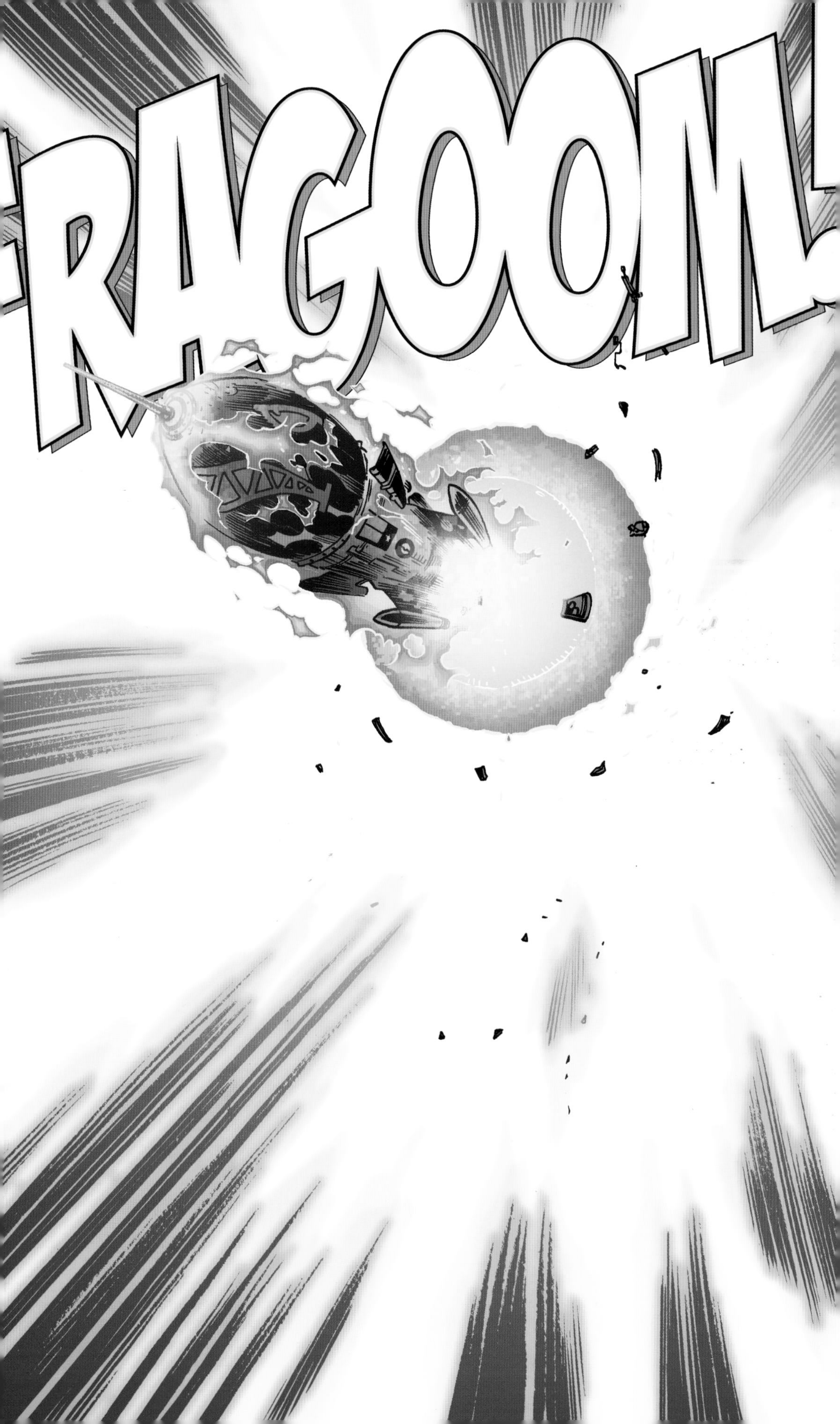
RAGOOM

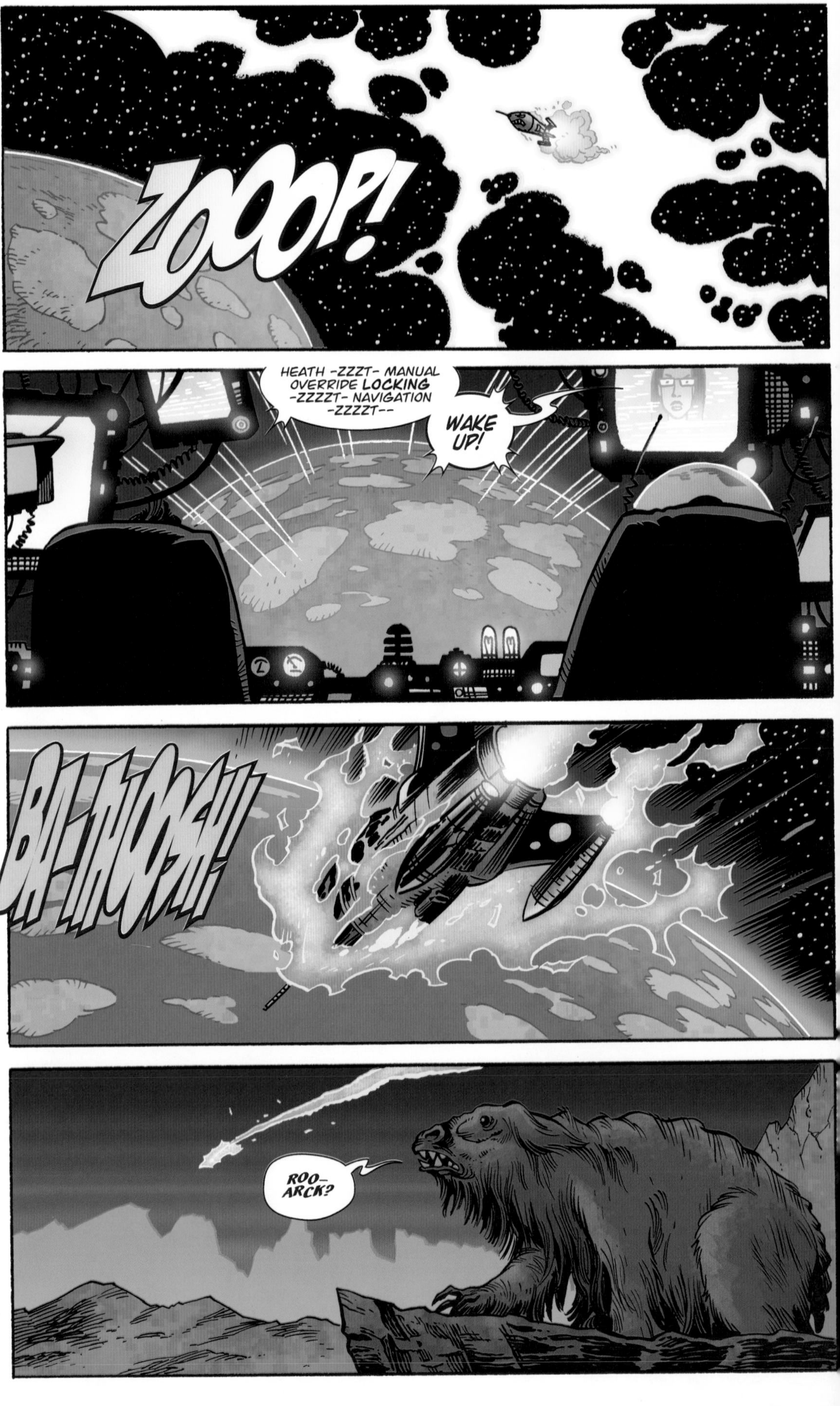
ZOOOP!
HEATH -ZZZT- MANUAL OVERRIDE LOCKING -ZZZZT- NAVIGATION -ZZZZT--
WAKE UP!
BA-THOOSH!!
ROO-ARCK?

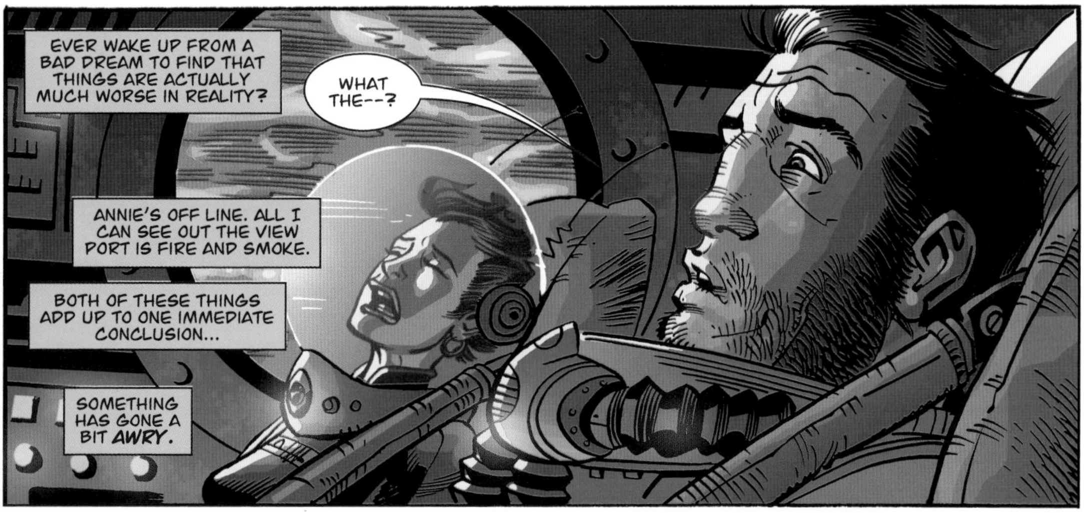
EVER WAKE UP FROM A BAD DREAM TO FIND THAT THINGS ARE ACTUALLY MUCH WORSE IN REALITY?
WHAT THE--?
ANNIE'S OFF LINE. ALL I CAN SEE OUT THE VIEW PORT IS FIRE AND SMOKE.
BOTH OF THESE THINGS ADD UP TO ONE IMMEDIATE CONCLUSION...
SOMETHING HAS GONE A BIT AWRY.

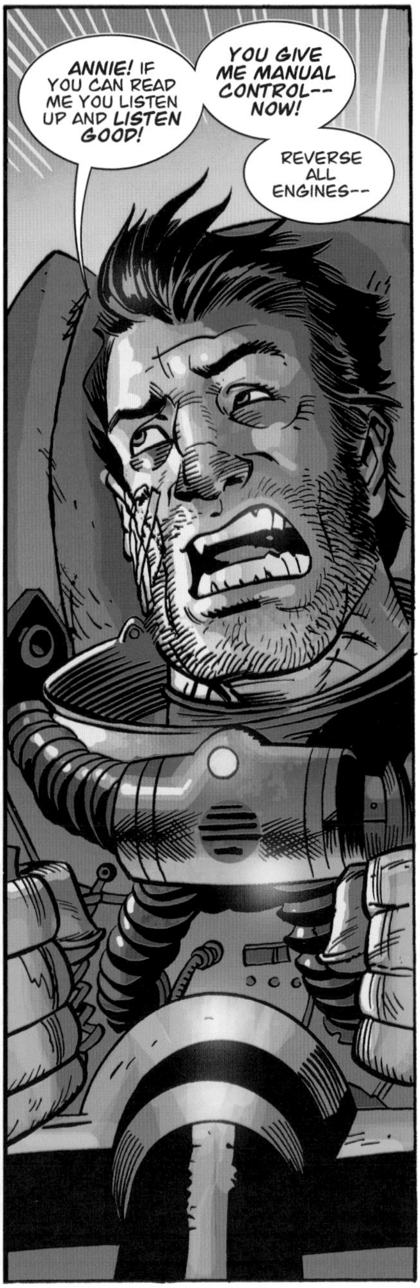
ANNIE! IF YOU CAN READ ME YOU LISTEN UP AND LISTEN GOOD!
YOU GIVE ME MANUAL CONTROL-- NOW!
REVERSE ALL ENGINES--

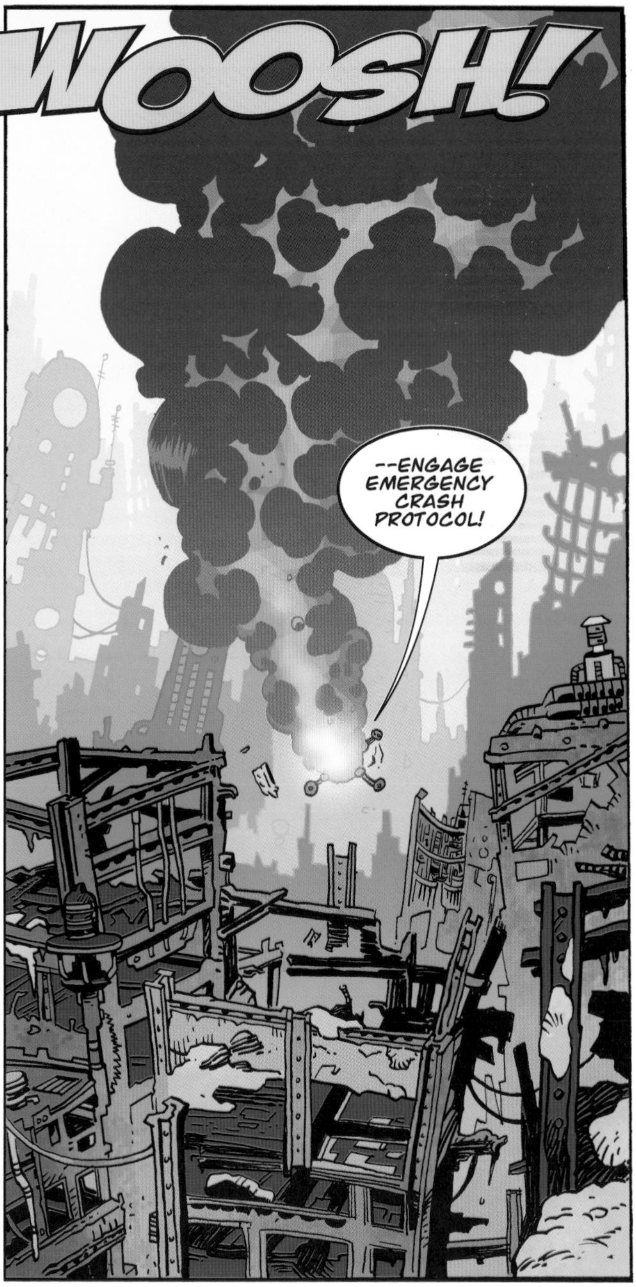
WOOSH!
--ENGAGE EMERGENCY CRASH PROTOCOL!

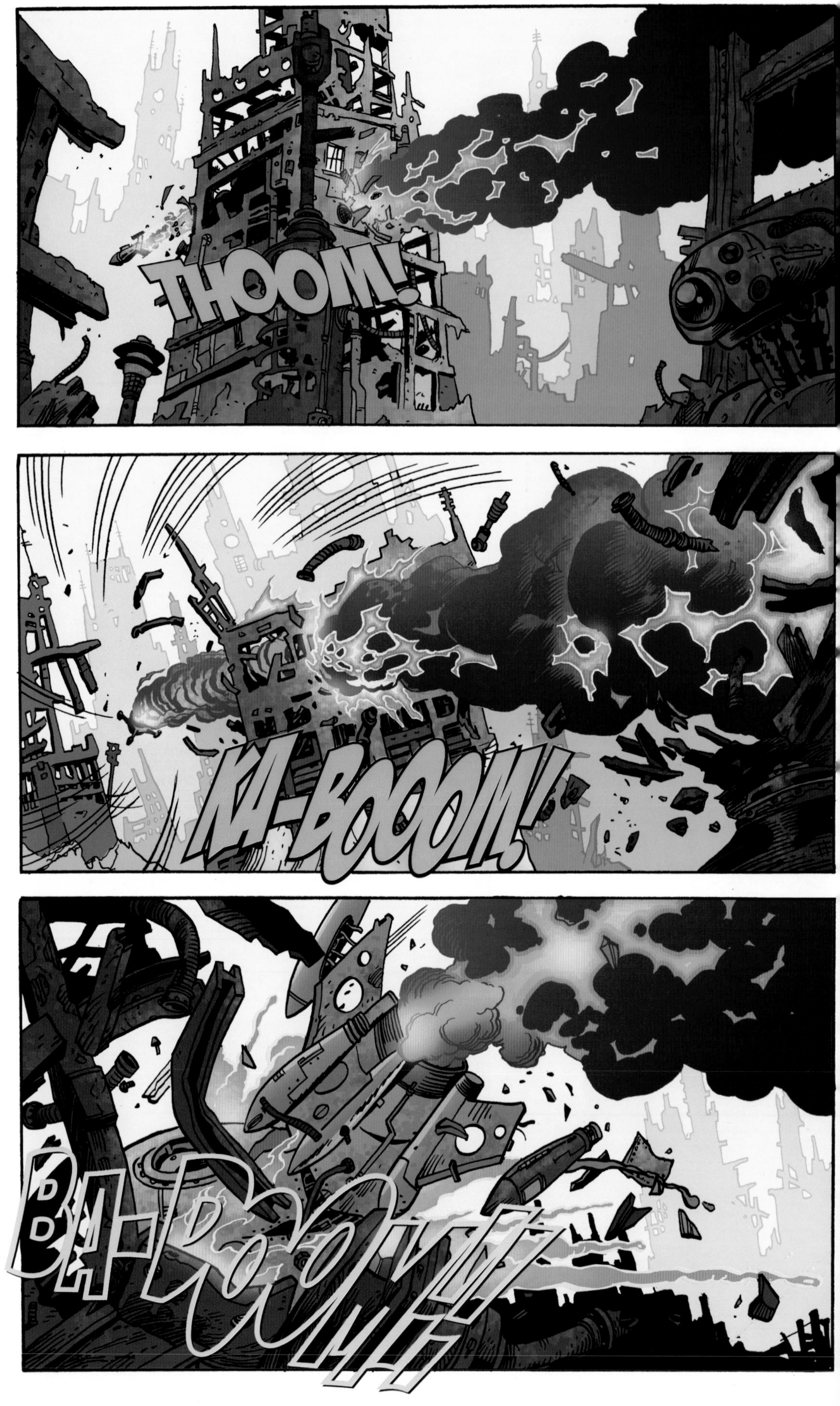
THOOM!
KA-BOOOM!

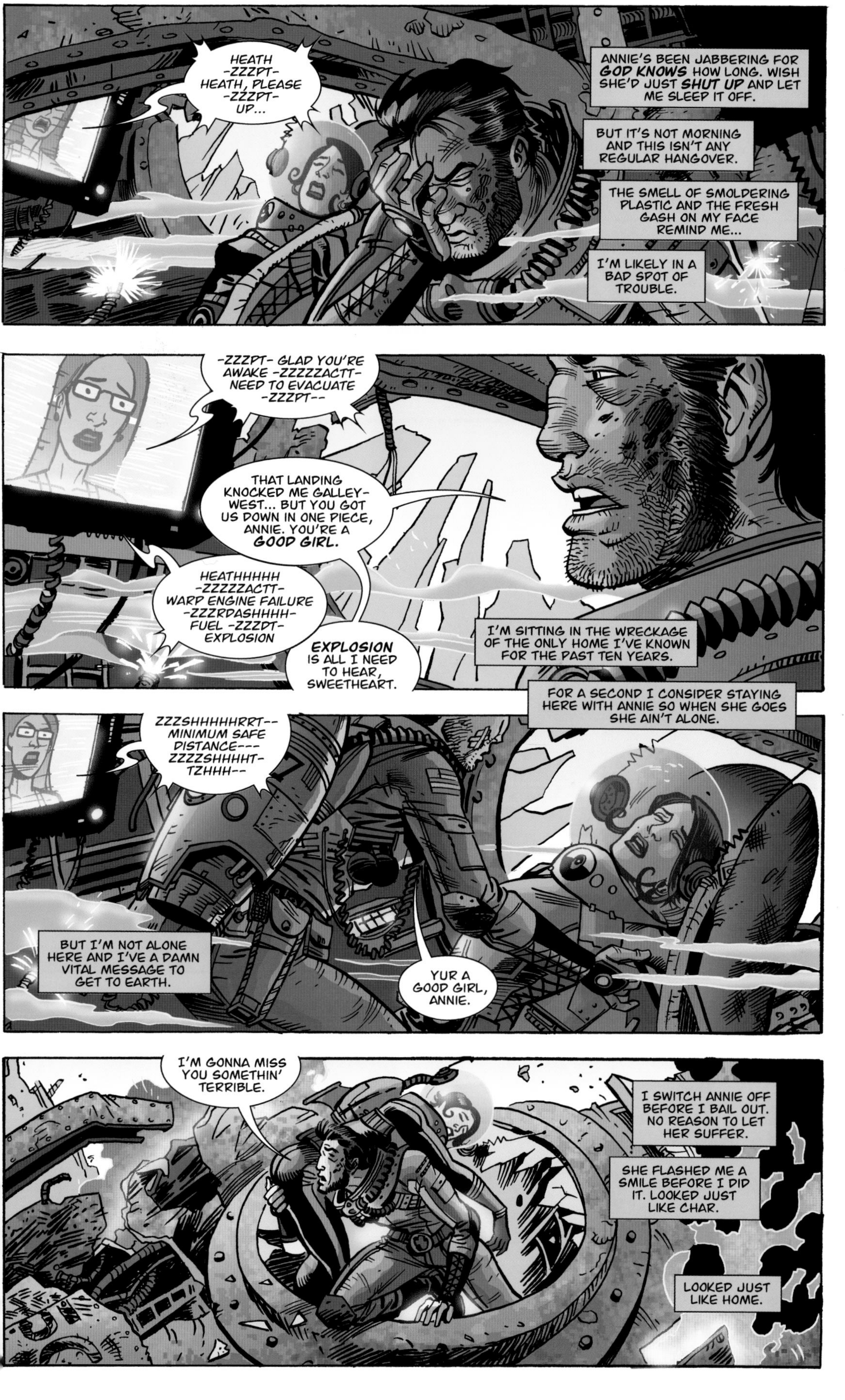

HEATH -ZZZPT- HEATH, PLEASE -ZZZPT- UP...
ANNIE'S BEEN JABBERING FOR GOD KNOWS HOW LONG. WISH SHE'D JUST SHUT UP AND LET ME SLEEP IT OFF.
BUT IT'S NOT MORNING AND THIS ISN'T ANY REGULAR HANGOVER.
THE SMELL OF SMOLDERING PLASTIC AND THE FRESH GASH ON MY FACE REMIND ME...
I'M LIKELY IN A BAD SPOT OF TROUBLE.
-ZZZPT- GLAD YOU'RE AWAKE -ZZZZZACTT- NEED TO EVACUATE -ZZZPT--
THAT LANDING KNOCKED ME GALLEY-WEST... BUT YOU GOT US DOWN IN ONE PIECE, ANNIE. YOU'RE A GOOD GIRL.
HEATHHHHH -ZZZZZACTT- WARP ENGINE FAILURE -ZZZRDASHHHH- FUEL -ZZZDT- EXPLOSION
EXPLOSION IS ALL I NEED TO HEAR, SWEETHEART.
I'M SITTING IN THE WRECKAGE OF THE ONLY HOME I'VE KNOWN FOR THE PAST TEN YEARS.
FOR A SECOND I CONSIDER STAYING HERE WITH ANNIE SO WHEN SHE GOES SHE AIN'T ALONE.
ZZZSHHHHHRRT-- MINIMUM SAFE DISTANCE--- ZZZZSHHHHT-TZHHH--
BUT I'M NOT ALONE HERE AND I'VE A DAMN VITAL MESSAGE TO GET TO EARTH.
YUR A GOOD GIRL, ANNIE.
I'M GONNA MISS YOU SOMETHIN' TERRIBLE.
I SWITCH ANNIE OFF BEFORE I BAIL OUT. NO REASON TO LET HER SUFFER.
SHE FLASHED ME A SMILE BEFORE I DID IT. LOOKED JUST LIKE CHAR.
LOOKED JUST LIKE HOME.

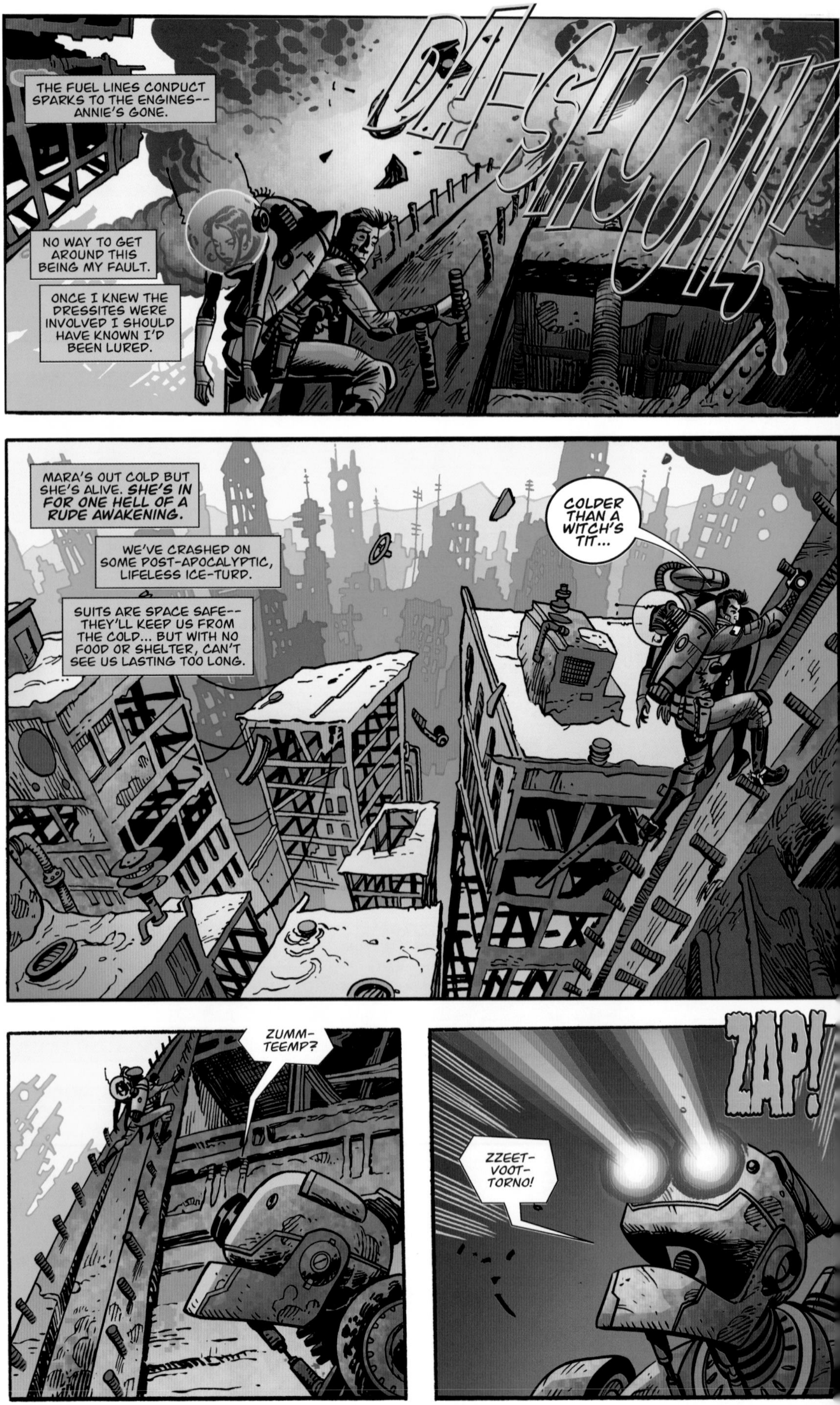

THE FUEL LINES CONDUCT SPARKS TO THE ENGINES-- ANNIE'S GONE.
NO WAY TO GET AROUND THIS BEING MY FAULT.
ONCE I KNEW THE DRESSITES WERE INVOLVED I SHOULD HAVE KNOWN I'D BEEN LURED.
MARA'S OUT COLD BUT SHE'S ALIVE. *SHE'S IN FOR ONE HELL OF A RUDE AWAKENING.*
WE'VE CRASHED ON SOME POST-APOCALYPTIC, LIFELESS ICE-TURD.
SUITS ARE SPACE SAFE-- THEY'LL KEEP US FROM THE COLD... BUT WITH NO FOOD OR SHELTER, CAN'T SEE US LASTING TOO LONG.
COLDER THAN A WITCH'S TIT...
ZUMM-TEEMP?
ZAP!
ZZEET-VOOT-TORNO!

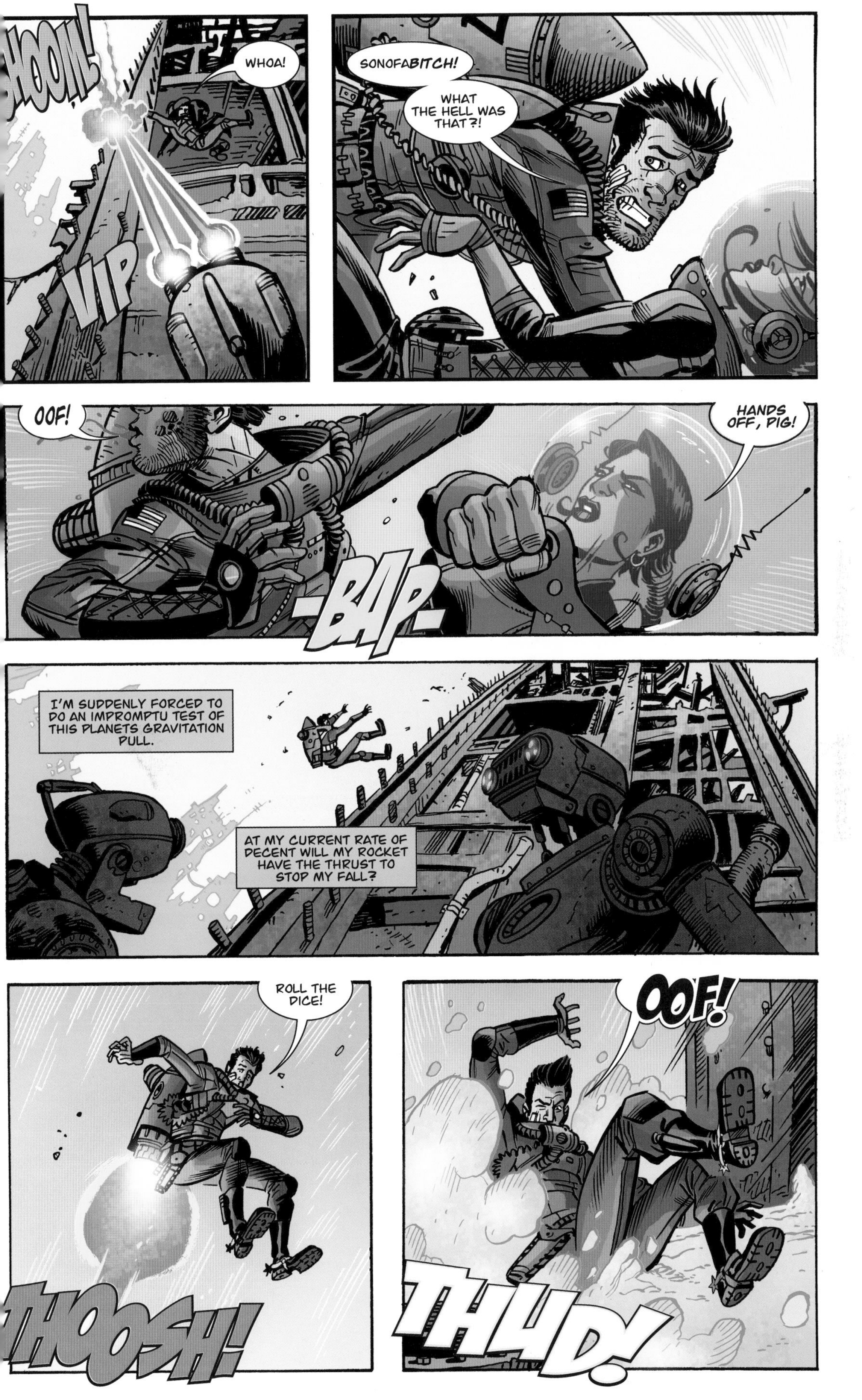
SHOOM!
WHOA!
VIP
SONOFABITCH!
WHAT THE HELL WAS THAT?!
OOF!
HANDS OFF, PIG!
-BAP-
I'M SUDDENLY FORCED TO DO AN IMPROMPTU TEST OF THIS PLANETS GRAVITATION PULL.
AT MY CURRENT RATE OF DECENT WILL MY ROCKET HAVE THE THRUST TO STOP MY FALL?
ROLL THE DICE!
THOOSH!
OOF!
THUD!

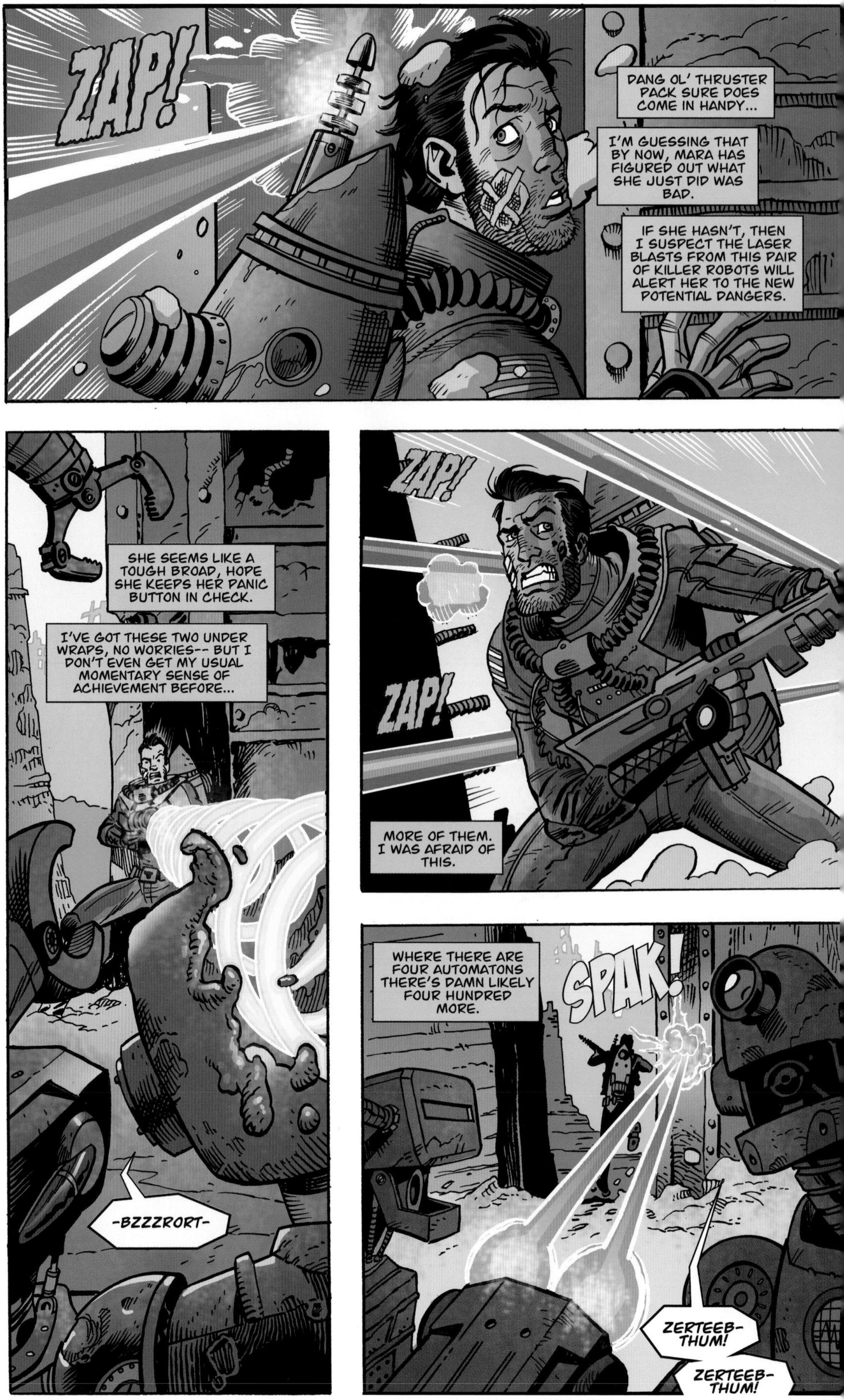
ZAP!
DANG OL' THRUSTER PACK SURE DOES COME IN HANDY...
I'M GUESSING THAT BY NOW, MARA HAS FIGURED OUT WHAT SHE JUST DID WAS BAD.
IF SHE HASN'T, THEN I SUSPECT THE LASER BLASTS FROM THIS PAIR OF KILLER ROBOTS WILL ALERT HER TO THE NEW POTENTIAL DANGERS.
SHE SEEMS LIKE A TOUGH BROAD, HOPE SHE KEEPS HER PANIC BUTTON IN CHECK.
I'VE GOT THESE TWO UNDER WRAPS, NO WORRIES-- BUT I DON'T EVEN GET MY USUAL MOMENTARY SENSE OF ACHIEVEMENT BEFORE...
-BZZZRORT-
ZAP!
ZAP!
MORE OF THEM. I WAS AFRAID OF THIS.
WHERE THERE ARE FOUR AUTOMATONS THERE'S DAMN LIKELY FOUR HUNDRED MORE.
SPAK!
ZERTEEB-THUM!
ZERTEEB-THUM!

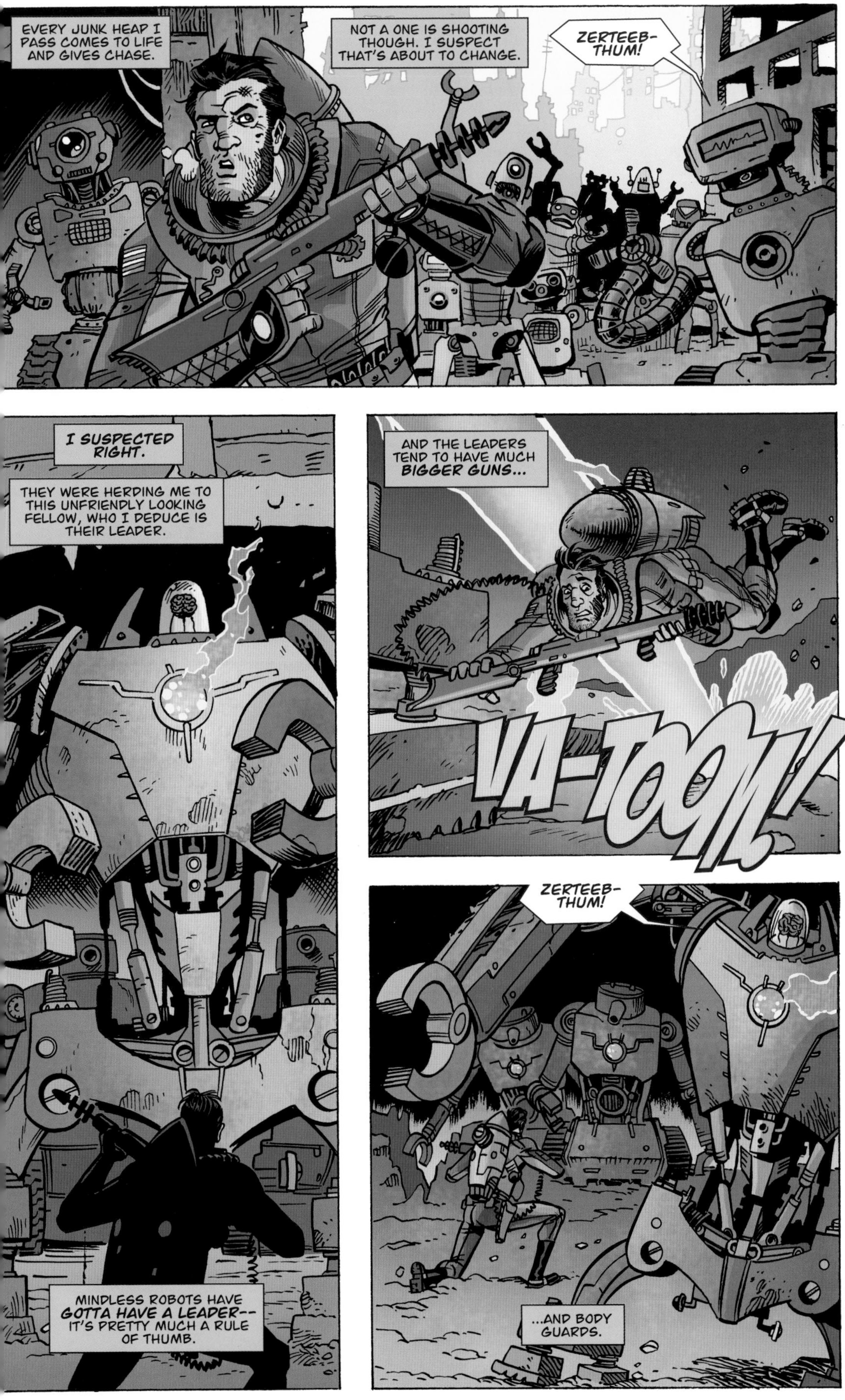
EVERY JUNK HEAP I PASS COMES TO LIFE AND GIVES CHASE.
NOT A ONE IS SHOOTING THOUGH. I SUSPECT THAT'S ABOUT TO CHANGE.
ZERTEEB-THUM!
I SUSPECTED RIGHT.
THEY WERE HERDING ME TO THIS UNFRIENDLY LOOKING FELLOW, WHO I DEDUCE IS THEIR LEADER.
MINDLESS ROBOTS HAVE GOTTA HAVE A LEADER-- IT'S PRETTY MUCH A RULE OF THUMB.
AND THE LEADERS TEND TO HAVE MUCH BIGGER GUNS...
VA-TOOM!
ZERTEEB-THUM!
...AND BODY GUARDS.

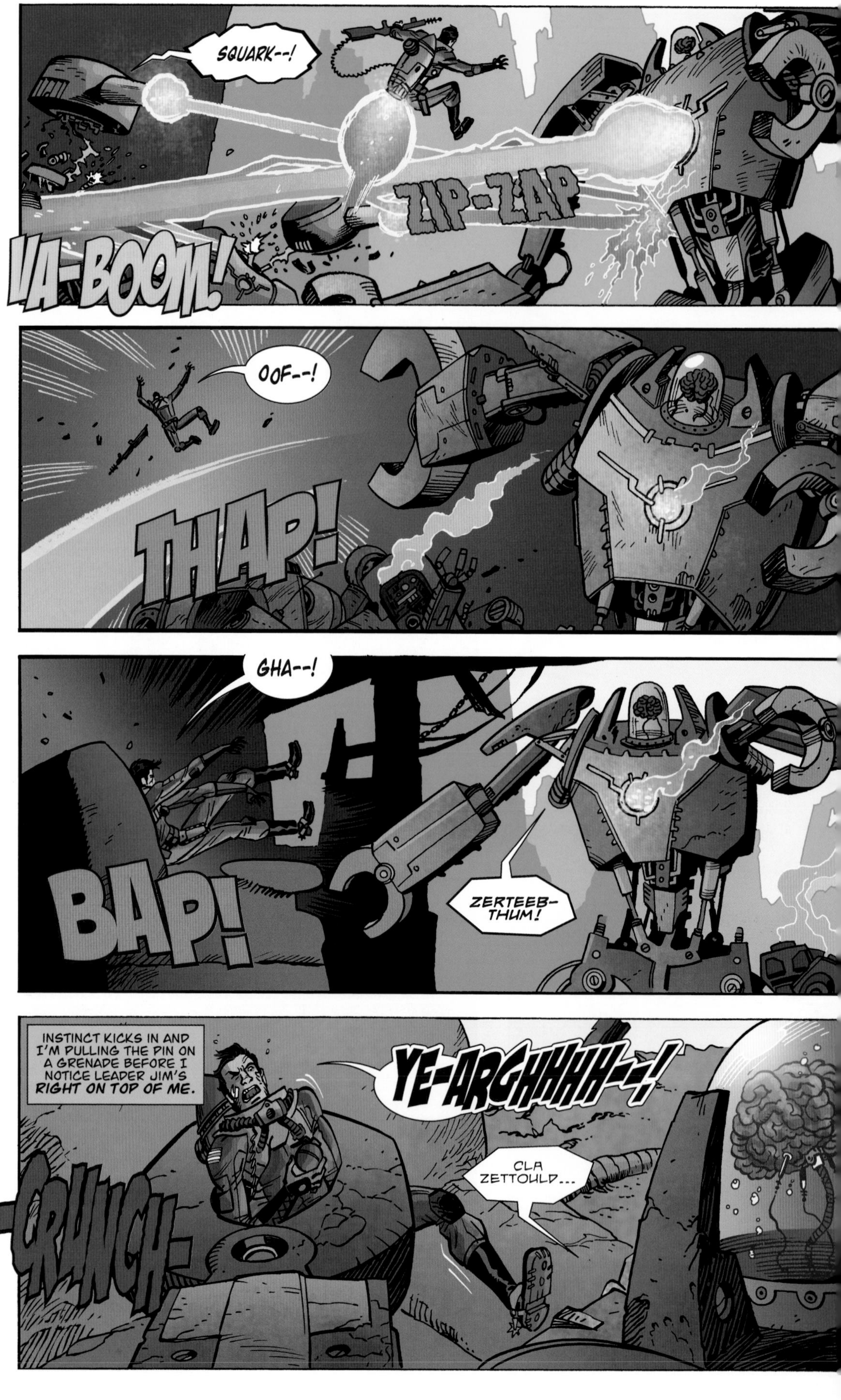
SQUARK--!
ZIP-ZAP
VA-BOOM!
OOF--!
THAP!
GHA--!
BAP!
ZERTEEB-THUM!
INSTINCT KICKS IN AND I'M PULLING THE PIN ON A GRENADE BEFORE I NOTICE LEADER JIM'S RIGHT ON TOP OF ME.
YE-ARGHHHH--!
-CRUNCH-
CLA ZETTOULD...

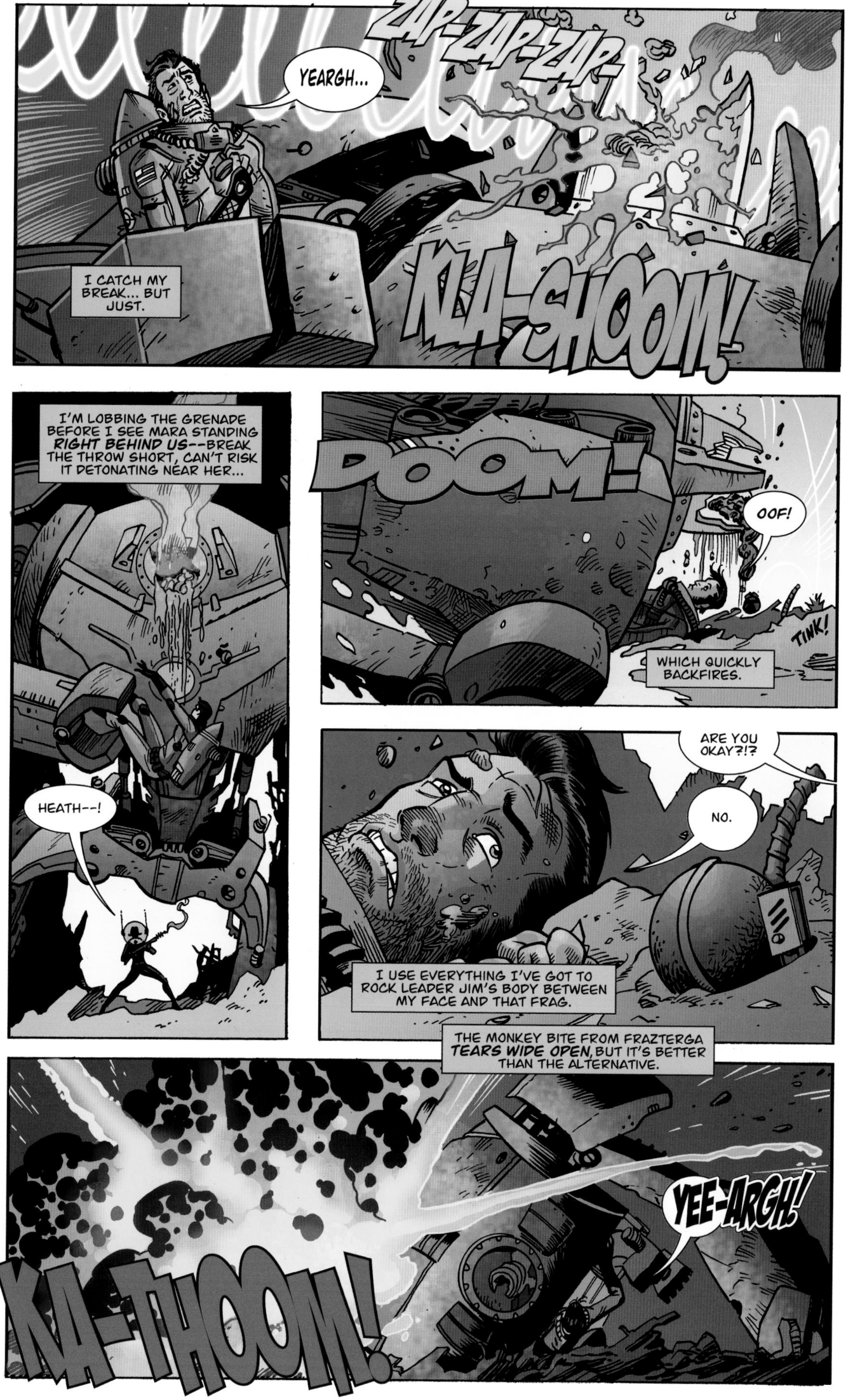
ZAP-ZAP-ZAP-
YEARGH...
I CATCH MY BREAK... BUT JUST.
KLA-SHOOM!
I'M LOBBING THE GRENADE BEFORE I SEE MARA STANDING RIGHT BEHIND US--BREAK THE THROW SHORT, CAN'T RISK IT DETONATING NEAR HER...
HEATH--!
DOOM!
OOF!
TINK!
WHICH QUICKLY BACKFIRES.
ARE YOU OKAY?!?
NO.
I USE EVERYTHING I'VE GOT TO ROCK LEADER JIM'S BODY BETWEEN MY FACE AND THAT FRAG.
THE MONKEY BITE FROM FRAZTERGA TEARS WIDE OPEN, BUT IT'S BETTER THAN THE ALTERNATIVE.
YEE-ARGH!
KA-THOOM!

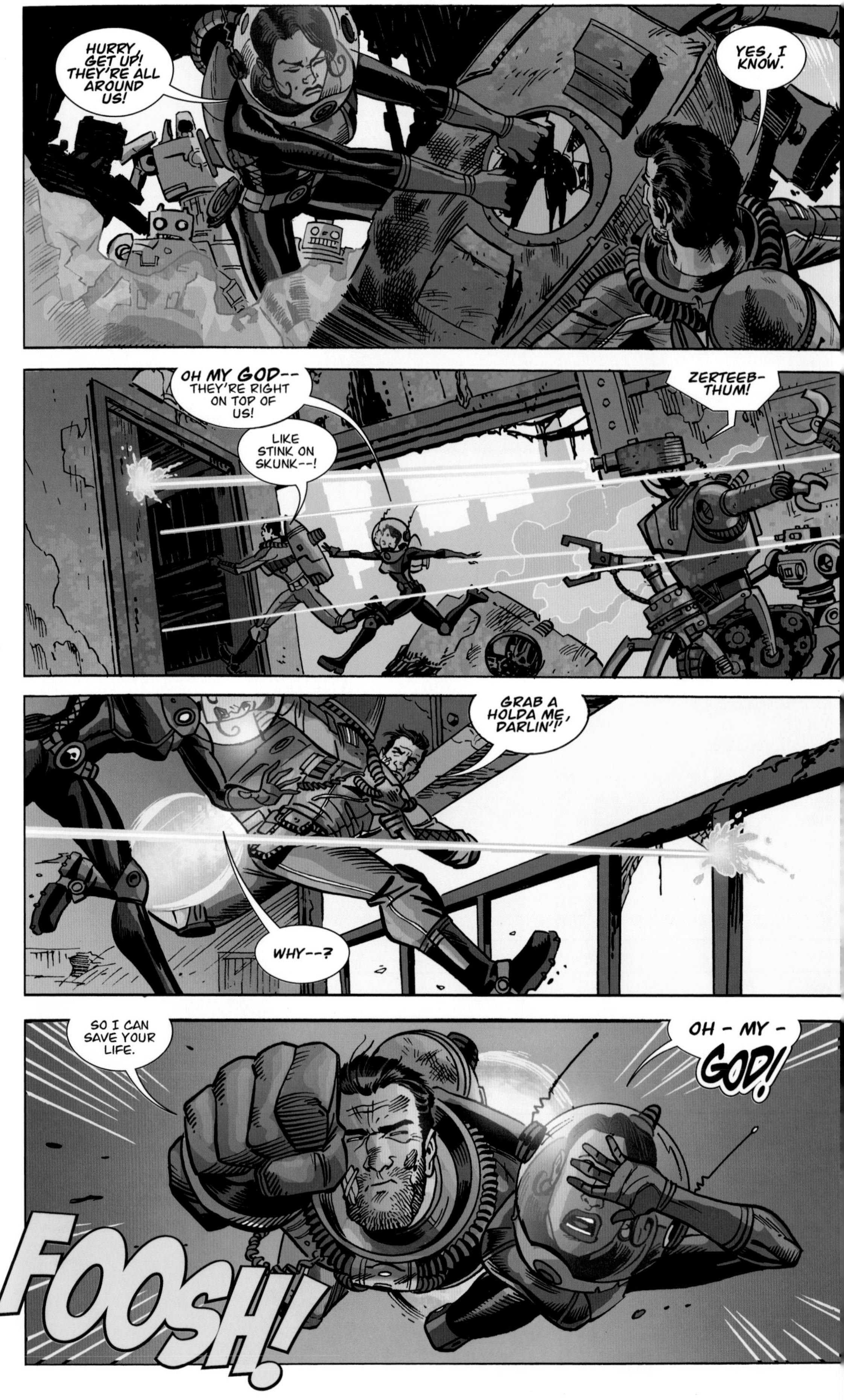
HURRY, GET UP! THEY'RE ALL AROUND US!
YES, I KNOW.
OH MY GOD-- THEY'RE RIGHT ON TOP OF US!
LIKE STINK ON SKUNK--!
ZERTEEB-THUM!
GRAB A HOLDA ME, DARLIN'!
WHY--?
SO I CAN SAVE YOUR LIFE.
OH - MY - GOD!
FOOSH!

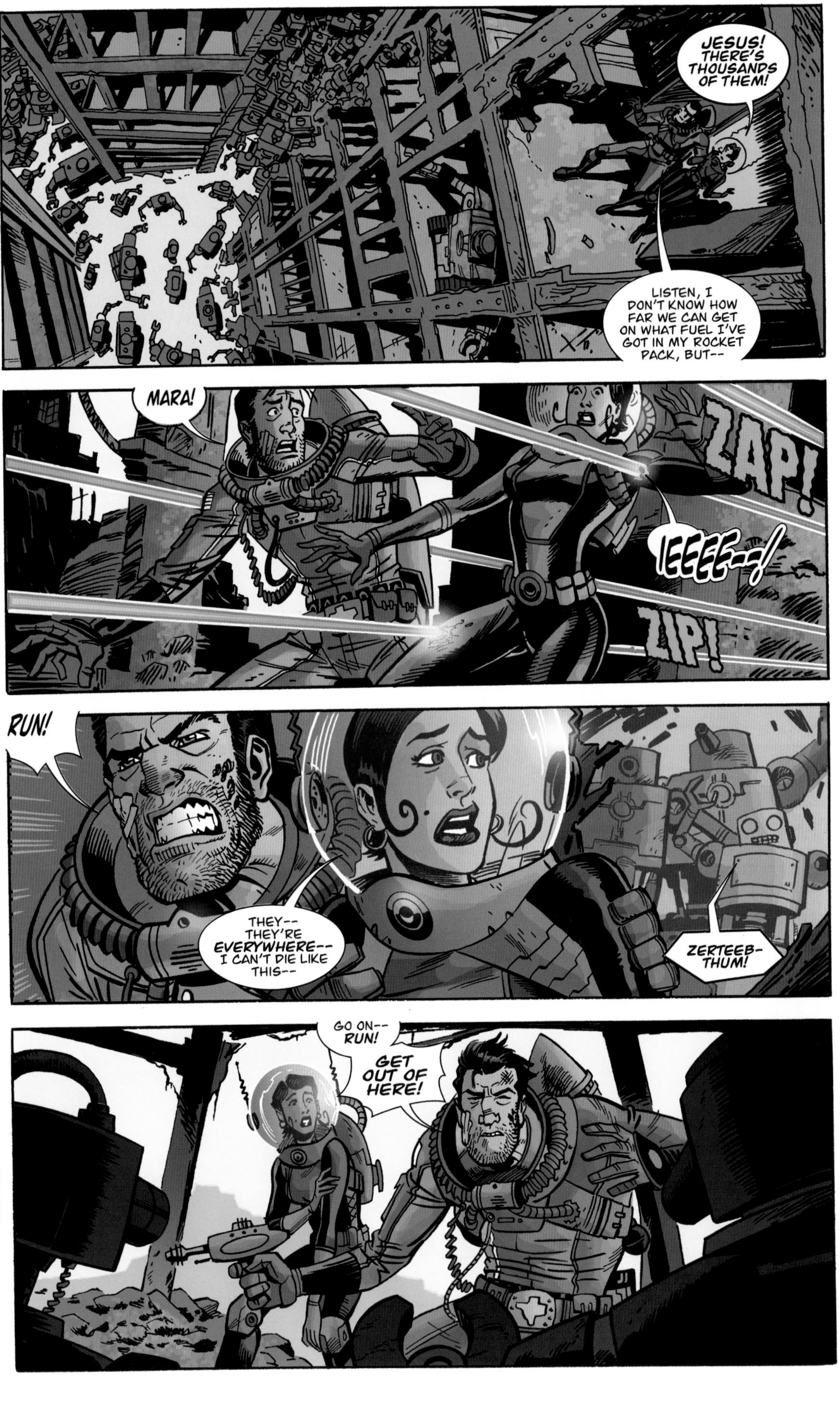

JESUS! THERE'S THOUSANDS OF THEM!
LISTEN, I DON'T KNOW HOW FAR WE CAN GET ON WHAT FUEL I'VE GOT IN MY ROCKET PACK, BUT--
MARA!
ZAP!
IEEEE--!
ZIP!
RUN!
THEY-- THEY'RE EVERYWHERE-- I CAN'T DIE LIKE THIS--
ZERTEEB-THUM!
GO ON-- RUN!
GET OUT OF HERE!

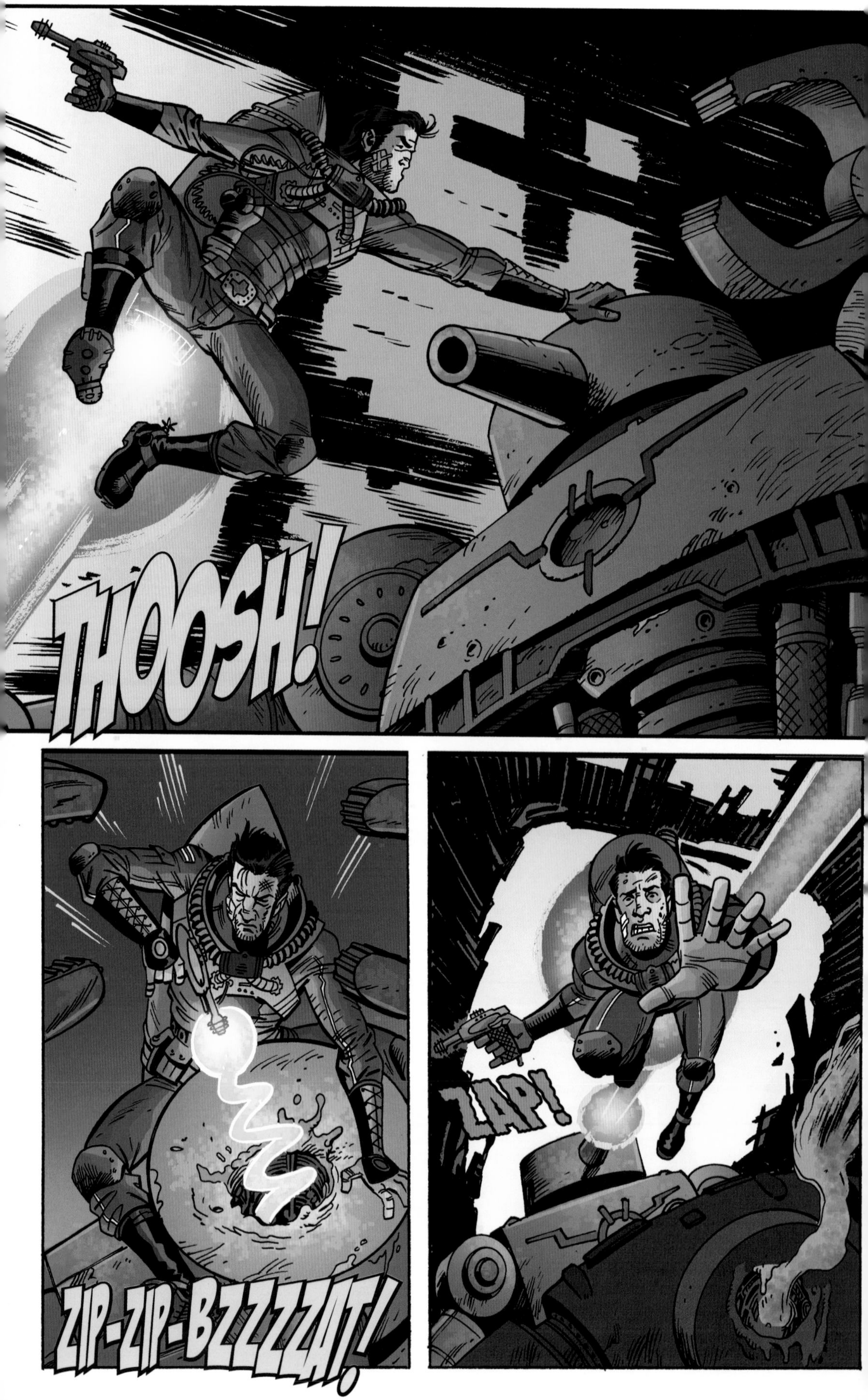
THOOSH!
ZIP-ZIP-BZZZZAT!
ZAP!

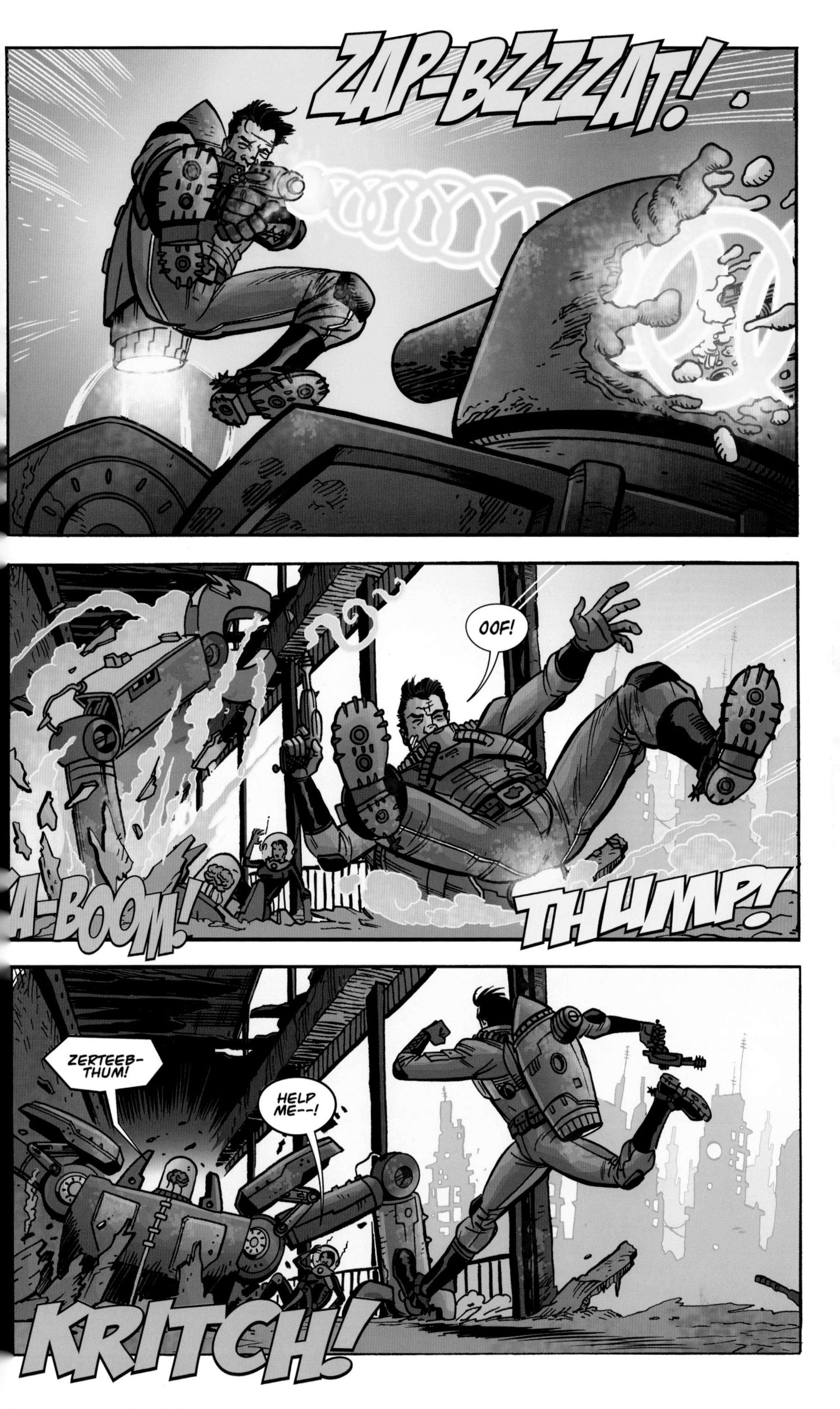
ZAP-BZZZAT!
OOF!
A-BOOM!
THUMP!
ZERTEEB-THUM!
HELP ME--!
KRITCH!

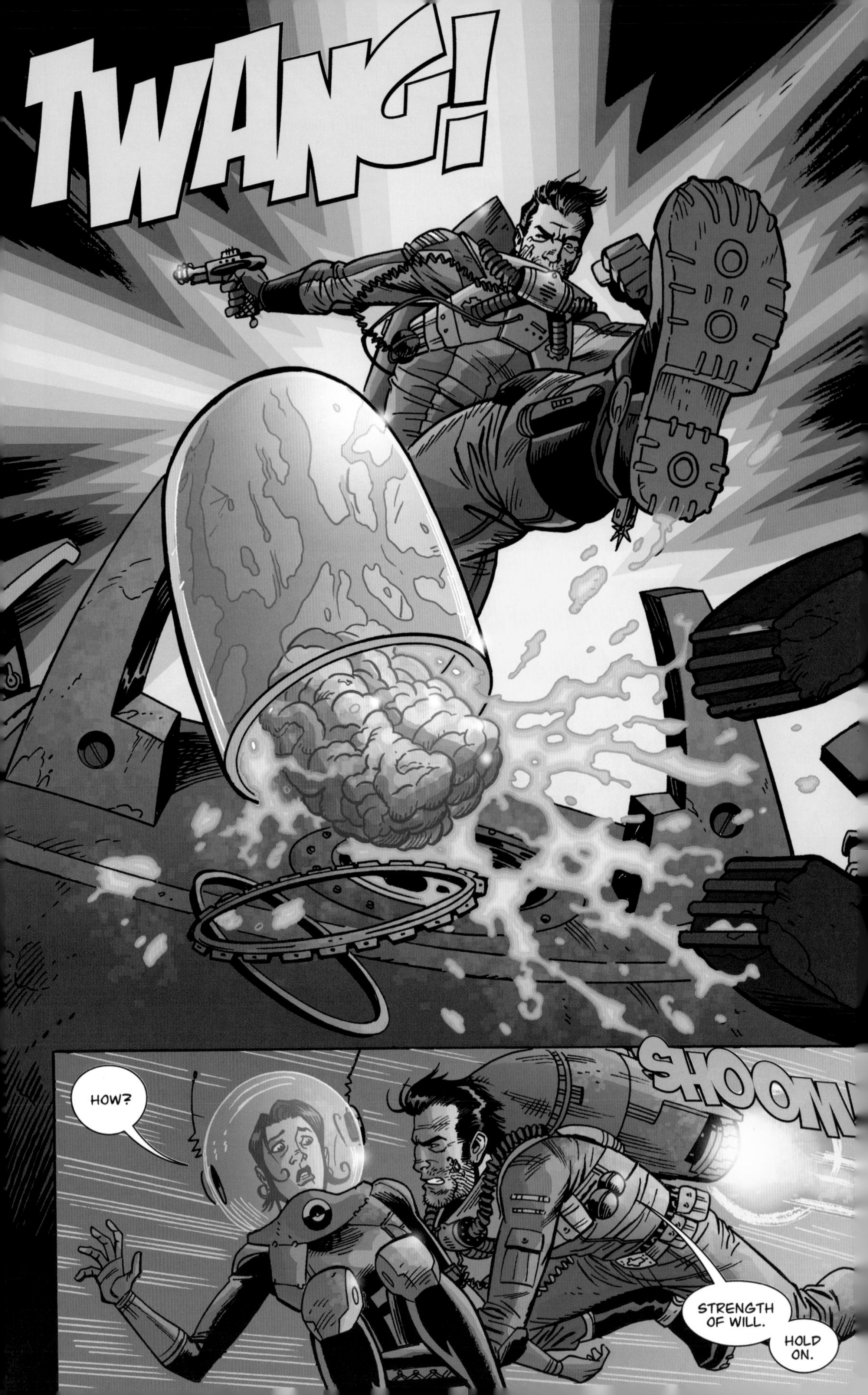
TWANG!
HOW?
SHOOM
STRENGTH OF WILL.
HOLD ON.

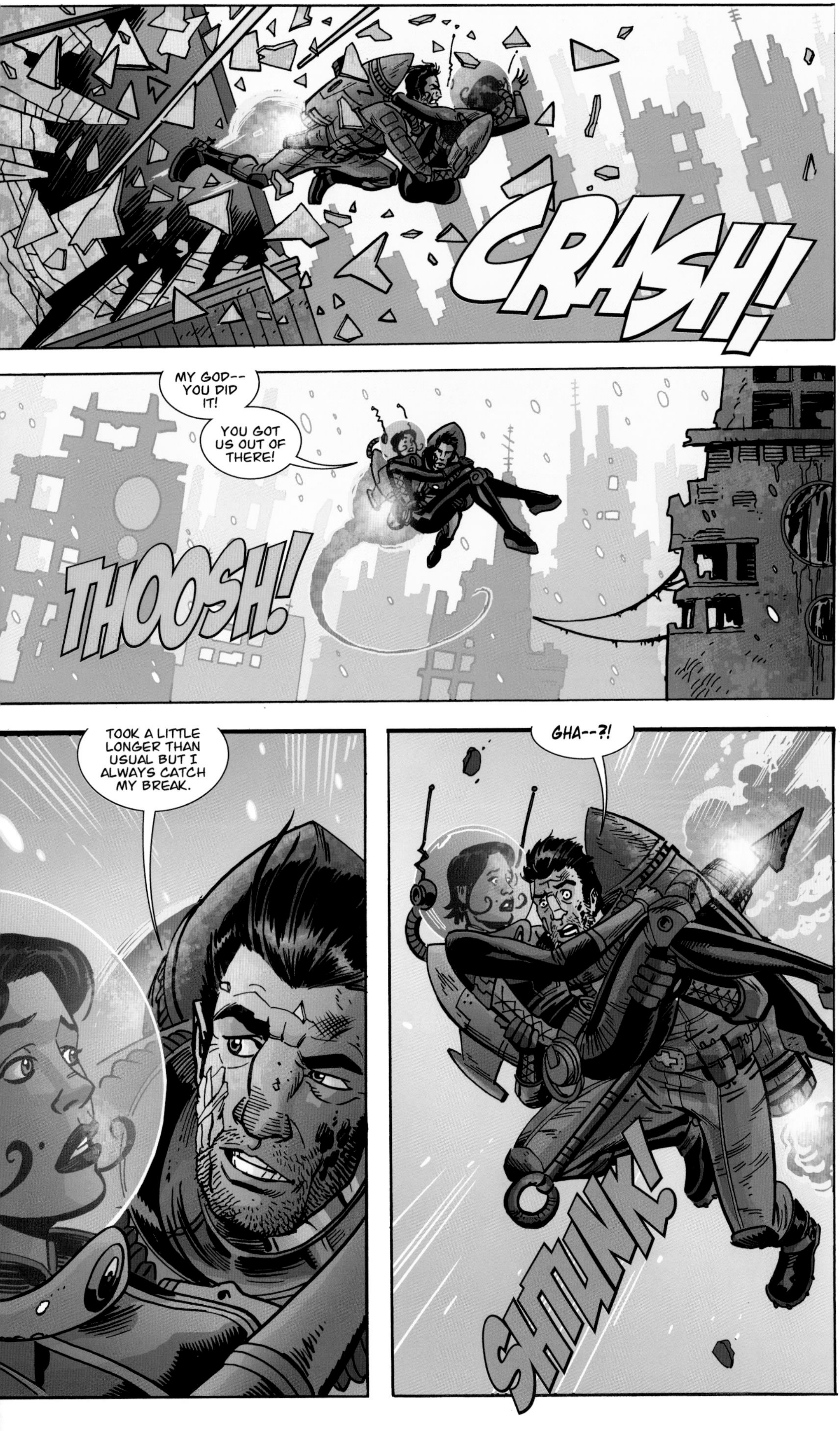
CRASH!
MY GOD-- YOU DID IT!
YOU GOT US OUT OF THERE!
THOOSH!
TOOK A LITTLE LONGER THAN USUAL BUT I ALWAYS CATCH MY BREAK.
GHA--?!
SHTUNK!

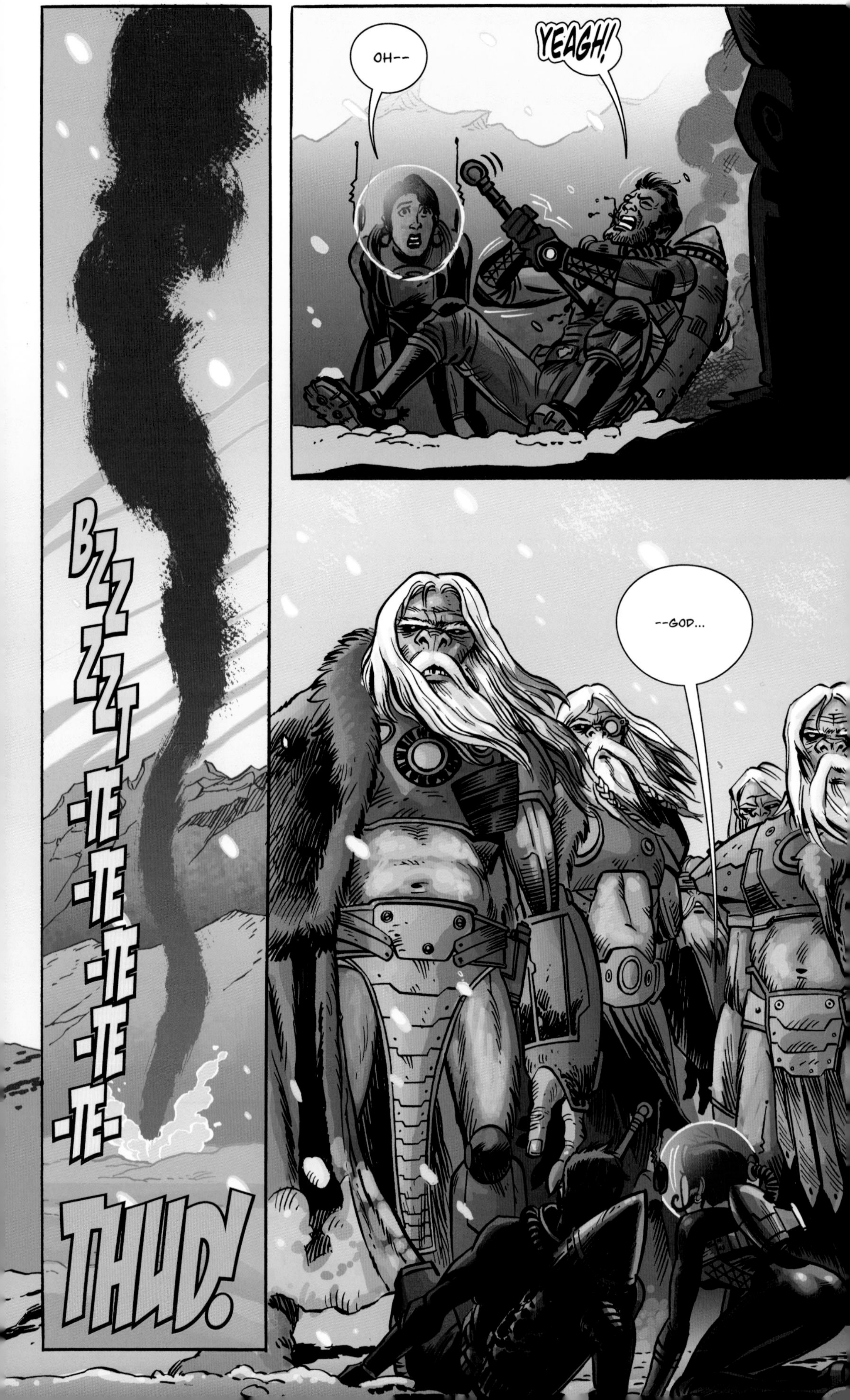
BZZZZT
-TE
-TE
-TE
-TE
-TE-
THUD!
OH--
YEAGH!
--GOD...

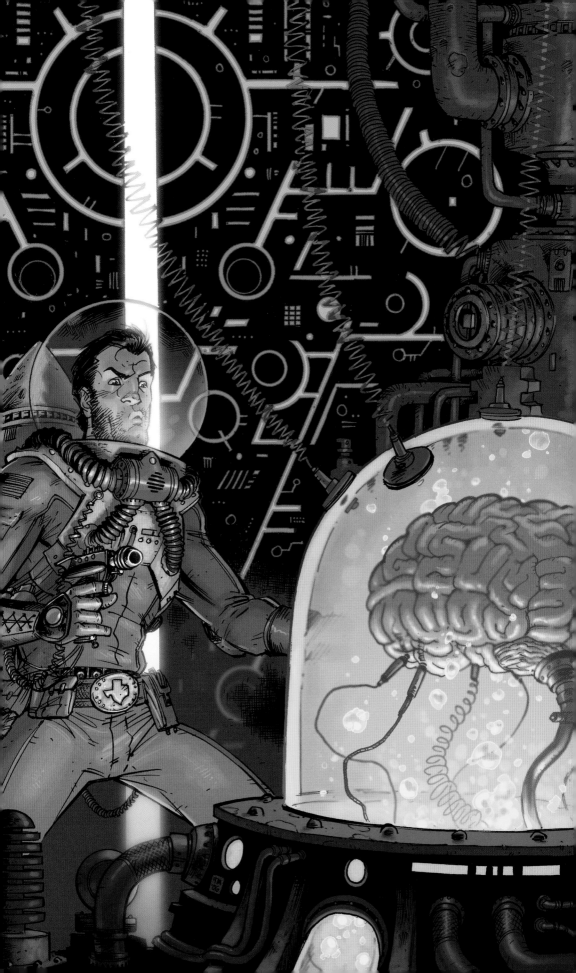

RE-IGNITION CHAPTER 4

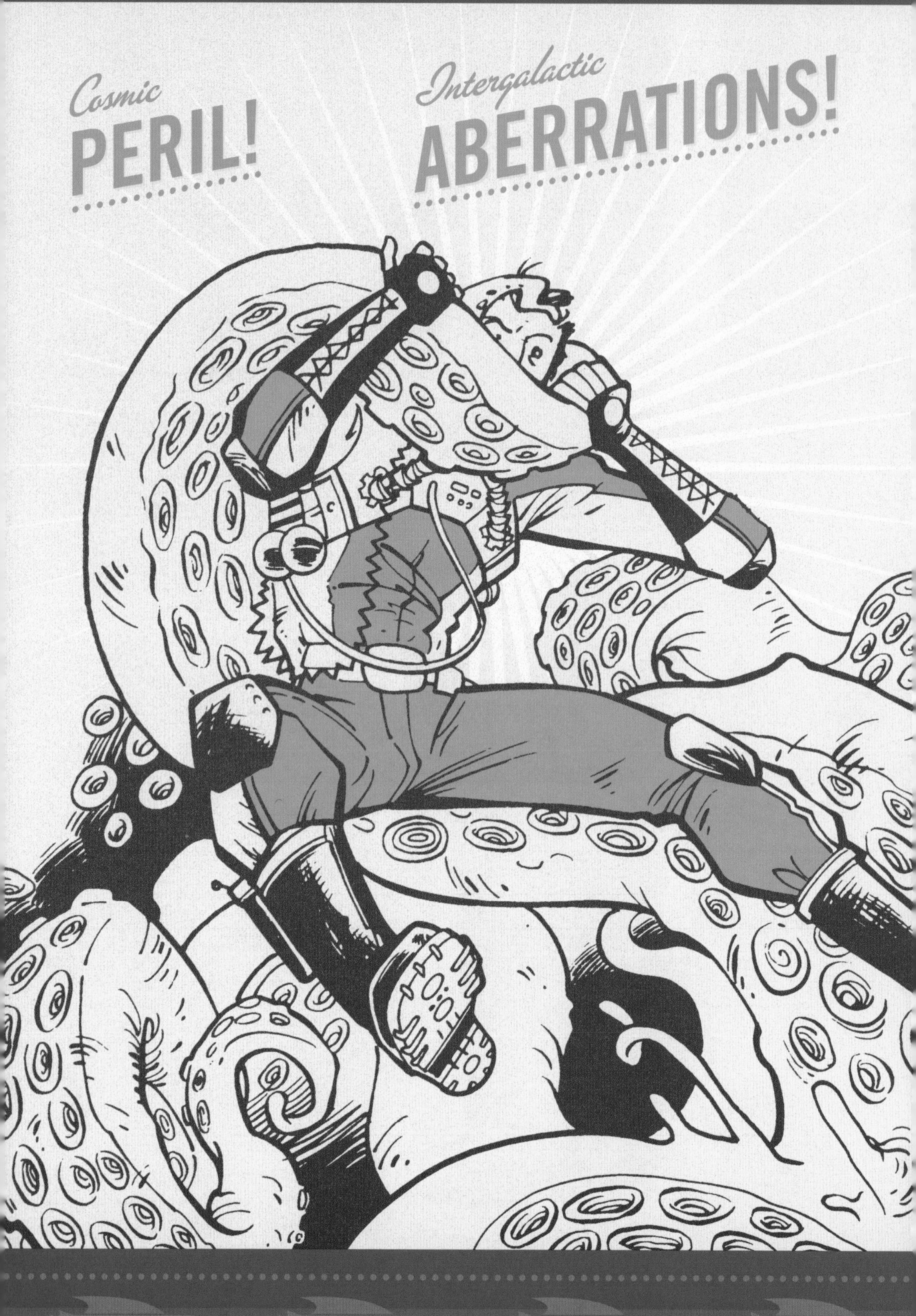
Cosmic
PERIL!
Intergalactic
ABERRATIONS!

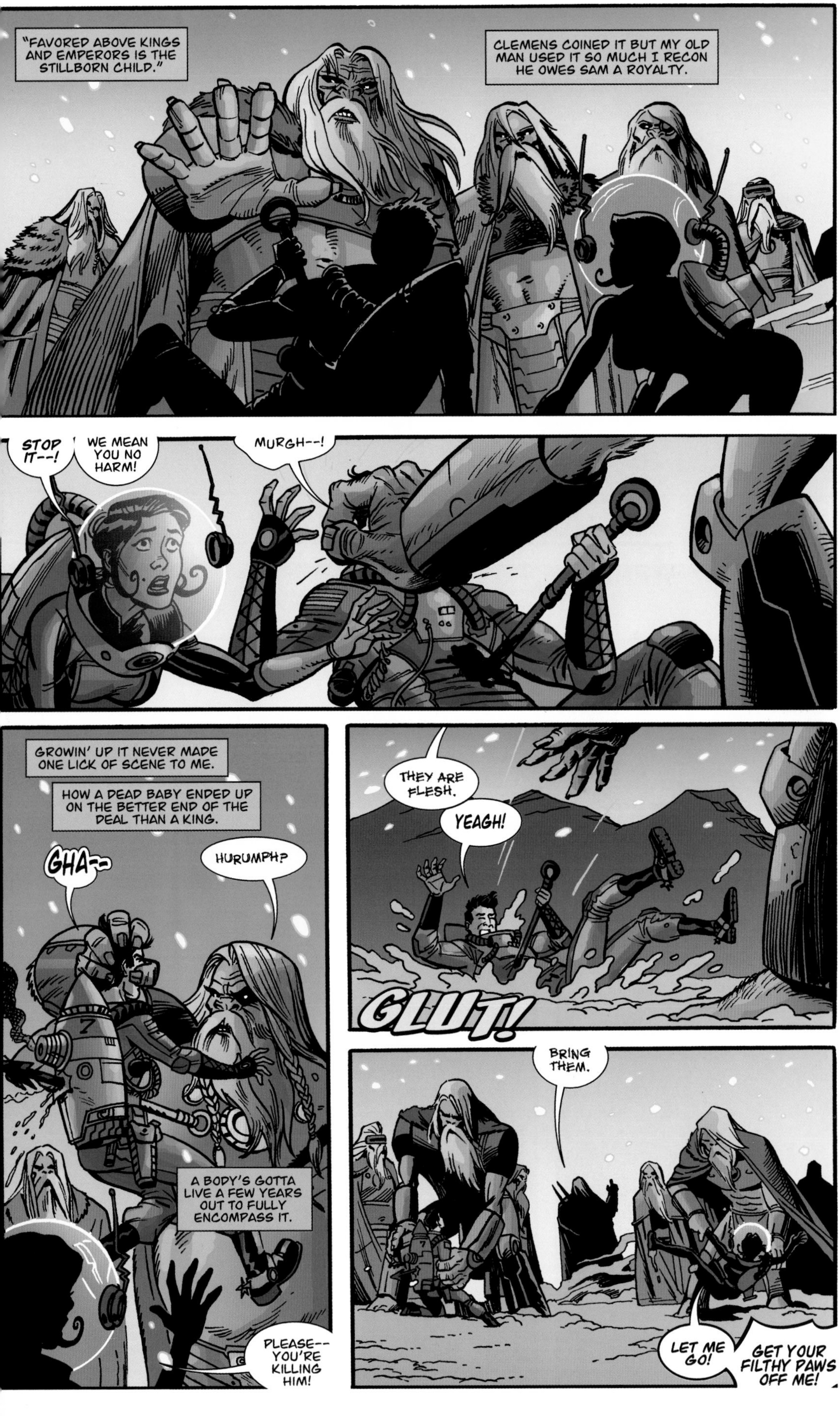
"FAVORED ABOVE KINGS AND EMPERORS IS THE STILLBORN CHILD."
CLEMENS COINED IT BUT MY OLD MAN USED IT SO MUCH I RECON HE OWES SAM A ROYALTY.
STOP IT--!
WE MEAN YOU NO HARM!
MURGH--!
GROWIN' UP IT NEVER MADE ONE LICK OF SCENE TO ME.
HOW A DEAD BABY ENDED UP ON THE BETTER END OF THE DEAL THAN A KING.
GHA--
HURUMPH?
A BODY'S GOTTA LIVE A FEW YEARS OUT TO FULLY ENCOMPASS IT.
PLEASE-- YOU'RE KILLING HIM!
THEY ARE FLESH.
YEAGH!
GLUT!
BRING THEM.
LET ME GO!
GET YOUR FILTHY PAWS OFF ME!

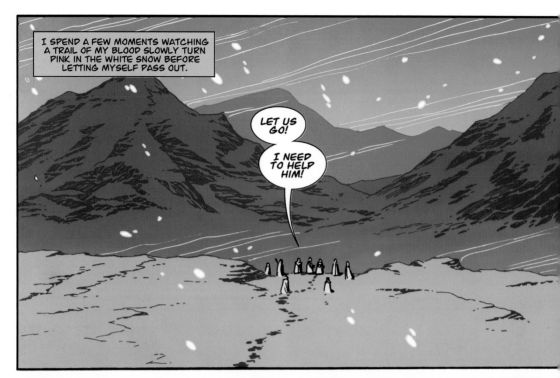

I SPEND A FEW MOMENTS WATCHING A TRAIL OF MY BLOOD SLOWLY TURN PINK IN THE WHITE SNOW BEFORE LETTING MYSELF PASS OUT.

LET US GO!

I NEED TO HELP HIM!

TEND TO HIM.

AS HE FELL BY MY SPEAR, I WISH TO BE UNHINDERED BY THE GUILT OF HIS DEATH.

NO RIGHT... TO TREAT...

BE STILL.

YOU HAVE LOST MUCH BLOOD.

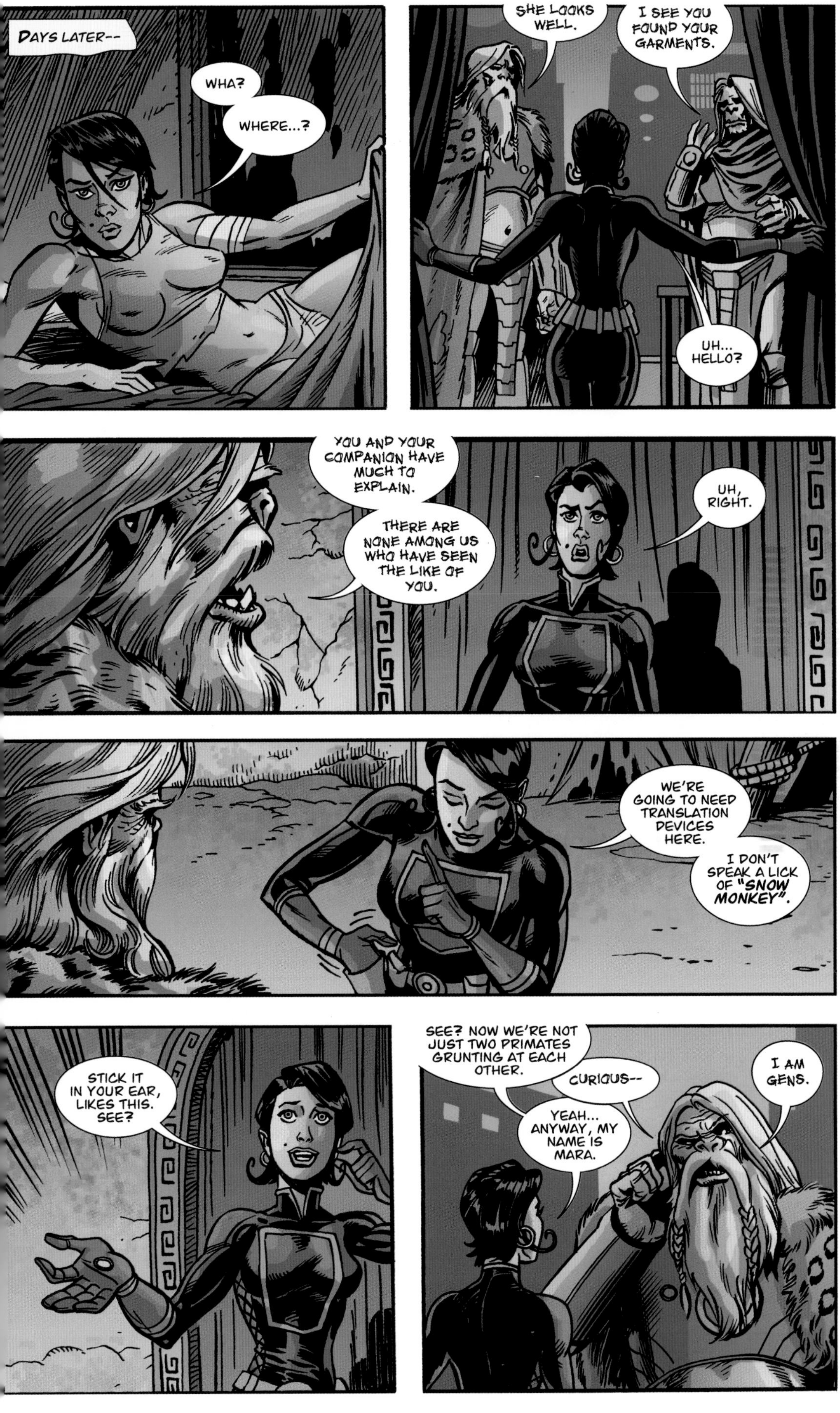
DAYS LATER--
WHA?
WHERE...?
SHE LOOKS WELL.
I SEE YOU FOUND YOUR GARMENTS.
UH... HELLO?
YOU AND YOUR COMPANION HAVE MUCH TO EXPLAIN.
THERE ARE NONE AMONG US WHO HAVE SEEN THE LIKE OF YOU.
UH, RIGHT.
WE'RE GOING TO NEED TRANSLATION DEVICES HERE.
I DON'T SPEAK A LICK OF "SNOW MONKEY".
STICK IT IN YOUR EAR, LIKES THIS. SEE?
SEE? NOW WE'RE NOT JUST TWO PRIMATES GRUNTING AT EACH OTHER.
CURIOUS--
YEAH... ANYWAY, MY NAME IS MARA.
I AM GENS.

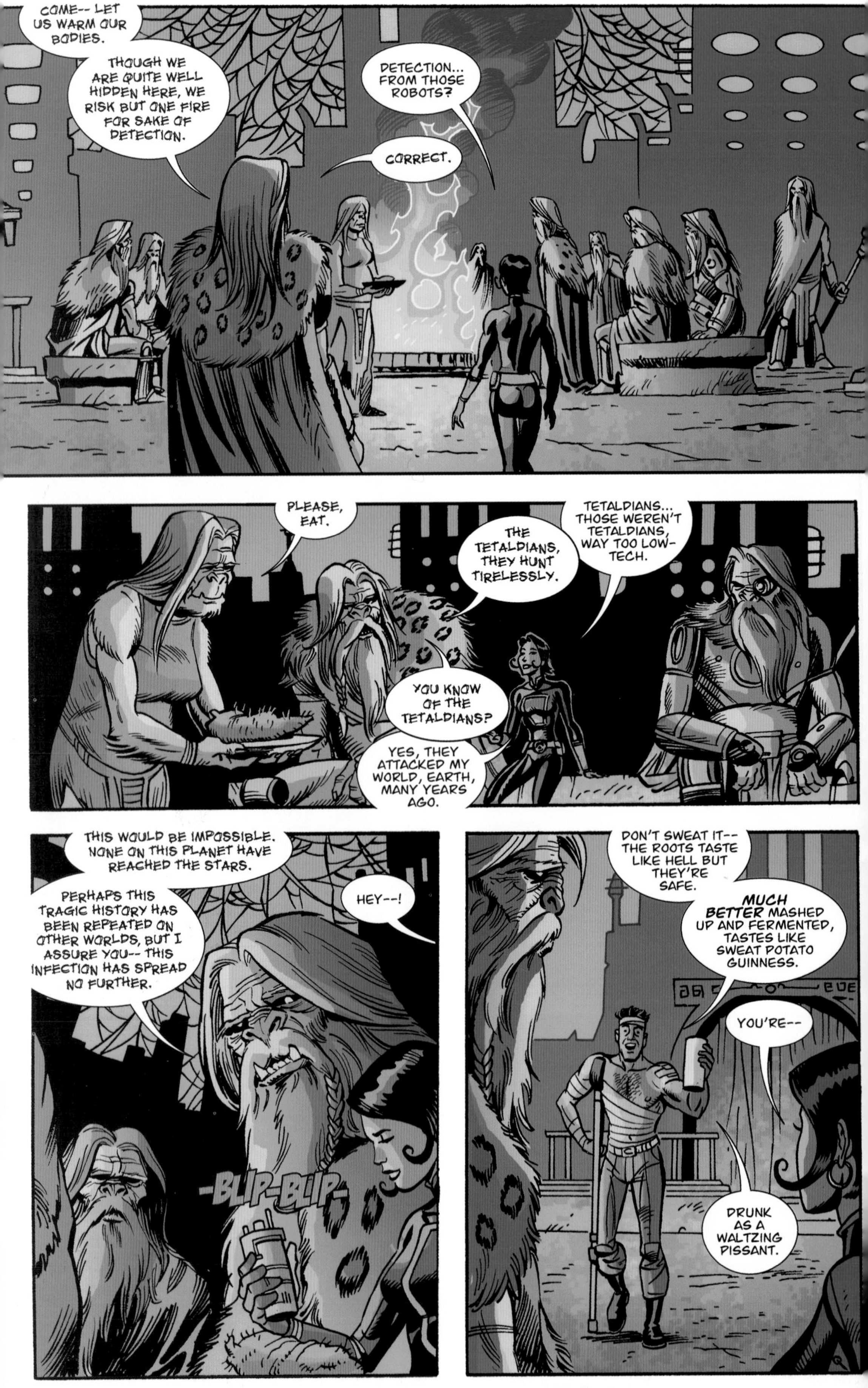
COME-- LET US WARM OUR BODIES.
THOUGH WE ARE QUITE WELL HIDDEN HERE, WE RISK BUT ONE FIRE FOR SAKE OF DETECTION.
DETECTION... FROM THOSE ROBOTS?
CORRECT.
PLEASE, EAT.
THE TETALDIANS, THEY HUNT TIRELESSLY.
TETALDIANS... THOSE WEREN'T TETALDIANS, WAY TOO LOW-TECH.
YOU KNOW OF THE TETALDIANS?
YES, THEY ATTACKED MY WORLD, EARTH, MANY YEARS AGO.
THIS WOULD BE IMPOSSIBLE. NONE ON THIS PLANET HAVE REACHED THE STARS.
PERHAPS THIS TRAGIC HISTORY HAS BEEN REPEATED ON OTHER WORLDS, BUT I ASSURE YOU-- THIS INFECTION HAS SPREAD NO FURTHER.
HEY--!
-BLIP-BLIP-
DON'T SWEAT IT-- THE ROOTS TASTE LIKE HELL BUT THEY'RE SAFE.
MUCH BETTER MASHED UP AND FERMENTED, TASTES LIKE SWEAT POTATO GUINNESS.
YOU'RE--
DRUNK AS A WALTZING PISSANT.

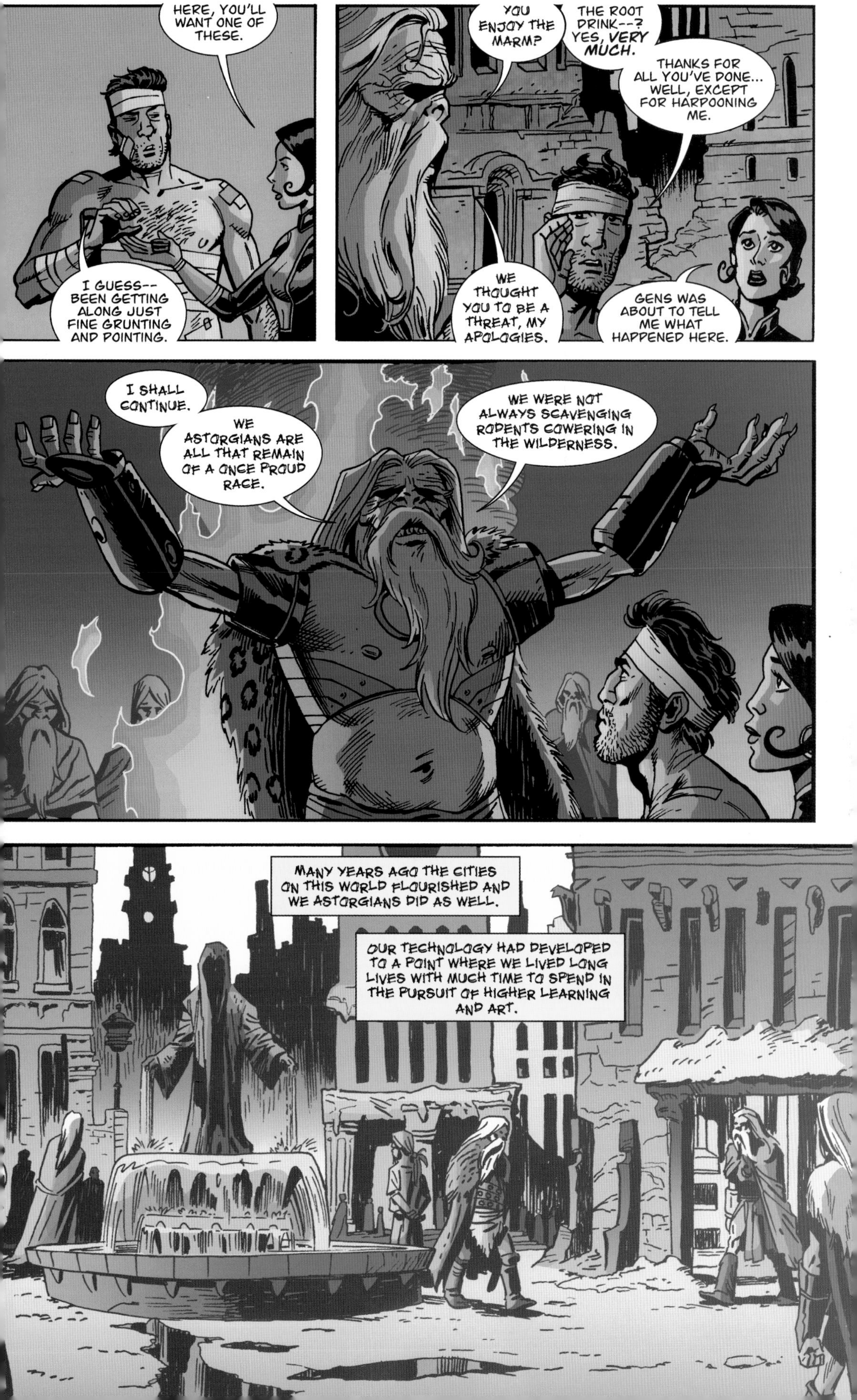

HERE, YOU'LL WANT ONE OF THESE.
I GUESS-- BEEN GETTING ALONG JUST FINE GRUNTING AND POINTING.
YOU ENJOY THE MARM?
THE ROOT DRINK--? YES, VERY MUCH.
THANKS FOR ALL YOU'VE DONE... WELL, EXCEPT FOR HARPOONING ME.
WE THOUGHT YOU TO BE A THREAT, MY APOLOGIES.
GENS WAS ABOUT TO TELL ME WHAT HAPPENED HERE.
I SHALL CONTINUE.
WE ASTORGIANS ARE ALL THAT REMAIN OF A ONCE PROUD RACE.
WE WERE NOT ALWAYS SCAVENGING RODENTS COWERING IN THE WILDERNESS.
MANY YEARS AGO THE CITIES ON THIS WORLD FLOURISHED AND WE ASTORGIANS DID AS WELL.
OUR TECHNOLOGY HAD DEVELOPED TO A POINT WHERE WE LIVED LONG LIVES WITH MUCH TIME TO SPEND IN THE PURSUIT OF HIGHER LEARNING AND ART.

WHEN OUR MOST BELOVED LEADER AND PHILOSOPHER, TETALD WAS COMING TO THE END OF HIS LIFE, THE GREATEST SCIENTIFIC MINDS OF THE TIME GATHERED IN HOPES THEY COULD DISCOVER A WAY TO GRANT HIM A REPRIEVE FROM DEATH.

I WILL ALLOW THE RESEARCH, FOR THE BETTERMENT OF ALL.

THEY SOON DISCOVERED THE TECHNOLOGY TO GRANT ETERNAL LIFE.

IT WAS RUDIMENTARY-- SIMPLY PLACING TETALD'S BRAIN IN AN ANDROID BODY.

TIME PASSED AND UNDER THE WATCHFUL EYE OF TETALD MANY OF THE HIGH COURT WERE GIVEN HIS BLESSING AS THEIR TIME CAME TO PASS.

TETALD BELIEVED IT WAS THE WILL OF THE TWO GODS THAT THE ASTORGIANS WOULD ONE DAY BECOME ADVANCED ENOUGH THAT ALL MIGHT BE IMMORTAL THROUGH TECHNOLOGY; CYBERNETICS WAS THOUGHT TO BE THE NEXT STAGE OF EVOLUTION.

AS TETALD'S TWO DISCIPLES, TROLEEN AND JENTU, CONTINUED TO TRANSFER THE DYING INTO THEIR NEW BODIES IT BECAME CLEAR THAT THERE WAS SIMPLY NOT ENOUGH METAL ON THE PLANET TO GIVE THE BLESSING TO ALL.

THERE WAS NOT NEARLY ENOUGH FOR EVEN A THIRD.

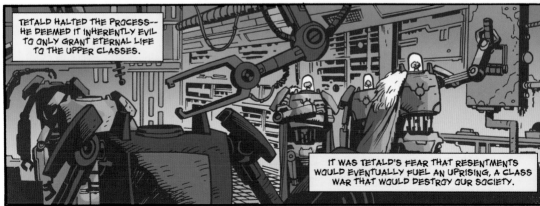

TETALD HALTED THE PROCESS-- HE DEEMED IT INHERENTLY EVIL TO ONLY GRANT ETERNAL LIFE TO THE UPPER CLASSES.

IT WAS TETALD'S FEAR THAT RESENTMENTS WOULD EVENTUALLY FUEL AN UPRISING, A CLASS WAR THAT WOULD DESTROY OUR SOCIETY.

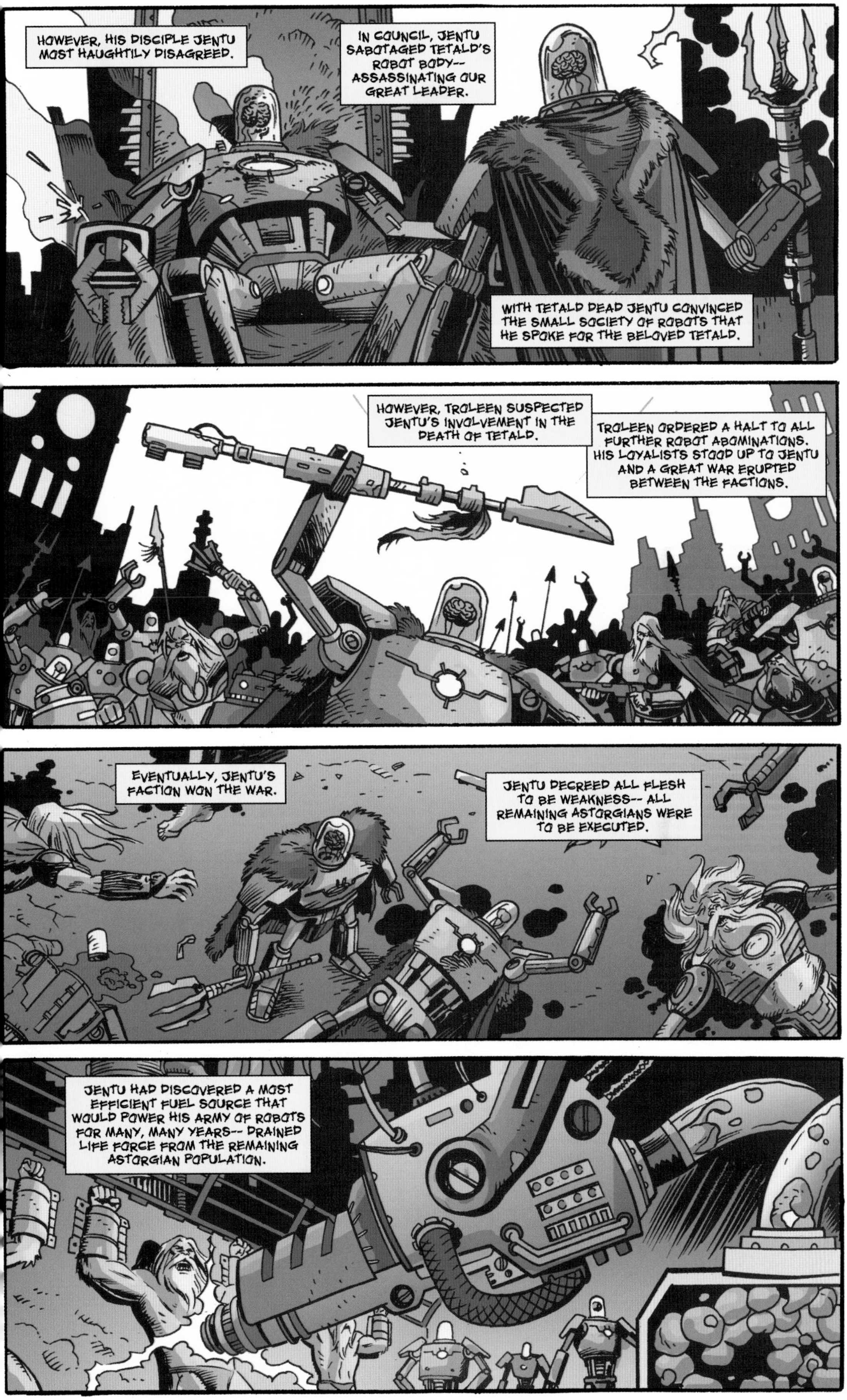
HOWEVER, HIS DISCIPLE JENTU MOST HAUGHTILY DISAGREED.
IN COUNCIL, JENTU SABOTAGED TETALD'S ROBOT BODY-- ASSASSINATING OUR GREAT LEADER.
WITH TETALD DEAD JENTU CONVINCED THE SMALL SOCIETY OF ROBOTS THAT HE SPOKE FOR THE BELOVED TETALD.
HOWEVER, TROLEEN SUSPECTED JENTU'S INVOLVEMENT IN THE DEATH OF TETALD.
TROLEEN ORDERED A HALT TO ALL FURTHER ROBOT ABOMINATIONS. HIS LOYALISTS STOOD UP TO JENTU AND A GREAT WAR ERUPTED BETWEEN THE FACTIONS.
EVENTUALLY, JENTU'S FACTION WON THE WAR.
JENTU DECREED ALL FLESH TO BE WEAKNESS-- ALL REMAINING ASTORGIANS WERE TO BE EXECUTED.
JENTU HAD DISCOVERED A MOST EFFICIENT FUEL SOURCE THAT WOULD POWER HIS ARMY OF ROBOTS FOR MANY, MANY YEARS-- DRAINED LIFE FORCE FROM THE REMAINING ASTORGIAN POPULATION.

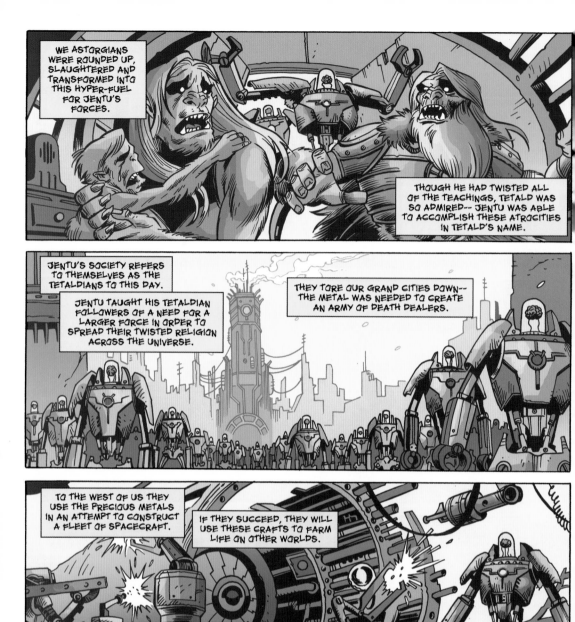

WE ASTORGIANS WERE ROUNDED UP, SLAUGHTERED AND TRANSFORMED INTO THIS HYPER-FUEL FOR JENTU'S FORCES.

THOUGH HE HAD TWISTED ALL OF THE TEACHINGS, TETALD WAS SO ADMIRED-- JENTU WAS ABLE TO ACCOMPLISH THESE ATROCITIES IN TETALD'S NAME.

JENTU'S SOCIETY REFERS TO THEMSELVES AS THE TETALDIANS TO THIS DAY.

JENTU TAUGHT HIS TETALDIAN FOLLOWERS OF A NEED FOR A LARGER FORCE IN ORDER TO SPREAD THEIR TWISTED RELIGION ACROSS THE UNIVERSE.

THEY TORE OUR GRAND CITIES DOWN-- THE METAL WAS NEEDED TO CREATE AN ARMY OF DEATH DEALERS.

TO THE WEST OF US THEY USE THE PRECIOUS METALS IN AN ATTEMPT TO CONSTRUCT A FLEET OF SPACECRAFT.

IF THEY SUCCEED, THEY WILL USE THESE CRAFTS TO FARM LIFE ON OTHER WORLDS.

HOWEVER, *THEY WILL NOT SUCCEED.* WE HAVE SACRIFICED MUCH IN ORDER TO SABOTAGE THESE EFFORTS-- THEY HAVE FAILED TO COMPLETE A SINGLE VESSEL.

AND WE WILL CONTINUE TO FIGHT THEM TO OUR VERY END. THIS PLAGUE IS OUR BURDEN-- IT *WILL NOT* BE PERMITTED TO SPREAD.

TETALDIANS...

I THOUGHT THE SAME THING, HEATH BUT IT'S IMPOSSIBLE.

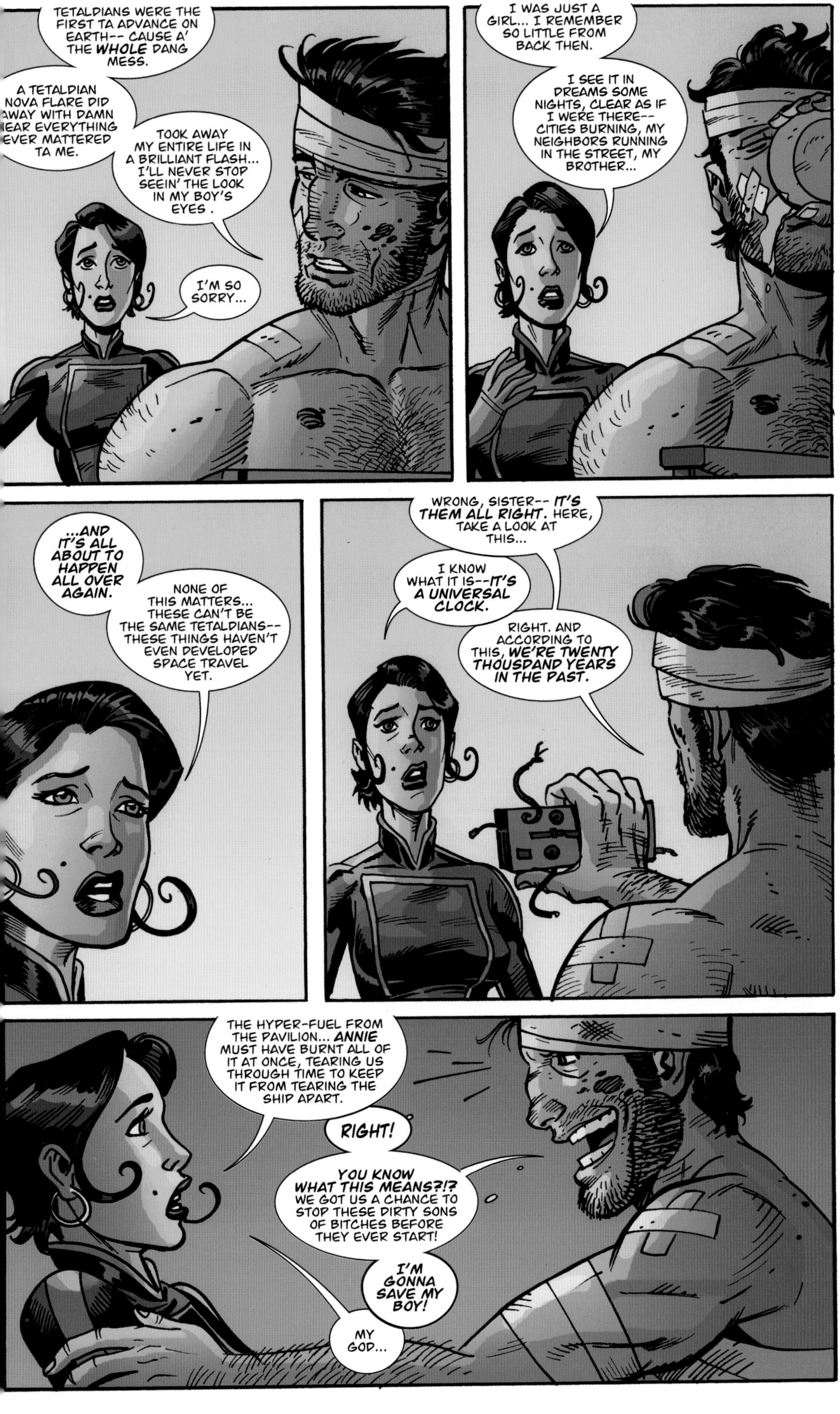
TETALDIANS WERE THE FIRST TA ADVANCE ON EARTH-- CAUSE A' THE WHOLE DANG MESS.
A TETALDIAN NOVA FLARE DID AWAY WITH DAMN NEAR EVERYTHING EVER MATTERED TA ME.
TOOK AWAY MY ENTIRE LIFE IN A BRILLIANT FLASH... I'LL NEVER STOP SEEIN' THE LOOK IN MY BOY'S EYES .
I'M SO SORRY...
I WAS JUST A GIRL... I REMEMBER SO LITTLE FROM BACK THEN.
I SEE IT IN DREAMS SOME NIGHTS, CLEAR AS IF I WERE THERE-- CITIES BURNING, MY NEIGHBORS RUNNING IN THE STREET, MY BROTHER...
...AND IT'S ALL ABOUT TO HAPPEN ALL OVER AGAIN.
NONE OF THIS MATTERS... THESE CAN'T BE THE SAME TETALDIANS-- THESE THINGS HAVEN'T EVEN DEVELOPED SPACE TRAVEL YET.
WRONG, SISTER-- IT'S THEM ALL RIGHT. HERE, TAKE A LOOK AT THIS...
I KNOW WHAT IT IS--IT'S A UNIVERSAL CLOCK.
RIGHT. AND ACCORDING TO THIS, WE'RE TWENTY THOUSAND YEARS IN THE PAST.
THE HYPER-FUEL FROM THE PAVILION... ANNIE MUST HAVE BURNT ALL OF IT AT ONCE, TEARING US THROUGH TIME TO KEEP IT FROM TEARING THE SHIP APART.
RIGHT!
YOU KNOW WHAT THIS MEANS?!? WE GOT US A CHANCE TO STOP THESE DIRTY SONS OF BITCHES BEFORE THEY EVER START!
I'M GONNA SAVE MY BOY!
MY GOD...

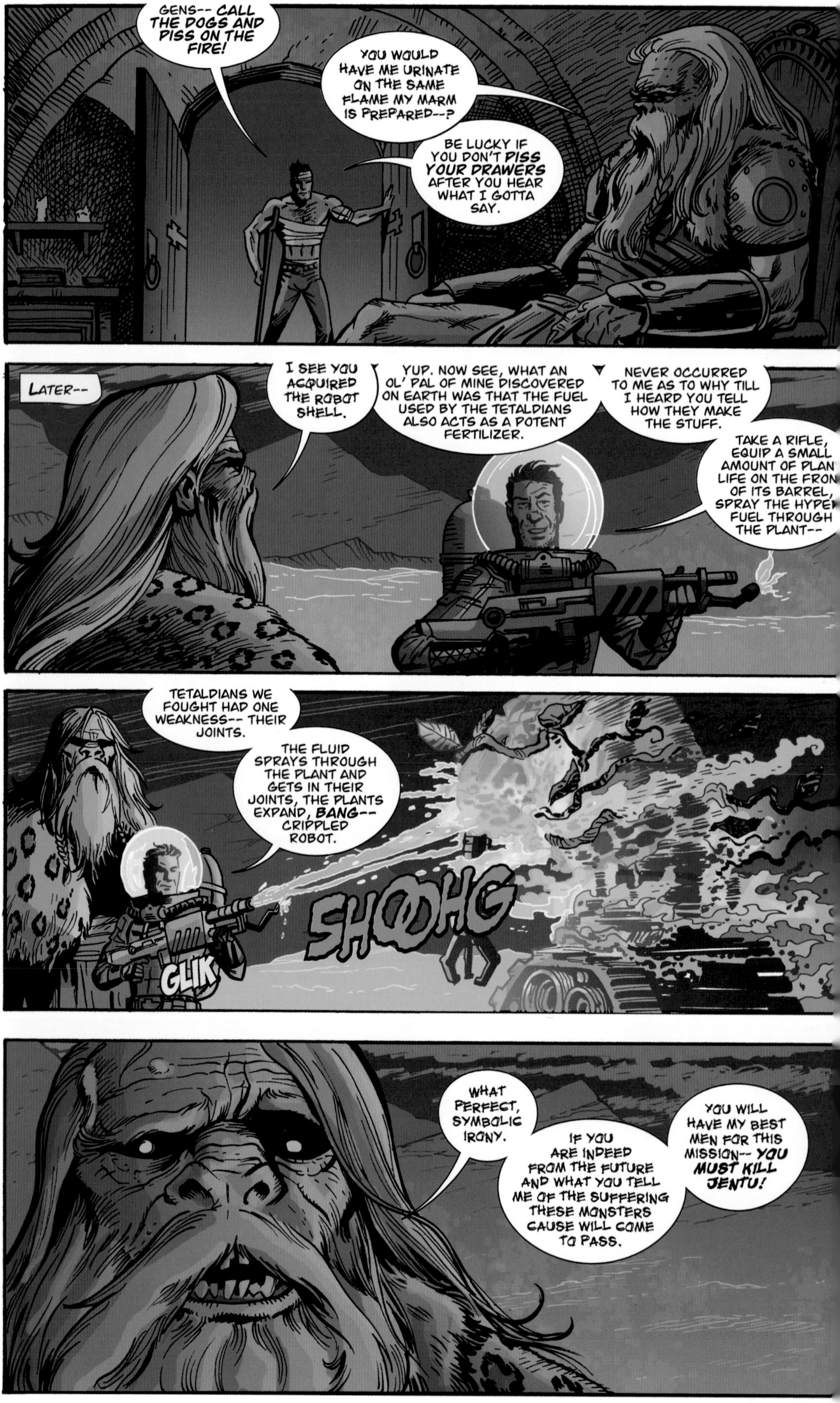
GENS-- CALL THE DOGS AND PISS ON THE FIRE!
YOU WOULD HAVE ME URINATE ON THE SAME FLAME MY MARM IS PREPARED--?
BE LUCKY IF YOU DON'T PISS YOUR DRAWERS AFTER YOU HEAR WHAT I GOTTA SAY.
LATER--
I SEE YOU ACQUIRED THE ROBOT SHELL.
YUP. NOW SEE, WHAT AN OL' PAL OF MINE DISCOVERED ON EARTH WAS THAT THE FUEL USED BY THE TETALDIANS ALSO ACTS AS A POTENT FERTILIZER.
NEVER OCCURRED TO ME AS TO WHY TILL I HEARD YOU TELL HOW THEY MAKE THE STUFF.
TAKE A RIFLE, EQUIP A SMALL AMOUNT OF PLAN LIFE ON THE FRON OF ITS BARREL, SPRAY THE HYPE FUEL THROUGH THE PLANT--
TETALDIANS WE FOUGHT HAD ONE WEAKNESS-- THEIR JOINTS.
THE FLUID SPRAYS THROUGH THE PLANT AND GETS IN THEIR JOINTS, THE PLANTS EXPAND, BANG-- CRIPPLED ROBOT.
SHOOHG
GLIK
WHAT PERFECT, SYMBOLIC IRONY.
IF YOU ARE INDEED FROM THE FUTURE AND WHAT YOU TELL ME OF THE SUFFERING THESE MONSTERS CAUSE WILL COME TO PASS.
YOU WILL HAVE MY BEST MEN FOR THIS MISSION-- YOU MUST KILL JENTU!

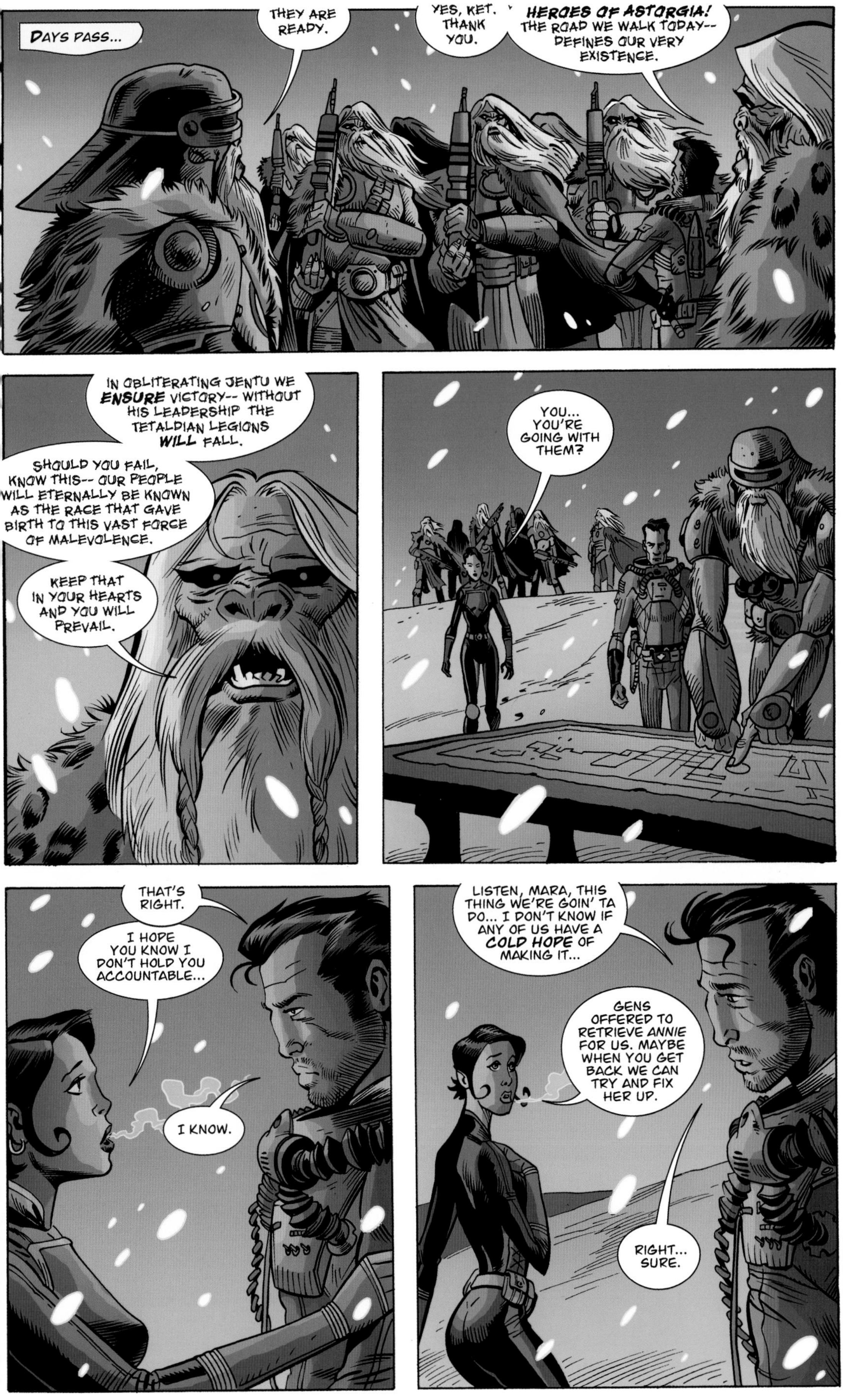
DAYS PASS...
THEY ARE READY.
YES, KET. THANK YOU.
HEROES OF ASTORGIA! THE ROAD WE WALK TODAY-- DEFINES OUR VERY EXISTENCE.
IN OBLITERATING JENTU WE ENSURE VICTORY-- WITHOUT HIS LEADERSHIP THE TETALDIAN LEGIONS WILL FALL.
SHOULD YOU FAIL, KNOW THIS-- OUR PEOPLE WILL ETERNALLY BE KNOWN AS THE RACE THAT GAVE BIRTH TO THIS VAST FORCE OF MALEVOLENCE.
KEEP THAT IN YOUR HEARTS AND YOU WILL PREVAIL.
YOU... YOU'RE GOING WITH THEM?
THAT'S RIGHT.
I HOPE YOU KNOW I DON'T HOLD YOU ACCOUNTABLE...
I KNOW.
LISTEN, MARA, THIS THING WE'RE GOIN' TA DO... I DON'T KNOW IF ANY OF US HAVE A COLD HOPE OF MAKING IT...
GENS OFFERED TO RETRIEVE ANNIE FOR US. MAYBE WHEN YOU GET BACK WE CAN TRY AND FIX HER UP.
RIGHT... SURE.

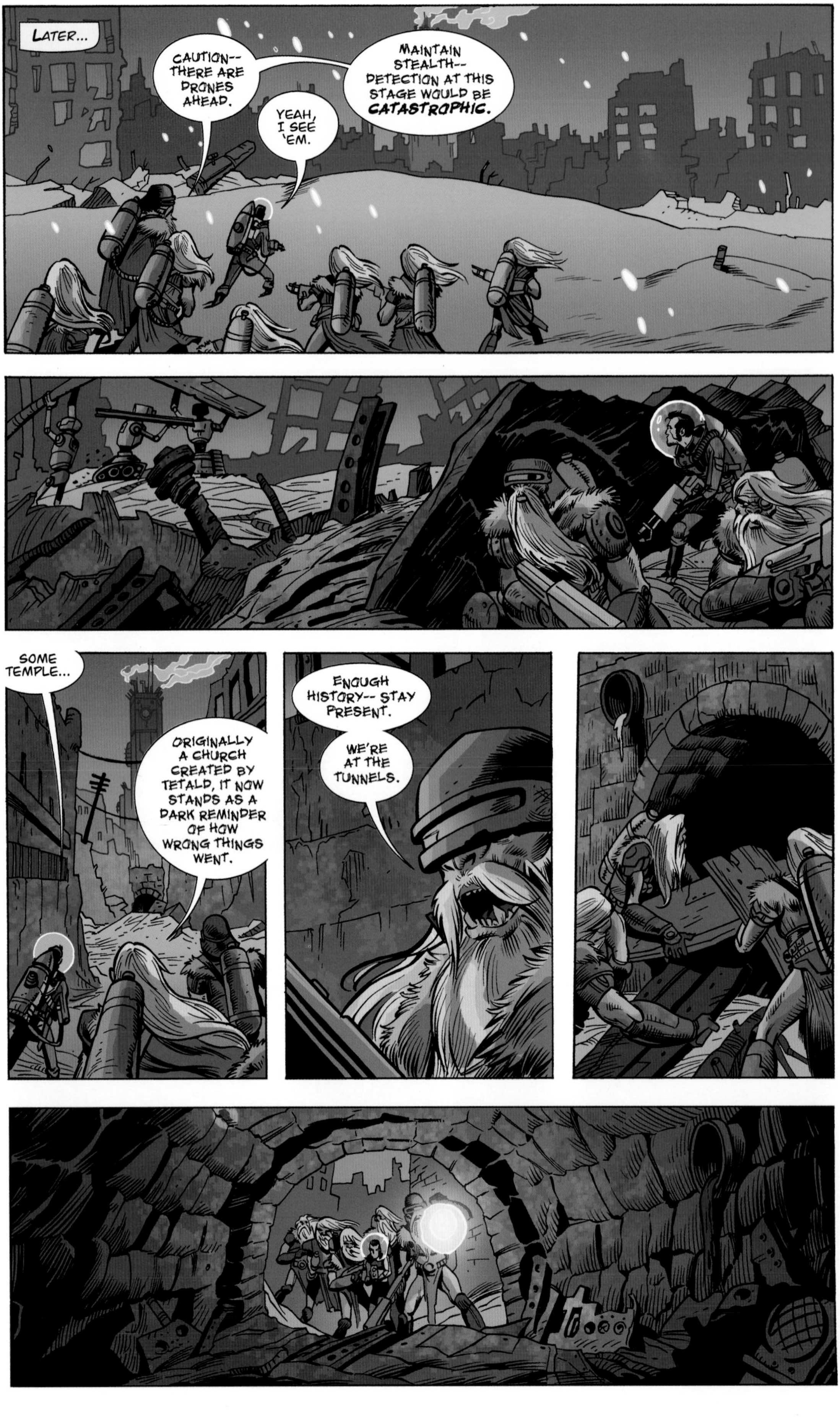
LATER...
CAUTION-- THERE ARE DRONES AHEAD.
MAINTAIN STEALTH-- DETECTION AT THIS STAGE WOULD BE CATASTROPHIC.
YEAH, I SEE 'EM.
SOME TEMPLE...
ORIGINALLY A CHURCH CREATED BY TETALD, IT NOW STANDS AS A DARK REMINDER OF HOW WRONG THINGS WENT.
ENOUGH HISTORY-- STAY PRESENT.
WE'RE AT THE TUNNELS.

UP AHEAD... LOTS MORE METAL, BUT NOTHING PROCESSING ENERGY.

THIS WILL SERVE LITTLE USE.

WHATEVER YOU SAY-- YOU'RE THE APE MAN...

WE NEAR THE TOWER ENTRANCE.

THE WALLS...

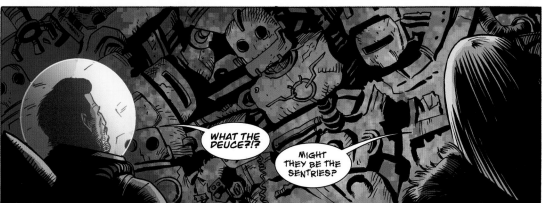

WHAT THE DEUCE?!?

MIGHT THEY BE THE SENTRIES?

QUIET YOUR FEARS-- THESE ARE LONG SINCE DISABLED AND POSE NO THREAT.

THEY WASTE NOTHING-- THE BODIES OF THE DEACTIVATED HAVE BEEN USED TO REINFORCE THE TOWER.

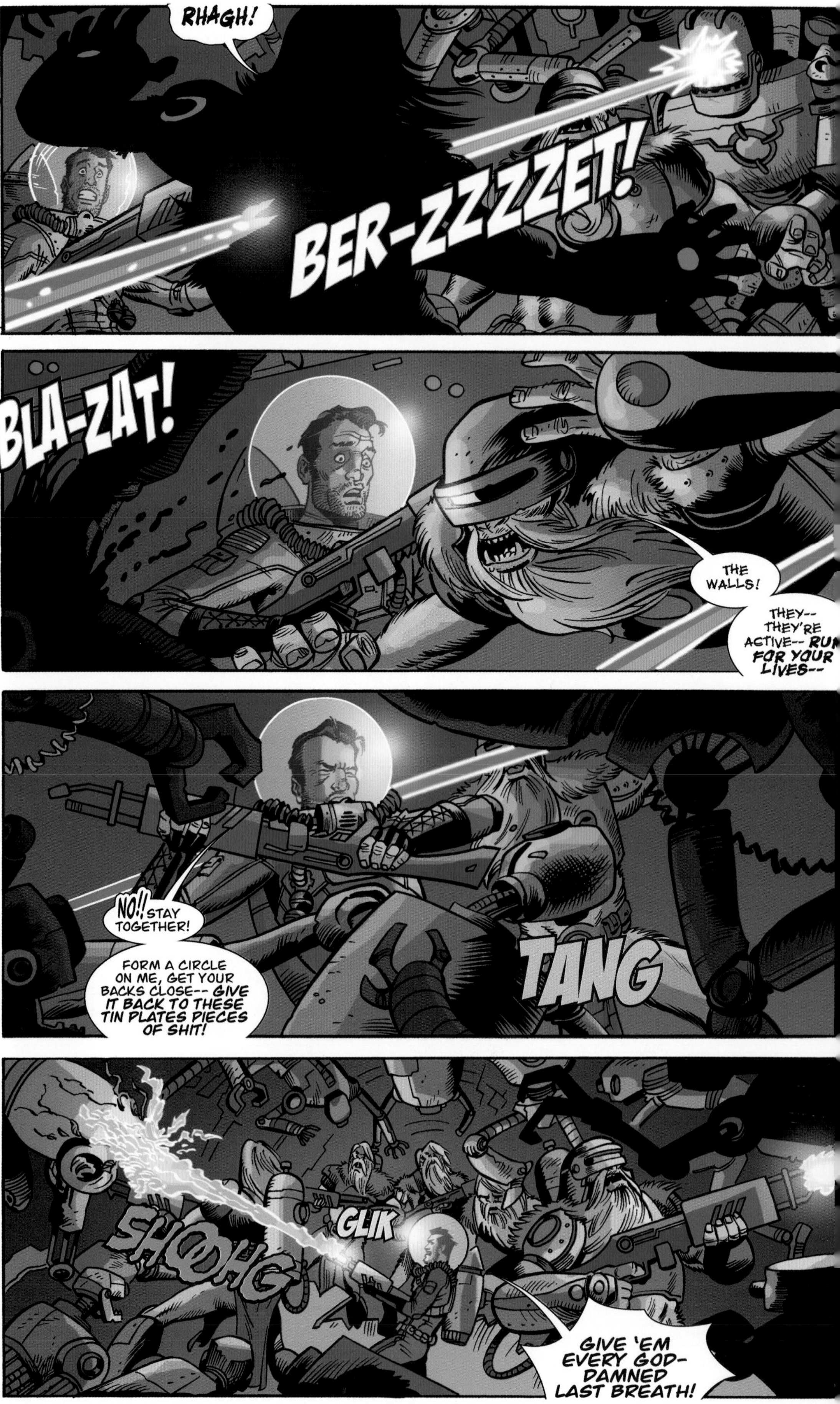

RHAGH!
BER-ZZZZZET!
BLA-ZAT!
THE WALLS!
THEY-- THEY'RE ACTIVE-- RU
FOR YOUR LIVES--
NO!! STAY TOGETHER!
FORM A CIRCLE ON ME, GET YOUR BACKS CLOSE-- GIVE IT BACK TO THESE TIN PLATES PIECES OF SHIT!
TANG
SHOOHG
GLIK
GIVE 'EM EVERY GOD-DAMNED LAST BREATH!

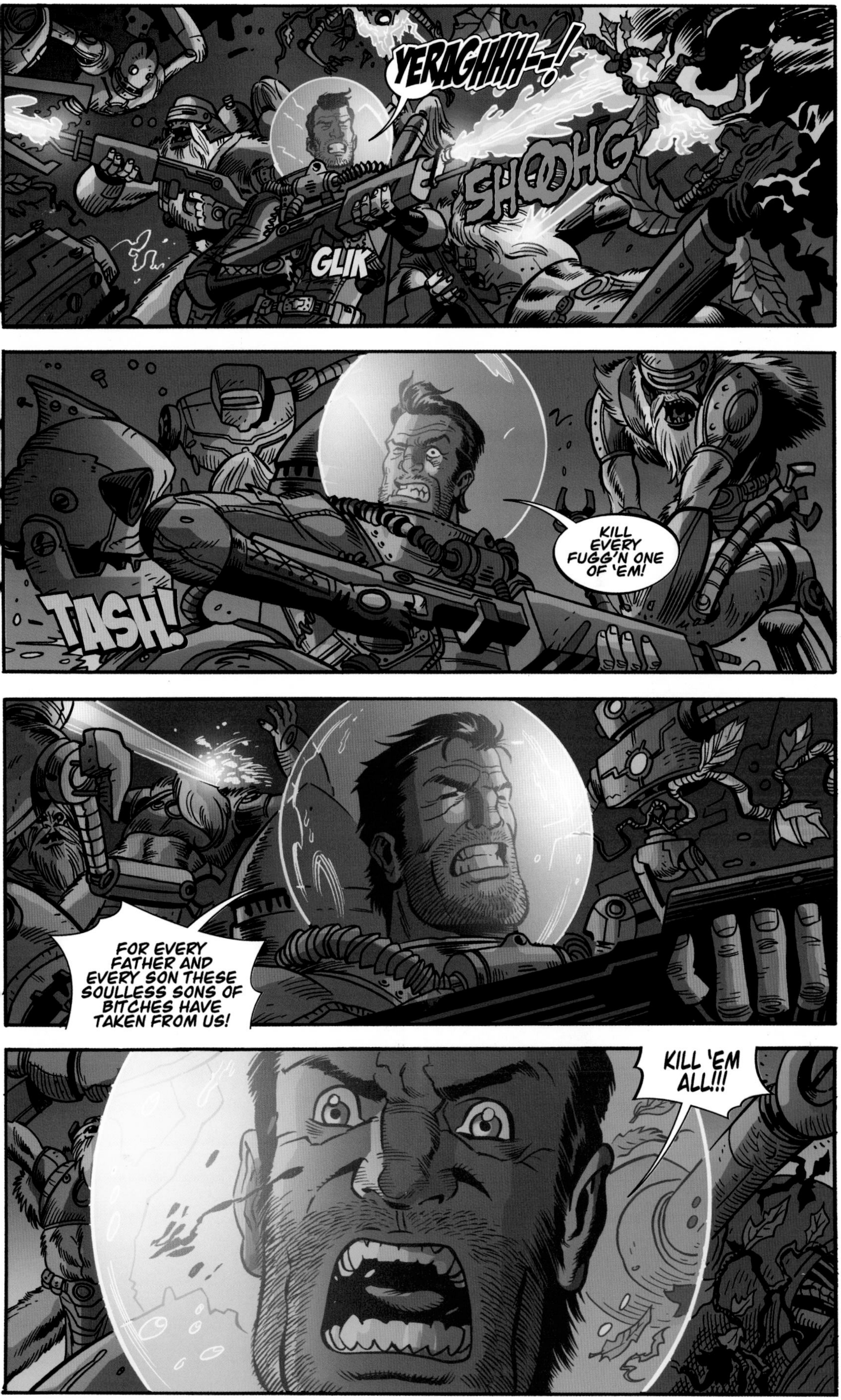
YERAGHHH--!
SHOOHG
GLIK
KILL EVERY FUGG'N ONE OF 'EM!
TASH!
FOR EVERY FATHER AND EVERY SON THESE SOULLESS SONS OF BITCHES HAVE TAKEN FROM US!
KILL 'EM ALL!!!

GO NOW--! WHILE THERE IS STILL TIME!

GET TO THE TOP OF THE TOWER-- KILL JENTU!

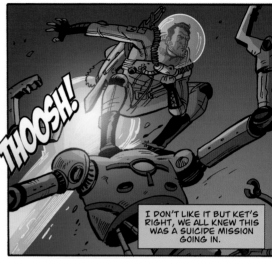

THOOSH!

I DON'T LIKE IT BUT KET'S RIGHT, WE ALL KNEW THIS WAS A SUICIDE MISSION GOING IN.

IF WE DON'T KILL JENTU IT WAS ALL A WASTE.

SHUNK

FOR THE GLORY OF TETALD!

FOR THE GLORY OF JENTU!

DOWN THE TUNNEL WHEN I HEAR THEIR SCREAMS.

WE ALL KNEW THIS WAS A SUICIDE MISSION.

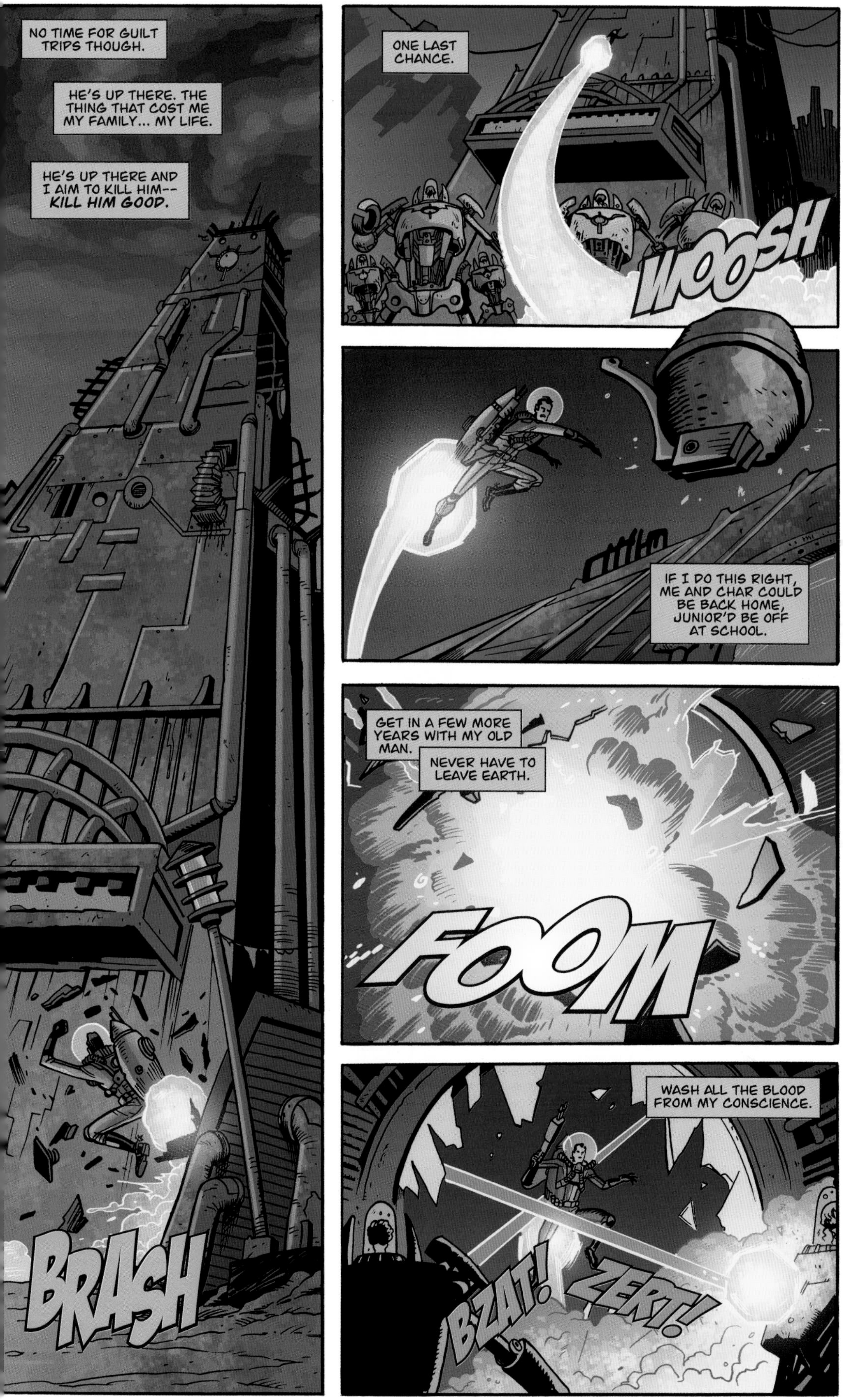
NO TIME FOR GUILT TRIPS THOUGH.
HE'S UP THERE. THE THING THAT COST ME MY FAMILY... MY LIFE.
HE'S UP THERE AND I AIM TO KILL HIM-- KILL HIM GOOD.
BRASH
ONE LAST CHANCE.
WOOSH
IF I DO THIS RIGHT, ME AND CHAR COULD BE BACK HOME, JUNIOR'D BE OFF AT SCHOOL.
GET IN A FEW MORE YEARS WITH MY OLD MAN.
NEVER HAVE TO LEAVE EARTH.
FOOM
WASH ALL THE BLOOD FROM MY CONSCIENCE.
BZAT!
ZERT!

THE GOOD LORD HAS SEEN FIT TA SHOW ME THE LOCK...

GLIK

SHOOOHG

...ALL I GOTTA DO IS TURN THE KEY.

KET DELIVERED YOU EARLIER THAN ANTICIPATED.

THAT SO?

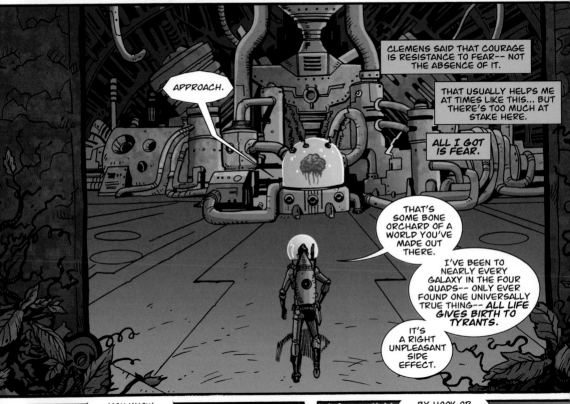

CLEMENS SAID THAT COURAGE IS RESISTANCE TO FEAR-- NOT THE ABSENCE OF IT.

THAT USUALLY HELPS ME AT TIMES LIKE THIS... BUT THERE'S TOO MUCH AT STAKE HERE.

ALL I GOT IS FEAR.

APPROACH.

THAT'S SOME BONE ORCHARD OF A WORLD YOU'VE MADE OUT THERE.

I'VE BEEN TO NEARLY EVERY GALAXY IN THE FOUR QUADS-- ONLY EVER FOUND ONE UNIVERSALLY TRUE THING-- *ALL LIFE GIVES BIRTH TO TYRANTS.*

IT'S A RIGHT UNPLEASANT SIDE EFFECT.

YOU KNOW ONLY THAT WHICH YOU ARE TOLD.

I KNOW THAT YOU KILLED MY FAMILY.

BY HOOK OR CROOK I'M GUNNA STOP YOU FROM DOING IT AGAIN.

TASH

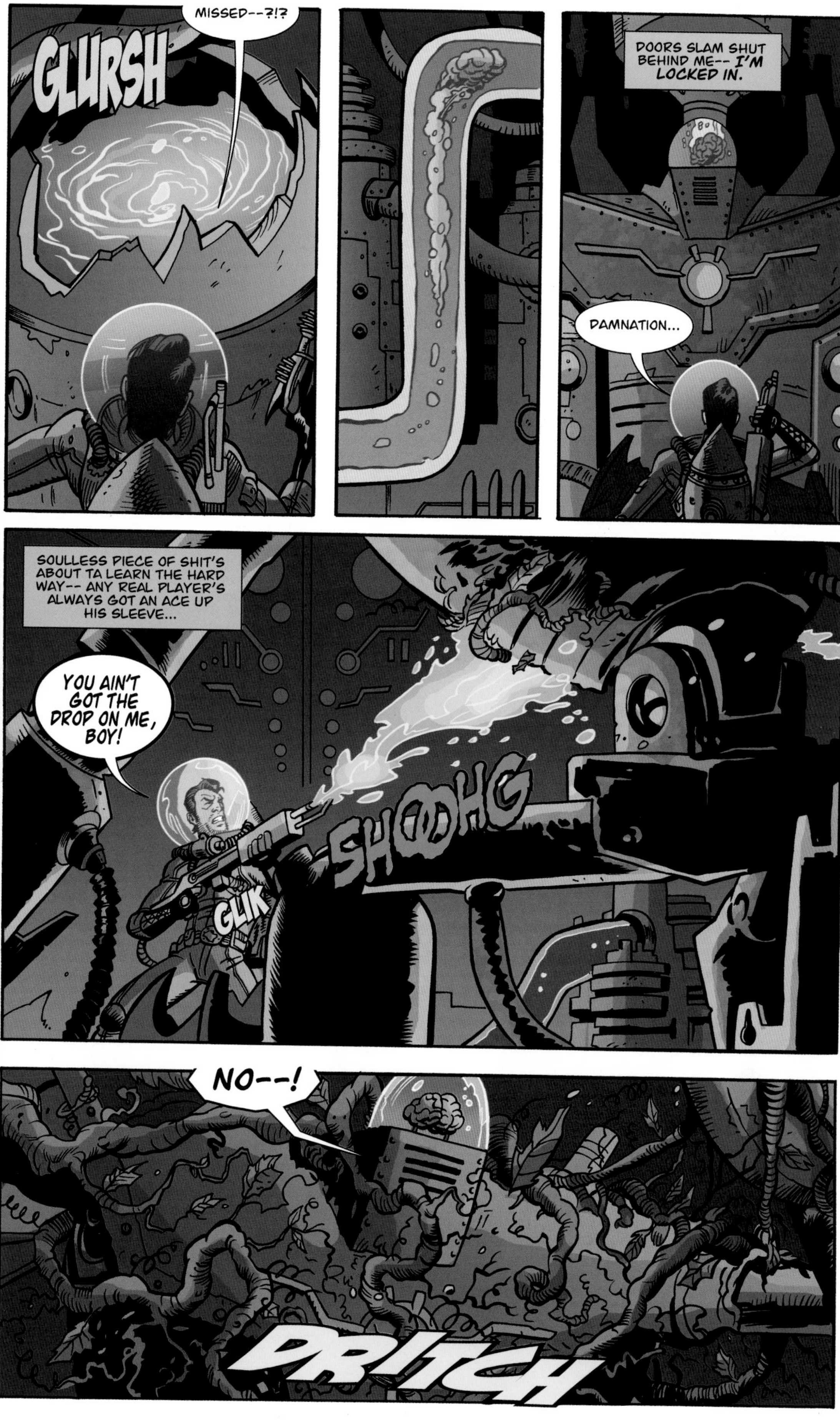
GLURSH
MISSED--?!?
DOORS SLAM SHUT BEHIND ME-- I'M LOCKED IN.
DAMNATION...
SOULLESS PIECE OF SHIT'S ABOUT TA LEARN THE HARD WAY-- ANY REAL PLAYER'S ALWAYS GOT AN ACE UP HIS SLEEVE...
YOU AIN'T GOT THE DROP ON ME, BOY!
SHOOHG
GLIK
NO--!
DRITCH

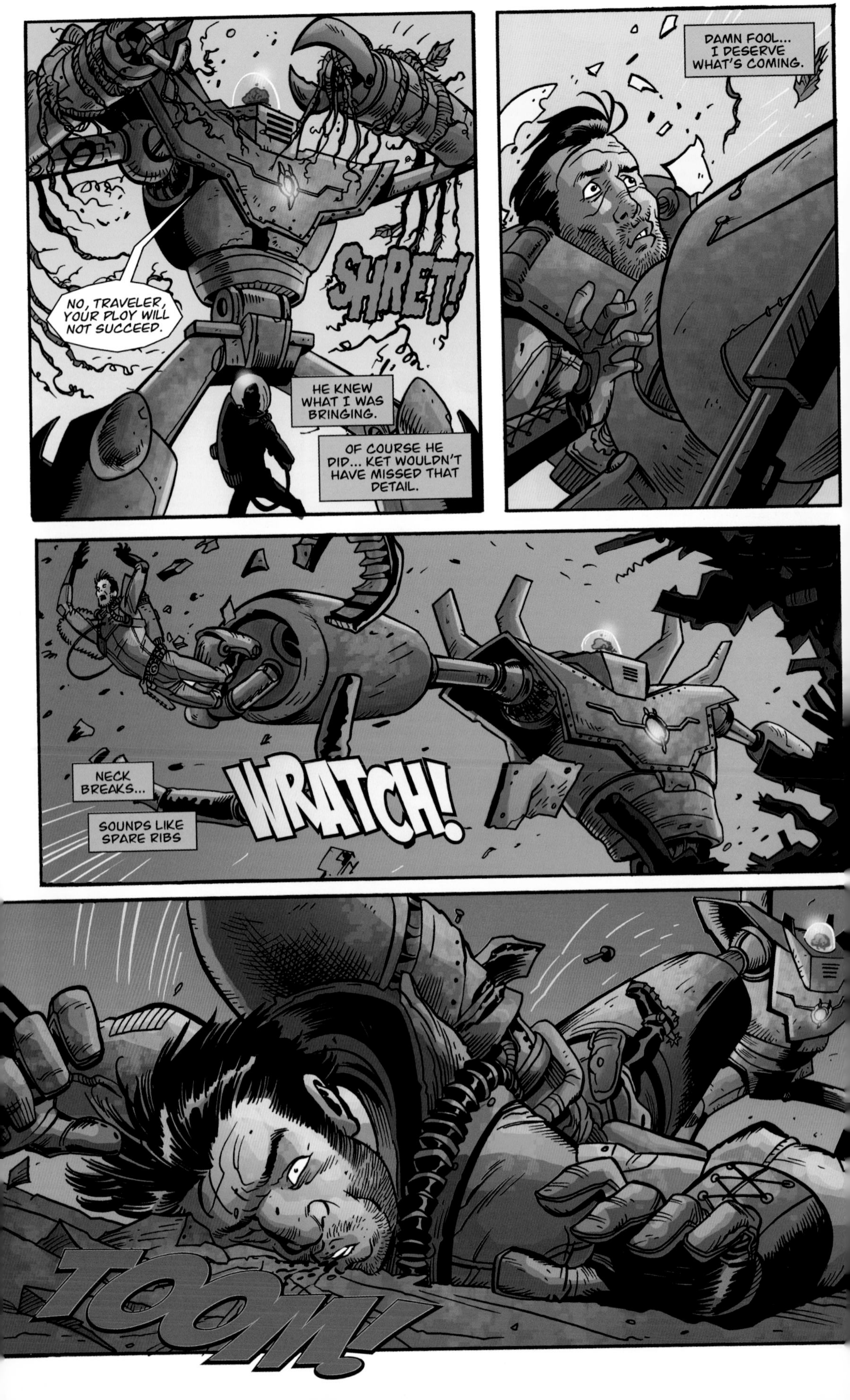
NO, TRAVELER, YOUR PLOY WILL NOT SUCCEED.
SHRET!
HE KNEW WHAT I WAS BRINGING.
OF COURSE HE DID... KET WOULDN'T HAVE MISSED THAT DETAIL.
DAMN FOOL... I DESERVE WHAT'S COMING.
NECK BREAKS...
SOUNDS LIKE SPARE RIBS
WRATCH!
TOOM!

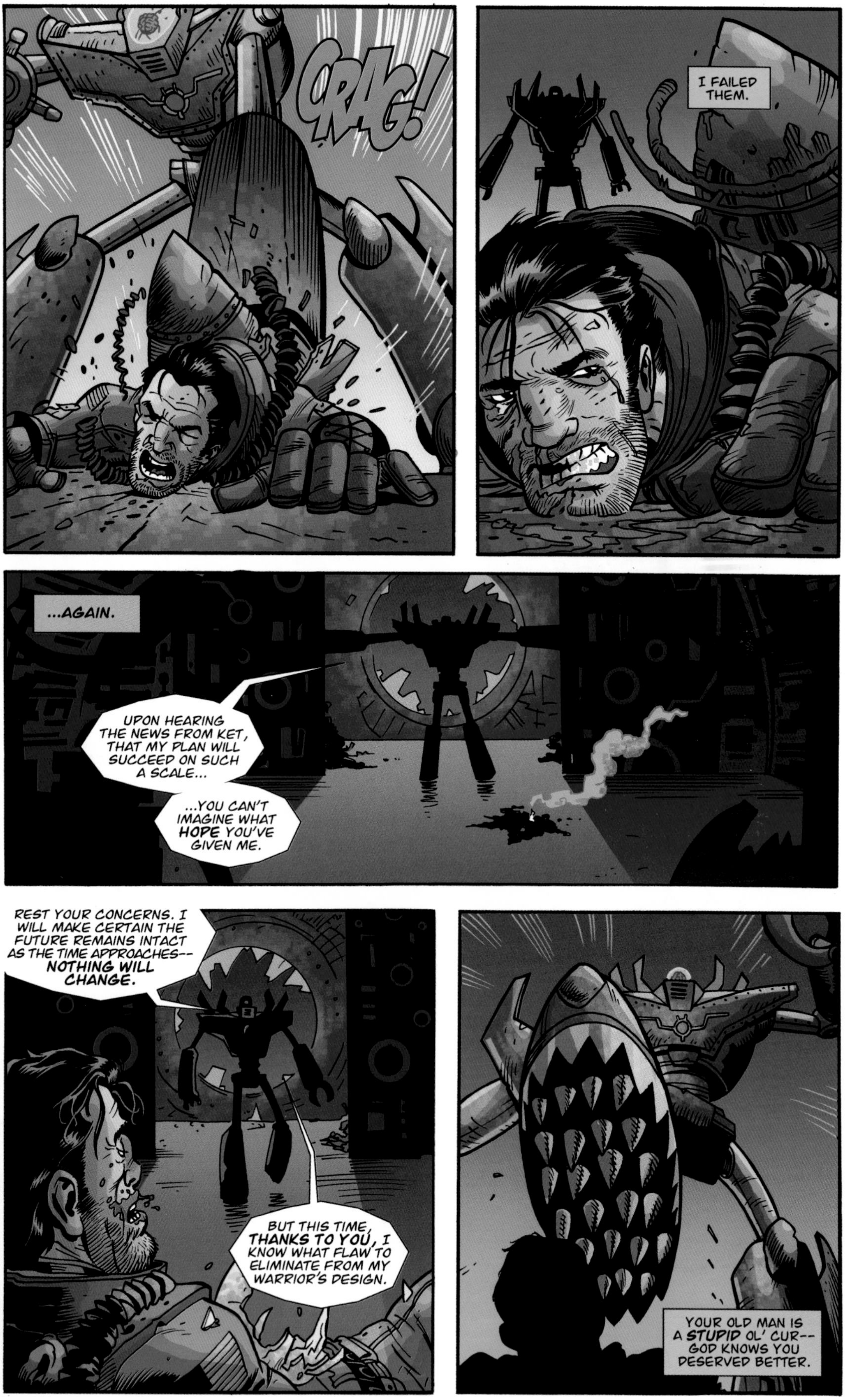
CRAG!
I FAILED THEM.
...AGAIN.
UPON HEARING THE NEWS FROM KET, THAT MY PLAN WILL SUCCEED ON SUCH A SCALE...
...YOU CAN'T IMAGINE WHAT HOPE YOU'VE GIVEN ME.
REST YOUR CONCERNS. I WILL MAKE CERTAIN THE FUTURE REMAINS INTACT AS THE TIME APPROACHES-- NOTHING WILL CHANGE.
BUT THIS TIME, THANKS TO YOU, I KNOW WHAT FLAW TO ELIMINATE FROM MY WARRIOR'S DESIGN.
YOUR OLD MAN IS A STUPID OL' CUR-- GOD KNOWS YOU DESERVED BETTER.

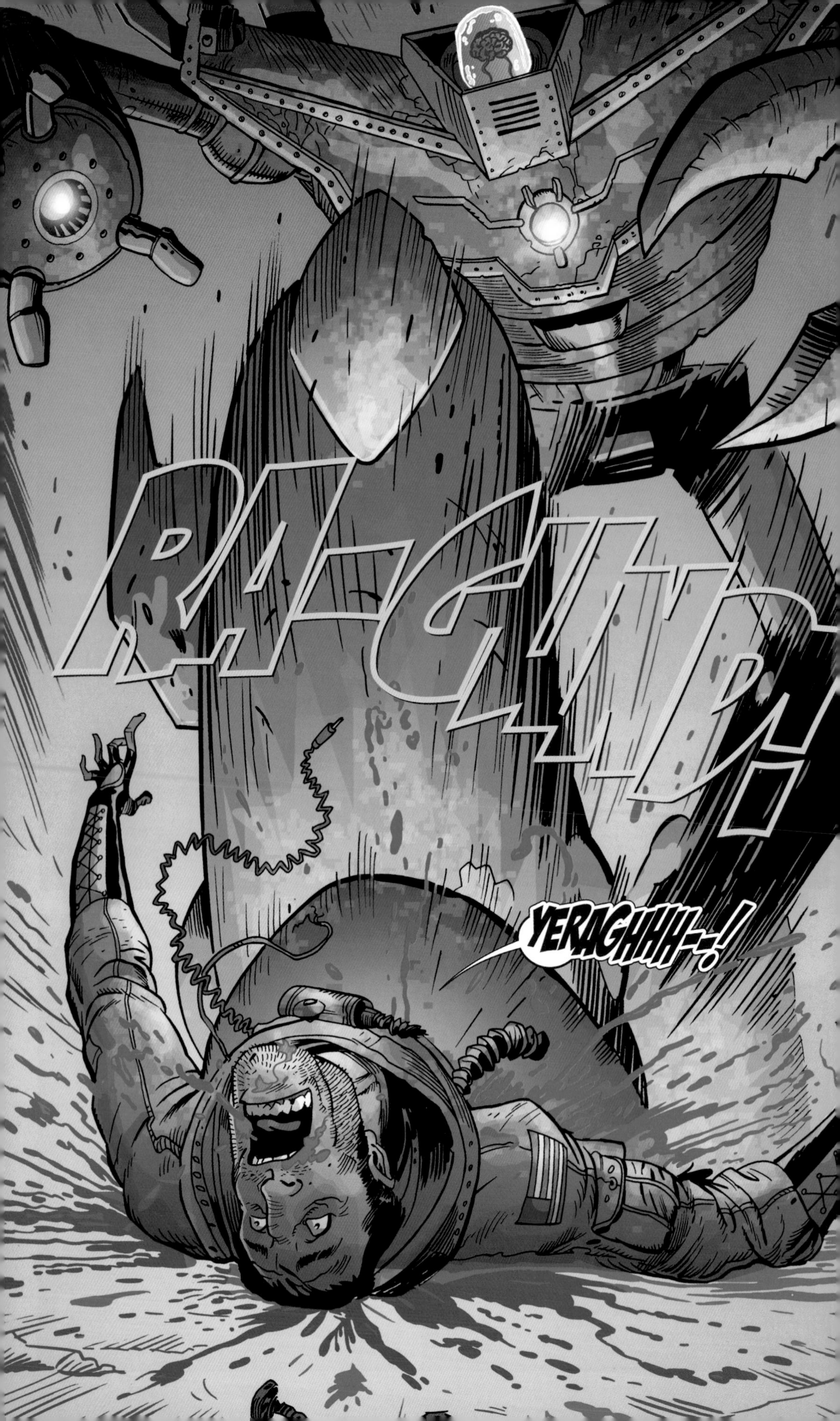
YERAGHHH--!